# Offshore Finance and State Power

# Offshore Finance and State Power

ANDREA BINDER

OXFORD
UNIVERSITY PRESS

Great Clarendon Street, Oxford, OX2 6DP,
United Kingdom

Oxford University Press is a department of the University of Oxford.
It furthers the University's objective of excellence in research, scholarship,
and education by publishing worldwide. Oxford is a registered trade mark of
Oxford University Press in the UK and in certain other countries

Published in the United States of America by Oxford University Press
198 Madison Avenue, New York, NY 10016, United States of America

British Library Cataloguing in Publication Data
Data available

Library of Congress Control Number: 2022945390

ISBN 978–0–19–287012–4

DOI: 10.1093/oso/9780192870124.001.0001

Printed and bound in the UK by
Clays Ltd, Elcograf S.p.A.

*To Carla and Maja*

# Acknowledgements

Virginia Woolf famously pointed out that 'a woman must have ... a room of her own if she is to write.'[1] Writing during a global pandemic, with two young children at home in never-ending successions of lockdowns and quarantines, is the exact opposite of *A Room of One's Own*. And so, finishing this book has been an extraordinary experience. It was extraordinarily taxing and painfully slow. Yet, there were also extraordinary moments of fun and togetherness. My family's insistence on *Feierabend* on Friday evenings, announced with electropop and accompanied by chips and drinks kept me sane. I owe them.

Luckily, most of the book's work had been done before the pandemic. It builds on my PhD research. That whole endeavour would have been impossible without the generous support of the Gates Cambridge Scholarship. In addition, the Department of Politics and International Studies, the Cambridge Political Economy Society Trust, the Simón Bolívar Fund, and Magdalene College contributed towards the field research that informs the book. My heartfelt thankfulness also goes to my interviewees. They shared their time and insights with me for nothing in return. Their generosity was a fine human experience, and it is a precondition for the research as I do it to exist.

I sincerely thank Juan Flores Zendejas and Gustavo del Ángel Mobarak for opening doors in Mexico. Javier Aparicio at CIDE provided a welcoming place while being there. In Brazil, I thank Oliver Stuenkel at FGV to provide a scholarly base and Paulo Savaget for inroads into Brazil's academic, financial, and corporate world. In Germany, I am grateful, as ever, to the team at the Global Public Policy Institute. Wolfgang Reinicke encouraged and supported my application to the Cambridge PhD programme. For a first-generation academic, the essential step. Thorsten Benner has been inspiring, helpful, and witty in so many ways since we first met in 2006. Katharina Nachbar turned my conceptual musings and Excel aesthetics into telling, elegant graphs. In Cambridge, my supervisors Helen Thompson and Jason Sharman made all the difference. Helen's scholarly rigour and her unwillingness to ever take the intellectually lazy route are academic qualities I aspire to. She taught me to understand when to persist and when to give up on an argument. Jason

---

[1] Woolf, Virginia. 2004 [1928]. *A Room of One's Own*. Revised edition. London: Penguin, p. 4.

joined along the way, supportive from day one. He brought with him a wealth of knowledge about the offshore world, probing questions, and an infectious optimism. I am deeply grateful for all of that.

I am indebted to Pieter van Houten and Kai Koddenbrock, who both suggested early on that the book needs a concept of the state. Jeremy Green and Jan Fichtner read the full thesis and made helpful suggestions for turning it into a manuscript. Thomas Rixen, Daniel Mügge, Lukas Hakelberg, Simon Linder, and Felicia Riethmüller, read different parts of the manuscript. They all provided helpful comments. As did the two reviewers at Oxford University Press. Louis Miebs helped meticulously with the preparation of the manuscript.

It is impossible to write a book, let alone to finish a PhD, without the enormous support of babysitters, friends, and family. Lauren Wilson and Luna Martinez Lopez were essential for lockdown survival. My friends were vital against cabin fever. My mum Hanni saved our souls countless times, from field research support in Brazil to mending teddies. My brother Martin shares in the good parts of life and the bad. My dad Richard instilled in me the interest in politics. I miss his warmth and our heated discussions. Finally, I am happy beyond words that my loves Carla, Maja, and Martin joined me on that journey. The girls generously spread their worldly wisdom. Martin shared the fun and the grind—all while following his own ambitions. He keeps it easy, no matter how rocky the ride.

Thank you all so much for being my village. How fortunate I am.

# Contents

# Acronyms

| | |
|---|---|
| BaFin | *Bundesanstalt für Finanzdienstleistungsaufsicht, Federal Financial Supervisory Authority* |
| Banamex | *Banco Nacional de México, National bank of Mexico* |
| BEPS | Base Erosion and Profit Shifting |
| BIS | Bank for International Settlements |
| BIS IDS | BIS International Debt Statistics |
| BNDES | *Banco Nacional de Desenvolvimento Econômico e Social, National Bank for Economic and Social Development* |
| BP | British Petroleum |
| CBE | Capitais Brasileiros no Exterior, Brazilian Capital Abroad |
| CD | compact disc |
| CDU | *Christlich Demokratische Union, Christian Democratic Party* |
| CPI | *Comissão Parlamentar de Inquérito, Parliamentary Committe of Inquiry* |
| DM | *Deutsche Mark* |
| ECB | European Central Bank |
| EU | European Union |
| FATCA | United States Foreign Account Tax Compliance Act |
| FDI | foreign direct investment |
| FDP | *Freie Demokratische Partei, Free Democratic Party* |
| GDP | gross domestic product |
| HMRC | Her Majesty's Revenues and Customs, Britain's tax authority |
| IDS | international debt statistics |
| IMF | International Monetary Fund |
| IPE | international political economy |
| IR | international relations |
| IRS | Inland Revenue Service, the United States' tax authority |
| NAFTA | North American Free Trade Agreement |
| NCA | National Crime Agency |
| OECD | Organization for Economic Co-operation and Development |
| PEMEX | *Petróleos Mexicanos* |
| PRI | *Partido Revolucionario Institucional, Institutional Revolutionary Party* |
| PT | Partido dos Trabalhadores, Workers' Party |
| RFB | *Secretaria da Receita Federal, Brazil's Federal Revenue Service* |
| SPD | Sozialdemokratische Partei Deutschlands, Social Democratic Party |
| UKIP | United Kingdom Independence Party |
| URV | *Unidade real de valor, Unit of Real Value* |
| VAT | value added tax |

# 1

# Introduction

The offshore world is like a house of mirrors. Offshore financial centres such as the City of London, Singapore, Luxembourg, or the Cayman Islands, provide non-residents with a legal framework that is strong on property rights and soft on taxation, banking regulation, and creative accounting techniques. As a result, documentation—from company registration to accounting—is scarce in offshore financial centres. The money that flows through them is thus largely invisible to official statistics. In this way, offshore financial services allow wealthy individuals and corporations to optimize their tax bills, legally or illegally. With the Pandora Papers in 2021, the Panama Papers in 2016, and previous leaks, these practices have made the headlines in newspapers around the world. What is not in the news, however, is that offshore financial services are paramount for banks to create money. Offshore finance extends the power to create money—since the seventeenth century a power shared between the state and banks within a given territory[1]—across borders.

Bringing together the wealthy, multinational corporations, banks, and governments, the offshore world reflects the international political economy and its underlying power relations. Yet, the reflection that offshore finance throws back is puzzling. The international economy's most fundamental elements seem bigger or smaller than usual. For instance, the volume of US dollars created offshore appears much bigger than what banking statistics suggest. Excluding offshore transactions, these statistics do not capture all that is there. Other elements, such as the volume of global foreign direct investment, appear to be much smaller than what economic statistics present. Counting virtual offshore investments the same way as substantial onshore ones, these statistics capture what, in essence, is not there.[2] If there is more US dollar credit in the world than we may think and substantially less foreign direct investment, if the regulations of the international banking system are not what they seem and neither are the tax rates imposed on multinational corporations, it raises

---

[1] Strange 1994; Vogl 2015.
[2] UNCTAD 2015; Damgaard, Elkjaer, and Johannesen 2019.

*Offshore Finance and State Power*. Andrea Binder, Oxford University Press. © Andrea Binder (2023).
DOI: 10.1093/oso/9780192870124.003.0001

the question how offshore finance affects the power of the state. This question entails an element that asks about the mechanism of the effect—how does it work?—and one that asks about its outcome—does offshore finance enhance or limit state power?

Asking about the relationship between offshore finance and state power is a form of the perennial question concerning relations between states and markets.[3] That question is not a theoretical one. Offshore financial services are exclusively available to the super-rich, to large multinational corporations, and to internationally active banks. They create rents for this exclusive circle of economic actors that are not available to everyone else. Offshore finance exacerbates wealth inequality.[4] Whether states are powerful and have, as Palan[5] holds, 'created offshore' or whether the offshore markets triumph and rob the state of power, as others contend,[6] determines whether the resulting inequality is a matter of political will or an instance of state capture.

Despite growing public attention in the past decade, academically and politically, offshore finance is still treated as a marginal phenomenon of the international economy. Practitioners—bankers, lawyers, and finance journalists—insist, however, that offshore finance *is* the global economy.[7] As far as we can trust the data, they seem to have a point. According to the estimates of Alstadsæter et al.,[8] the world's well-to-dos keep private wealth totalling US$7.6 trillion or about 10 per cent of the world's gross domestic product (GDP) offshore. Multinational corporations are estimated to shift another US$600 billion annually in corporate profits there.[9] Yet, the volume of money that is created offshore likely surpasses all those offshore assets. There are no global estimates for credit denominated in so-called Eurocurrencies, national currencies created outside their home country.[10] At the eve of the 2007–09 global financial crisis, the four countries studied in this book—Britain, Germany, Mexico, and Brazil—alone accumulated, according to data from the Bank for International Settlements (BIS) over US$3.2 trillion in offshore dollar liabilities. It might not be *the* international economy, but

---

[3] See Strange 1994.
[4] Alstadsæter, Johannesen, and Zucman 2019.
[5] Palan 1998, 625.
[6] Genschel 2005; Shaxson 2012; Zucman 2015.
[7] Obermayer and Obermaier 2016; MacIntosh 2017.
[8] Alstadsæter, Johannesen, and Zucman 2018.
[9] Tørsløv, Wier, and Zucman 2018, 13.
[10] The most important Eurocurrencies are the Eurodollar and the Euroeuro. Despite the name, Eurocurrencies are not necessarily created in Europe or denominated in US dollars or euro. Hong Kong, for instance, is an important offshore centre for Asian currencies. Since most of what is happening offshore is denominated in US dollars, unless otherwise specified I refer to the Eurodollar markets and system. I use the terms Eurodollar and offshore dollar interchangeably.

offshore finance clearly is a substantial part of it. Offshore financial centres are by no means far-flung tropical islands involved in obscure financial transactions. Rather, they play a crucial role in the creation and intermediation of global financial flows. They are the machine room of the international financial system, creating global liquidity. To understand offshore finance better means to understand the international political economy better.

## 1 Researching the offshore world

However, studying the effect of offshore finance on state power comes with a double challenge. One is conceptual, the other empirical.

The conceptual challenge concerns the notions of state power and that of offshore finance. State power is an essentially contested concept.[11] It cannot be given definitive meaning. Nevertheless, we need to pin it down in the real world to find out how it relates to offshore finance. Offshore finance, on the other hand, is a rather new concept in international studies. We need to spell out what exactly it is and how far it influences the international political economy.

The empirical challenge concerns the opacity of offshore financial services. Their arcane nature makes quantification difficult. Standard macroeconomic data, such as national accounts and investment data, miss offshore transactions.[12] More problematic still, they lose quality over time, precisely because of the offshore phenomenon.[13]

To address this twin challenge, the book develops an analytical perspective that I call 'the money view'[14] (Chapter 2). I argue that money is inherent to and important for both state power and offshore finance. Money is what holds these two phenomena together, making them relevant for the international political economy. Consequently, the book approaches the *meaning* of state power and offshore finance from the perspective of money.

Three propositions are central to the money view. First, money, in essence, is a social relation. It is a means to account for and to settle debt, most importantly tax and sovereign debt. The state cannot create money without going into debt. Phrased differently, money is a set of debtor–creditor relationships between the state, its financiers, and taxpayers. Money creation is

---

[11] Gallie 1956.
[12] Zucman 2013.
[13] Linsi and Mügge 2019.
[14] I borrow the term 'the money view' from Mehrling (2011). See Chapter 2, footnote 1.

underpinned by the struggle between the state, financiers, and taxpayers over how to raise and spend state finances.[15] Second, the state is—in line with Max Weber's[16] thought—a *Herrschaftsverband*, an institutional association of rule. It is marked by mutual dependency between ruler and ruled. From the money view, the relationship between ruler and ruled can be specified as the creditor–debtor relationships that constitute money. These relationships are institutionalized in a country's tax and bank institutions. Third, the power position of the state in its relations with financiers and taxpayers depends on its ability to mediate successfully the political conflict about the distribution of the costs and benefits of taxation and money creation between different groups of society.[17]

State power, from this perspective, is the state's ability to mobilize and centralize resources to finance its political goals. This notion of state power emphasizes state autonomy over state influence[18] and material over ideational perspectives. It highlights the relational nature of power, while being agnostic towards its purpose. Offshore finance, in turn, exhibits three central features:[19] (1) Underlying offshore financial services are exclusively offered to non-residents of the respective jurisdiction. (2) They entail zero or low taxation and regulation. (3) They make financial flows, ownership, and liabilities invisible.[20] The contracts underlying offshore financial services are deliberately designed to keep the financial flows out of sight.[21] That is, offshore finance is not simply a new expression for foreign financial flows, including in the form of capital flight. It has a more precise meaning. Offshore finance is a specific set of cross-border financial flows adhering to a legal code that obscures them and makes them exclusive.

This perspective on state power and offshore finance is new insofar as state power is commonly addressed from the angle of territorial control, economic, or ideational might. Offshore finance, on the other hand, is usually addressed from the perspective of taxation. The money view, in contrast, highlights the shared power of states and banks to create money as a crucial feature of

---

[15] Ingham 2004.
[16] Weber 1994.
[17] Levi 1989; Calomiris and Haber 2014.
[18] Cohen 2013.
[19] Palan, Murphy, and Chavagneux 2010; Sharman 2010.
[20] The terms used in the literature are usually 'secrecy' or 'anonymity'. I prefer invisibility over those terms because it better encapsulates the intentions of the provider and consumer of offshore services. Whether invisibility is achieved through secrecy, anonymity, or by other means is changing across time and context. See Chapter 2.
[21] Pistor 2020.

modern statehood,[22] and the bifurcation of that power across borders as a key element of offshore finance.

Empirically, the book traces the social relations that underpin money creation from a historical-institutionalist perspective. It combines the insights from sixty elite interviews with bankers, lawyers, central bankers, government representatives, and other experts in matters of offshore finance with descriptive statistics from the BIS. Linking these two sources is done fully consciously of the fact that macroeconomic data are 'political artefacts', as Mügge[23] points out. It never fully reflects the real-world phenomenon it is supposed to measure. Likewise, interviews run the risk that interviewees, no matter how carefully and systematically selected, conflate *their* world with *the* world. Therefore, this book combines a concept analysis of state power and offshore finance with a case comparison that embeds the data from the interviews and banking statistics into an historical account based on secondary sources.

Starting in the nineteenth century, the beginning of modern taxation and banking, the book scrutinizes in each case the determinants of state power: the institutional association of rule and how it evolves over time; the changing nature of money creation and taxation; and the distribution of the related costs and benefits across different groups in society. It determines the contemporary exposure to offshore financial services of the respective countries. It then explains what happens if state power encounters offshore finance. Historicizing the analysis allows the book to overcome a teleologic notion of countries' shared path to modern state financing. It thereby opens the possibility to account for the historical and geographical contingencies of each state's relationship with offshore finance. The comparative nature of the study allows the identification of common patterns across countries. Such an approach prioritizes empirical depth over theoretical parsimony and the identification of larger patterns over forensic detail. It explains the relationship between offshore finance and state power in historical rather than law-like terms.

Four countries take centre stage in this book: Britain, Germany, Brazil, and Mexico. Britain is considered the first Western state to develop modern ways to finance itself through sovereign debt and taxation.[24] Moreover, the country is the birthplace of offshore banking and a considerable number of classical offshore tax havens—from the Channel Islands to the Cayman Islands—are British Overseas Territories.[25] As a result, Britain holds a special

---

[22] Vogl 2015.
[23] Mügge 2020, 2.
[24] Bonney 1999.
[25] Hampton 1996a; Tax Justice Network 2013.

place in the offshore world (Chapter 3). Germany, on the other hand, is Europe's largest economy and shares a border with three of the globally most important offshore financial centres: the Netherlands, Switzerland, and Luxembourg. Consequently, it is said to be among the prime 'victims' of offshore tax planning[26] (Chapter 4). Next to Europe, Latin America is also significantly exposed to offshore finance. Moreover, many Latin American states explicitly crafted their post-independence constitutions on European models.[27] While uneven, Europe and Latin America's paths to the modern state have enough parallels to be compared and analysed from the proposed 'money view'. Within Latin America, Brazil and Mexico are two insightful cases to study. Brazil is the world's second largest borrower in offshore financial markets. Offshore financial services are deeply ingrained in Brazilian economy and society (Chapter 5). Mexico was historically also strongly exposed to offshore finance. However, it largely withdrew from the offshore money markets after the double financial crises of 1982 and 1994. Today, Mexican firms and individuals make comparatively little use of offshore financial services, not least because the informal economy provides space for tax evasion and money laundering (Chapter 6). These cases are first and foremost crucial cases.[28] All four countries are significant for the offshore markets—in the past and, with the puzzling exception of Mexico, in the present. Without these states, it is unlikely offshore finance would have developed the way it did. Britain invented offshore finance, Germany fuelled it, Brazil and Mexico have long been among its largest borrowers. If we are to see the relationship between offshore finance and state power, it is in these cases.

With this approach, the book builds on but deviates from the literature on offshore finance.[29] First, it presents in-depth case studies that make it possible to account for differences and change within and between countries and across time. The current research, on the contrary, remains mostly at the aggregate level and focuses on the short-term. Second, the book argues that given the interlinked nature of debt and tax underlying the process of sovereign money creation, we must study offshore banking and offshore tax planning in tandem. The literature, thus far, tells two separate stories about offshore finance. One story is about offshore financial centres as a hub where wealthy individuals and multinational corporations can minimize their tax bills, legally or illegally.

[26] Alstadsæter, Johannesen, and Zucman 2019.
[27] Centeno and Ferraro 2013.
[28] Gerring 2009.
[29] See Palan 1998; Sharman 2010; Fichtner 2016; Alstadsæter, Johannesen, and Zucman 2018.

This is a story about tax havens.[30] The other, less well-researched, and less well-known story is about offshore financial centres as a hub for banking. This story is about how banks extend their power to create money offshore.[31] The literatures on offshore tax planning and offshore banking rarely speak to each other. On closer examination, however, the two stories of offshore tax havens and offshore banking are strikingly similar.

Most obviously, offshore banking and offshore tax planning happen in the same geographical locations. The Netherlands, Switzerland, the Cayman Islands, and many of the smaller offshore financial centres, are usually both tax havens and a hub for offshore banking. Additionally, in both stories offshore financial services share the same characteristics: they are cross-border services marked by the non-resident principle, low or no taxation and regulation, and invisibility.[32]

The literature's two separate offshore stories also share a common plot. Wealthy individuals, firms, and banks go offshore to avoid rules and regulations while mostly following the letter, but not the spirit of the law.

Lastly, although addressing the question only implicitly, the two strands of offshore literature agree that offshore finance undermines state power. The research on international tax competition—of which offshore tax planning is the proverbial tip of the iceberg—finds that offshore financial centres create substantial tax losses for the state through illegal tax evasion and legal tax avoidance. Offshore finance undermines the state's power to tax.[33] The research on offshore banking highlights the potentially harmful effect of offshore money creation on financial stability.[34] Offshore finance limits the state's power to regulate financial flows. Taken together, the literature holds that offshore finance robs the state of power.

## 2 The argument in brief

This book, on the contrary, argues that the effect of offshore finance on state power is not straightforward. The book demonstrates theoretically (Chapter 2) and empirically (Chapters 3 to 6) that the undermining effect of offshore finance on state power, so prevalent in academic and public debates, is but one outcome. Offshore finance can also enhance the ability of the state to finance

---

[30] Palan, Murphy, and Chavagneux 2010; Sharman 2010; Zucman 2015.
[31] See Helleiner 1994; Burn 1999, 199; McCauley, McGuire, and Sushko 2015.
[32] Palan 1998; He and McCauley 2012.
[33] OECD 1998; Zucman 2013a; IMF 2014; Crivelli, De Mooij, and Keen 2015.
[34] Black and Munro 2010; He and McCauley 2010; Avdjiev, Chui, and Shin 2014; Altamura 2017.

its political goals. Both effects occur in succession, and sometimes even in parallel.

Offshore finance can strengthen state power for two principal reasons—the provision of preferential liquidity and the possibility for a politics of the invisible. Preferential liquidity means that offshore finance can provide direct financing to the state and its large economic actors via offshore credit-money that comes at better conditions than in the domestic or in onshore foreign economies. It provides access to investors that is otherwise not available. It is issued under a more debtor-friendly legal framework. It is also usually cheaper as rates and transaction costs (including tax) are lower.[35] As such, offshore liquidity can be a source of sovereign debt when money creation at home or in regular foreign economies is not sufficient. Likewise, it increases access to foreign currency, first among them the US dollar, for internationally active corporations—again with preferential conditions.

Next, the politics of the invisible is the trump card of the offshore game. The obscure nature of offshore financial services allows the state to pursue contradictory economic policies simultaneously without being called out on it. For instance, offshore banking allows the state to regulate its domestic banking system while tolerating loose financial conditions offshore.[36] Or the state can tax corporations at nominally high rates, while keeping their effective tax burden low. The politics of the invisible hides the true nature of the tax and bank bargains. The constitution of state power is, thanks to offshore finance, no longer exclusively rooted in domestic factors and subject to external influences. Instead, the institutional association of rule can tap into the offshore world to advance its domestic goals.

On the other hand, offshore finance can indeed undermine state power. Again, offshore money creation is the core mechanism between the offshore world and state power. Offshore money creation undermines state power in times of financial crises and their aftermath when its costs outpace the benefits. During the crisis, the volatility of unregulated offshore markets is transmitted into the domestic economy and preferential liquidity dries up. The response to the crisis exposes the true nature of the bank and tax bargains. It makes transparent who benefits from money creation and who must foot the bill for bailing out the banks. Cancelling the politics of the invisible, the power of the state becomes contested economically and politically in the crises' aftermath.

---

[35] Black and Munro 2010.
[36] Palan 1998.

The same reasons that enhance state power through offshore finance in good times, unfold destructive forces in bad times.

Importantly, the propensity to generate crises is inherent to offshore finance. Offshore finance allows credit-money to be created across borders and beyond what is possible onshore. It therefore increases the opportunity for capitalist expansion but also the chances for broken promises of repayment in the absence of a lender of last resort. Offshore finance holds its own undoing.

Nevertheless, states have agency in the offshore game. They can make offshore finance work in their interest. Most notably, in the contemporary period, all four countries found ways to mitigate the potentially power-limiting effects of offshore tax planning. Britain, Germany, Brazil, and Mexico protected themselves against levels of offshore tax planning that would threaten state power. They did so through a combination of measures, including the shift from direct to indirect taxation and from taxation to social security contributions. The measures also entailed domestic law enforcement, and multilateral initiatives to curb offshore tax planning.

Regarding offshore money creation, the mitigation strategy and effectiveness of the different states varied widely. Germany and Brazil ring-fenced their banking systems. Germany allowed only a select number of banks to engage in offshore money creation. Offshore money creation took place mainly in London and Luxembourg and so the fallout happened quite literally elsewhere. Brazil established, over time, an effective system backing up offshore money creation through regulation, foreign reserves, and central bank swaps.[37] Pre-1982 Mexico, on the other hand, did not have a strategy to mitigate the effects of offshore banking on its ability to finance its politics. As the crises hit, Mexican state power was destroyed. Mexico then opted for the ultimate approach to ensure that offshore finance does not undermine state power— it withdrew from the offshore markets. In Britain, the heartland of offshore finance, running the system was in the interest of the state. It therefore took limited measures to mitigate the effects of offshore finance on state power. The Bank of England, when first allowing offshore banking in the City of London, made it clear that, should the business go wrong, the banks would not be bailed out. When it finally did go wrong in 2007–09, the banks had become so exposed to the offshore markets that the Bank of England could not stick to its word. It bailed out the banks. The fallout for the British state was enormous.

The extent to which a country aims to mitigate the effects of offshore finance are a function of the unique constellation of political and economic elites in

---

[37] Alami 2019; Alvarez 2020.

a country, the tax and bank bargains they have struck, and the role offshore finance plays herein. Take Germany and Britain as examples. In the post-war years, Germany's money elite—rooted in industrial production—succeeded in preserving its interests in how the state financed its political programme. The social security system was not overly distributive, and state spending was aligned with the interests of the economic elite: support for industry and labour welfare. Offshore finance, then, was simply a means for the political elite to sweeten the deal for the moneyed classes. In Britain, the post-war tax and bank bargains were less aligned with the interests of an economic elite rooted in finance. The more strongly tax-based financing of the welfare state and tax policies in general were strongly redistributive. Moreover, bank regulations and the growing importance of US American finance undermined the financial elites' traditional way of making money. Offshore finance was a means to uphold the old order: decreasing taxation outside of wartime and maintaining the primacy of the City of London.

Theoretically, offshore finance can affect state power through both sides of the balance sheet—claims (tax) and liabilities (debt). In practice, because of the strategies taken by states to mitigate the effects of offshore tax planning, it is offshore banking that has been the central mechanism linking offshore finance with state power. Given the central importance of offshore banking for the power of the state, the offshore literature's focus on tax planning led to a false understanding of the *raison d'être* of offshore finance. The main purpose of offshore finance is not simply to *shelter* the money of the wealthy and the multinational corporations. Its main purpose is to *create* that money in the first place. Offshore finance's potency in affecting state power lies in its ability to create global credit-money at preferential conditions. The markets for offshore dollar, or Eurodollar, drive offshoring.

Given that money creation is a shared power between the state and banks, if follows that an encounter with the offshore world does not happen against the state's will. It happens with its support or at least in tacit agreement.[38] This does not mean, however, that the state has always been in control. In times of crisis, offshore finance can turn the state into the sorcerer's apprentice who no longer commands the spirits that it called upon.

The effect of offshore finance on state power is, indeed, not straightforward. Its power-enhancing effects are attractive for the state until—in times of financial crises—the costs of offshore money creation and tax planning outweigh the benefits. Offshore money creation persistently enhanced the power of the

---

[38] Palan 1998; Altamura 2017; Braun, Krampf, and Murau 2020.

state to unite resources between the 1950s and the early 1980s. Yet, it did so to a differing degree, depending on the unique constellation of political and economic elites in a country, the strategy to finance the state, and the role off-shore finance played therein. In Latin America, the price of offshore money creation—the limited ability of the state to do anything effectively to halt the problems that had been created offshore—became clear with the debt crises of the 1980s and 1990s. In Europe, it took until the global financial crisis 2007–09 for this price to materialize. Yet, by then, the size of the global Eurodollar markets had grown so big and had become so intrinsic to government and corporate financing that none of the case study countries, apart from Mexico, found a way to get out of it. As a result, Britain, Germany, and Brazil are now stuck with a system of offshore money creation that is at once indispensable and highly volatile. Propping up offshore money creation and making it work for state power ties up political and economic capital in increasing proportions.

# 2

# State power in the age of offshore finance

Studying the relationship between state power and offshore finance creates a twin challenge. There are, first, conceptual issues. As Quentin Skinner points out, 'there has never been any agreed concept to which the word *state* has answered.'[1] State power is an essentially contested concept.[2] It cannot be given definitive meaning. It can only be interpreted in its historical and geographical context.[3] For instance, the German state and its sources of power are different today than they were, say, in the 1920s or 1970s. They also differ, as we shall see, in fundamental aspects from the Brazilian, Mexican, or British states and their sources of power.

Offshore finance, on the other hand, is a new concept in international studies. We thus need to spell out what exactly it is and to what extent it is a specific and influential phenomenon in the international political economy.

From these conceptual issues follows, second, an empirical challenge. We must pinpoint where and how we see state power in the real world, despite its contested nature. Likewise, we must find a way to make offshore financial flows visible despite their obscure legal nature.[4]

This chapter is dedicated to addressing the first of the two challenges: the analysis of the concepts of state power and offshore finance. It creates the foundation for the empirical analysis in subsequent chapters. The aim of this concept analysis is to lessen the tension between the quest for identifying enduring patterns through comparative analysis, and the necessity to account for the unique historical and geographical contingencies of different states. Getting this balance right is particularly important in research that compares, as this book does, states from different regions that have come to modern statehood by different paths.[5] To do so, it is paramount to carefully analyse and reassess our concepts. For they may become indistinct or stretched thin as they travel across time and space.[6] Without conceptual reassessment, our empirical

---

[1] Skinner 2009, 326.
[2] Gallie 1956.
[3] Berenskoetter 2016.
[4] Sharman 2010; Pistor 2020.
[5] Tilly 1990; Centeno 2002.
[6] Sartori 1970.

*Offshore Finance and State Power*. Andrea Binder, Oxford University Press. © Andrea Binder (2023).
DOI: 10.1093/oso/9780192870124.003.0002

analyses risk being out of sync with the real world. We also fall more easily for a teleological reading of the past. A concept analysis is thus more than a simple definition. It determines, in the words of Goertz and Mahoney, 'what is inherent and important'[7] in the object under study.

I argue in the following that what is inherent in and important for both state power and offshore finance—the glue that holds them together and makes their relationship relevant for the international political economy—is *money*.

Yet, money is rarely at the forefront of the minds of scholars of international studies. One reason for that omission is that dominant economic thought frames money as a neutral veil of real economic activity.[8] Money has long been portrayed as natural, politically neutral, and scarce. Following the 2008 financial crisis and its response, this framing of money has been unveiled as mythical.[9] Central bankers reluctantly admitted that they create money simply by crediting someone's account.[10] Quantitative easing pushed up share prices, increasing the wealth of shareholders.[11] Money creation thus has redistributive effects.[12] Also, Western governments' monetary response to the economic shocks caused by the COVID-19 pandemic reached unprecedented levels. In short, post-2008 money has neither been natural, nor politically neutral, nor scarce. Rather, framing money that way has been an intellectual and political project rooted in John Lock's monetary thought of the late seventeenth century.[13] The success of that project made scholars disregard money's social and constitutional nature.[14] They stopped interrogating how money's nature changes across time and space and how that affects politics. As Mehrling points out, the discipline misses a 'money view'.[15]

In the following, I put forth such a 'money view' on state power and offshore finance by taking the nature of money and the process of creating it seriously. If Charles Tilly famously argued that war made states and states made war,[16] the money view contends that money creates states and states create money.

This shift in perspective is not to argue that war did not play a significant role in the development of modern states across Europe. It is simply to say that next

---

[7] Goertz and Mahoney 2012, 206.
[8] Borio and Disyatat 2011.
[9] Eich 2020; van 't Klooster and Fontan 2020.
[10] McLeay, Radia, and Thomas 2014; Deutsche Bundesbank 2017.
[11] https://www.bankofengland.co.uk/monetary-policy/quantitative-easing, last accessed 10 January 2022.
[12] Desan 2014; Sahr 2017; Koddenbrock 2019.
[13] Eich 2020.
[14] On money as a social relationship see Ingham (2004); on money as a constitutional project, see Desan 2014.
[15] Mehrling 2011, 1–10.
[16] Tilly 1990, ch. 3.

to security, money creation is essential for the development and survival of the modern state—in Europe and beyond. Yet, while security and war receive a lot of attention in international studies, money creation does not. Surely, there is little controversy that revenue is a matter of life and death for the modern state.[17] Taxation[18] and sovereign debt[19] hence preoccupy scholars of international political economy. What constitutes the money that exchanges hands and crosses borders, and how it is created, has received much less attention however. The money view is one way to address this conceptual lacuna.

In the following, I spell it out in three steps. I first discuss the nature of money to overcome the dominant depoliticized and ahistorical treatment of money so widespread in international studies. I then analyse state power and offshore finance respectively from a perspective that centres on the nature of money and its creation. Finally, I discuss what happens theoretically when one encounters the other.

# 1 Money

Money is a liability for the issuer and a credit for the user.[20] Creating it is a shared power between states and banks.[21] The state and banks cannot create money without simultaneously creating debt. The issuing of notes, coins, or bonds is a liability on the government's balance sheet. A note in a national currency, say a £10 note, is nothing other than a promise by the British government to pay back £10 to whomever holds the note. The same is true for the government bond, only its value is much larger. That is, those same coins, notes, and bonds that are liabilities for the British government are an asset for their owners. Therefore, as Ingham argues, all money is credit.[22] Obviously, a government can only create money by going into debt if it has an asset on the other side of its balance sheet. Otherwise, no creditor (small or large) would be willing to extend credit to the government. These assets are the citizens' tax debt. That is, a citizen in possession of our £10 note can, for instance, use it to buy a paperback book. Or she can use the £10 note to discharge £10 of her tax

[17] Tilly 1990; Schumpeter 1991; Centeno 2002; Macdonald 2003.
[18] see Swank 2003, 2016; Genschel and Schwarz 2011; Hakelberg and Seelkopf 2021.
[19] see Krasner 1999; Tomz 2007; Tomz and Wright 2013.
[20] In the following, I strongly rely on Ingham's notion of credit-money. As with all theories of money, credit-money is contested. However, as the aim of the analysis is to align concepts with the real world, the credit theory of money is best suited for it is closest to how practitioners describe money creation, McLeay, Radia, and Thomas 2014; Deutsche Bundesbank 2016.
[21] Strange 1994.
[22] Ingham 2004.

debt. By exclusively accepting the money that the state itself issues as a means to discharge tax debt, the state ensures the validity of sovereign money. This is why, simply put, one cannot repay a tax bill with a life insurance.

The circle of money, tax, and debt closes when the state's financiers extend credit to the government only if there is a valid money that can reliably account for how much the government owes them. Ultimately, money is a means to account for and to settle debt, most importantly tax and sovereign debt.[23] At first, taxation and sovereign debt developed in Europe throughout the fifteenth–seventeenth centuries as two separate state practices. Yet, over time, they came to reinforce each other, creating modern money and constructing a net of social relations between issuer (the state) and users (the citizens) in its wake.

The social relations constructed by money are organized in a hierarchy (Figure 2.1).[24] At the top of the hierarchy is sovereign money, the state's promise to pay. It is the most sought-after credit because it is backed by tax revenue and the state's monopoly power of issue. Sovereign money is followed in the hierarchy by deposits, loans, and all sorts of financial instruments. These various forms of private debt constitute, in the words of Ingham, 'near money'.[25] They entail not only the promise to pay back but also the promise to be transferable into sovereign money at some point in the future.

The hierarchy is organized by differential rates of interest, expressing the differing degree of the risk of broken promises to pay back inherent in the

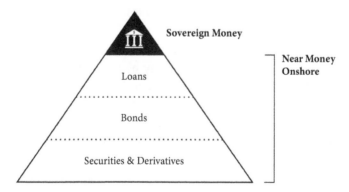

**Figure 2.1** The hierarchy of money
*Source*: Own illustration, based on Ingham (2004).

---

[23] Ibid.
[24] Knapp 1924; Ingham 2004; Mehrling 2012.
[25] Ingham 2004, 30.

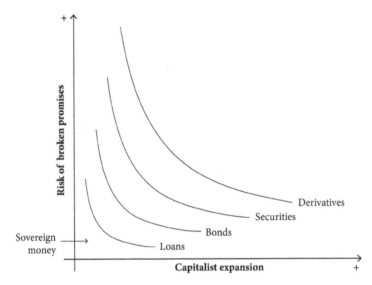

**Figure 2.2** Risk of broken promises and capitalist expansion
*Source*: Own illustration.

different forms of money (Figure 2.2). The nearer it is to the top, the more transferable is one form of credit into another. The distinctiveness of sovereign money is that it alone is transferable into any other form of credit. Near money—in the form of loans, bonds, securities, other financial instruments—becomes monetized once it is exchanged 'for sovereign promises to pay that are fully transferable and acceptable anywhere within the monetary space defined by the money of account' as Ingham states.[26]

The central bank plays an important role in the transferability of different forms of private debt into sovereign money by taking the banking system's liabilities—in times of financial distress—onto its balance sheet.[27] Transferring near money into sovereign money, the central bank becomes the interface between the financial markets and the state. However, private debt is usually not monetized. Rather, the proliferation of debt instruments allows for capitalist expansion via private money creation hooked to sovereign money.[28] In other words, modern money hinges on the state authority that accepts its existence and thereby guarantees its validity.[29]

---

[26] Ibid., 138.
[27] Ingham 2004; Mehrling 2016.
[28] Ingham 2004; Pistor 2020.
[29] Knapp 1924.

## 2  State power

Unlike the nature of money, the state, and its sources of power figure promi-
nently in international studies. Yet, most scholars do not spell out what the state
is. They assume that, for their analytical purposes, the state can be treated as a
unitary actor. This assumption is an analytical shortcut to deal with the trade-
off between theoretical parsimony and empirical richness.[30] That shortcut
is sensible in the context of security. The modern state, at least in its ideal-
type incarnation, enjoys within its territory a 'monopoly of legitimate physical
violence',[31] as Weber famously put it.

When it comes to money, however, the modern state does not enjoy a
monopoly. Historically, the governments of nascent modern states in Europe
and the merchant classes struggled over the power to create money. The merchant classes dominated the system of private debt while the state possessed
a monopoly over coinage and currency issue.[32] The foundation of the Bank
of England in 1694 represented the first institutionalized compromise in that
struggle. It divided monetary sovereignty between the state and banks.[33]

That is, next to a monopoly on violence, the modern state is characterized
by the shared power of money creation. When it comes to money, the state
cannot be framed as a unitary actor. Any analysis that takes money seriously
thus needs to spell out what the modern state and its sources of power are.

### Associating to rule and mobilizing resources

From the money view too, Weber can be a central point of reference. For
the monopoly on violence and territoriality are only the starting points in
his deliberations on the nature of the modern state.[34] He adds a third and, in
his own judgement 'fundamental',[35] characteristic to his concept of the modern state: the material means necessary for administration. Taking these three
critical elements together, Weber says:

> [T]he modern state is an institutional association of rule (*Herrschaftsver-
> band*) which has successfully established the monopoly of physical violence

[30] Lake 2008.
[31] Weber 1994, 310p.
[32] Ingham 2004; Vogl 2015.
[33] Strange 1994; Ingham 2004; Vogl 2015.
[34] Weber 1994, 310f.
[35] Ibid., 315.

as a means of rule within a territory, for which purpose it unites in the hands of its leaders the material means of operation.[36]

Weber's notion of the modern state as an 'institutional association of rule' and the fact that in order to rule, the state needs to 'unite ... the material means of operation' are often neglected in the reception of Weber in international studies. The meaning of 'institutional association of rule' is not relevant to those who consider the state a unitary actor. And the need to accumulate 'the material means of operation' are, if at all considered, usually reduced to taxation. One of the reasons for that neglect may be that the German original is difficult to translate elegantly into English.

Nevertheless, both elements—the idea of the state as an institutional association of rule (*Herrschaftsverband*) and the emphasis on mobilizing and centralizing resources for its operation (*Betriebsmittel vereinigen*)—are helpful for analysing the relationship between state power and offshore finance across different countries. I therefore explain them here in more detail.

The term *Herrschaftsverband* (institutional association of rule) is a neologism Weber created for the purpose of defining the modern state. The compound noun brings together *Herrschaft* with *Verband*. The term *Herrschaft* has a historical and a sociological meaning. In the historical sense, a *Herrschaft* was the fiefdom of a nobleman; it was the lowest rank with full feudal rights. It constitutes the institutionalized relationship between *Herr* and *Vasall*, between lord and liege. This feudal relationship was characterized by a clear hierarchy but also by mutual support. The notion of a hierarchical but mutually beneficial relationship lives on in the sociological meaning of the term *Herrschaft* (rule), which describes a hierarchical power relationship that sets itself apart from sheer power insofar as the ruler can only rule if considered legitimate by the ruled. A *Verband* is an association, a group of people coming together for a specific purpose akin to a club, a society, or an otherwise privately organized group. The term lives on in professional or business associations.

The emphasis on the need for the state to accumulate resources, in turn, is Weber's way of recognizing that revenue is crucial for the modern state's existence. With his phrasing, he highlights that the *Herrschaftsverband* must mobilize and centralize these resources. Unlike in the pre-modern era, the material means of operation are impersonal. They come from the collective.[37]

---

[36] Ibid., 316.
[37] Ibid., 315–317.

Weber's notion of the *Herrschaftsverband* allows us to understand the modern state as elite rule, institutionalized through centralizing administration and through mutualizing the resources necessary to finance the rulers' political goals. The individual character of any given state, he argues, is shaped by the question from which social strata members of the *Herrschaftsverband* are recruited[38] and what their strategy is to mobilize and centralize resources for financing their politics. Importantly, the power of the ruling elites is not absolute. It is marked by a mutual dependency between ruler and ruled.

The money view specifies this relationship between the ruler and ruled as creditor–debtor relations between the state, financiers, and taxpayers. It points to the intimate relation between modern money and the state. The creation of money is a power shared between states and financiers and it is dependent on tax payments. Consequently, state power is relational and contested. The contestation happens within the institutional association of rule and between those inside and outside of it. All states face the 'fundamental political problem of legitimating rule that arises out of the clash of interests and beliefs among their citizens' as Thompson puts it.[39]

The money view identifies the conflict over how to mobilize and centralize resources as one key conflict creating issues of legitimacy for the exercise of state power. Given that the issuance of money is a liability for the state that can only work in relation to an asset—tax income—the conflict over how to finance the state affects both sides of the state's balance sheet. On the liabilities side is the conflict over who is allowed to create money and how the resulting costs (risks) and benefits are distributed. The outcome of that conflict is a country's bank bargain.[40] On the asset side of the state's balance sheet, is the conflict over who must pay how much tax on which elements of their wealth and income as well as the question of how the revenue is spent. The outcome is a country's tax bargain. Through money, the two bargains are intrinsically linked.

## Bank and tax bargains

The bank bargain reflects the struggle in which the state and financiers wrestle over market entry (who can open a bank), access to credit, the price of debt, bank regulation, and the allocation of losses in case of default.[41] These rules, in turn, determine the competitive structure and size of the

---

[38] Ibid., 318pp.
[39] Thompson 2010, 145f.
[40] Calomiris and Haber 2014.
[41] Ibid.

banking sector in the respective country. Access to credit determines who in a society can spend today and repay in the future. The price of debt comprises the economic, political, and social costs the different actors face when going into debt. Bank regulation determines what banks can do and at what level of risk. Finally, the allocation of losses determines which social groups must bear the costs of sovereign debt, sovereign default, and bank failures. The central bank, indeed, plays a central role in that struggle. A central bank makes it possible for financiers to extend private credit to the state. At the same time, creating central bank reserves through the issuing of government bonds, the state is—since Bagehot's days—the 'lender of last resort' to its own financiers.[42]

The tax bargain reflects the struggle in which the state and citizens wrestle over who must pay how much tax. In that struggle, the government must mediate between the interests of different groups in society. Generally, the state taxes capital by putting a levy on the value of capital stock (e.g. real estate, estate, and wealth taxes) or on the flow of capital income (e.g. the capital income tax). Levies on labour are wage taxes and social security contributions. In addition, the state collects indirect taxes (e.g. value added tax (VAT) and other consumption taxes). Indirect taxes are not linked to the source and level of income of the taxpayer. They are thus a particularly heavy burden for those with lower incomes because they accumulate to a larger share of their disposable income than they do for wealthier groups.[43] The struggle between the different groups of taxpayers, then, is about how the different sources of tax are balanced and how the revenue is spent—most centrally to fight wars, to finance the welfare state, or to service sovereign debt. For the government to be successful, the tax bargain must create trust among taxpayers that each group pays its fair share. In addition, to sustain tax compliance, the state must ensure that taxpayers are confident that they will receive the promised, although not guaranteed, material returns for their contributions.[44]

The nature of the bank and tax bargains is fundamental for the state's legitimacy because the expectations of taxpayers are irreconcilable with those of the financiers: Individual taxpayers expect public goods in return for their payments. Firms expect low interest rates and favourable bankruptcy laws to sustain company financing. Financiers, on the other hand, request that tax money is spent on serving interest payments and debt. They aim for interest rates that make their lending profitable. And so, to cite Thompson, '[t]he state cannot possibly, at any given moment, act as the guardian of all its citizens'

---

[42] Ingham 2004; Vogl 2015; Mehrling 2016.
[43] Piketty 2014, ch. 13.
[44] Levi 1989.

material interests. It has to side with some over others.'[45] Underneath the struggle between the state, taxpayers, and financiers over how to finance the state lies the question of class.[46]

## State power from the money view

Starting from Weber's notion of the state and taking the political and constitutional nature of money seriously, state power is the ability of the institutional association of rule to mobilize and centralize resources to finance its political goals. This power is not absolute. For the state to be able to accumulate resources in the form of money, it must enter a creditor–debtor relationship with financiers and taxpayers. State power is thus a function of the state's ability to mediate successfully the central political conflict over how the costs and benefits of money creation and taxation are distributed between different groups of society. The conflict is institutionalized in a country's banking and tax systems. The banking system is the institutionalized expression of the power relationship between the state and its financiers. It articulates who creates credit, who has access to credit, and under which conditions.[47] The tax system is the institutional expression of the power relationship between the state and taxpayers. It articulates who must pay how much based on what principles. Borrowing from and taxing citizens are an expression of, and a limit to, state power. Modern money makes state power relational and contested.

The notion of state power as articulated here emphasizes state autonomy (the ability of the state to act without external constraints) over state influence (the ability of the state to make others do what it wants).[48] This emphasis reflects that the state's ability to unite and use resources in an autonomous way is a precondition for it to exert influence. Furthermore, the notion highlights the relational nature of state power,[49] while being agnostic towards its purpose. It is based on the premise that, fundamentally, politics is about the conflict over the interests of different groups. These conflicts are reflected in and shaped through historically grown political and economic institutions such that inescapably—though not unchangeably—some interests are privileged over others.[50] Finally, seeing the state from the money view also puts a spotlight on the material dimension of state power, de-emphasizing other,

[45] Thompson 2010, 145.
[46] Macdonald 2003; Ingham 2004.
[47] Calomiris and Haber 2014.
[48] Cohen 2013.
[49] Dahl 1957.
[50] Hall and Taylor 1996.

equally important dimensions such as military or ideational might. Such a focused perspective is understood to be complimentary to other approaches. It is warranted because the shared power of money creation and the role of taxation herein has received insufficient attention in the study of international political economy.

## 3 Offshore finance

Compared to state power, offshore finance is a new concept in international studies. In the past decade, scholars carved out three characteristics that sets offshore finance apart from onshore or regular cross-border financial flows: (1) The underlying offshore financial services are exclusively offered to non-residents of the respective jurisdiction. (2) They entail zero or low taxation and regulation. (3) They make financial flows, ownership, and liabilities invisible.[51]

The non-resident principle evolved as economic and political actors have innovated offshore financial services. Whilst regulators were open to the new financial products, they were also keen to ring-fence their domestic economies from potentially harmful effects. So, they allowed these services to be offered exclusively to non-residents.[52] Had Switzerland, say, applied the same tax regime to its residents as it has to non-residents since the 1920s, it is unlikely the country's infrastructure would be in the good shape it is today. Yet, offering low regulatory hurdles and tax rates to non-residents has been a welcome opportunity to attract inward financial flows as a means of economic development.[53] The lax regulatory and tax environments are, in turn, a precondition for those non-residents to rout financial flows through offshore financial centres. Otherwise, the transaction costs for going offshore would be too high.

Next to the non-resident principle and a lax tax and regulatory environment, invisibility is a third characteristic of offshore financial services. Most scholars of offshore finance use the terms secrecy or anonymity to describe the obscure nature of offshore finance. Yet, secrecy and anonymity are only two ways of obscuring economic realities. Other means include, for instance, trusts and accounting techniques. A trust is a legal construct that allows the owner of something, say shares in a company, to give away these shares for the benefit of a third person, without making this beneficiary the new owner of the shares. Rather, the trust holds and manages them according to the will of the original

---

[51] Palan, Murphy, and Chavagneux 2010; Sharman 2010.
[52] Palan, Murphy, and Chavagneux 2010; O'Malley 2015.
[53] Hampton 1996a. Genschel 2005; Ogle 2017.

owner. That is, the original owner gives up legal ownership but retains control over their assets. The third person, in turn, can enjoy the benefits, for instance the dividend payments, without being their legal owner. The wealth, private or commercial, and its owner become invisible.[54] Or take banks' accounting techniques. Banks can keep certain financial instruments or transactions, such as trust or fiduciary funds, off their balance sheet.[55] They can also book certain transactions as taking place offshore when they really take place onshore. This way whole asset classes or financial flows can disappear from the books. That is, offshore financial services become invisible because of the logic of 'calculated ambiguity', to use Jason Sharman's fitting term.[56] Calculated ambiguity means that, thanks to offshoring, a company or an individual can appear simultaneously rich and poor, here and far away, as the owner of something or not. It can give two diametrically opposed answers to the same question depending on who is asking and both answers are legally correct.[57] Take the question about the financial health of a company as an example. A German multinational company can shift its profits via shell companies to, say, Luxembourg and then claim to be loss-making to the tax authorities while at the same time present the companies' annual profits to its shareholders. Likewise, a bank can shift its debt via special purpose vehicles incorporated in the Cayman Islands off its balance sheet in the country where it is under regulatory supervision, say in the City of London. The bank can be highly leveraged and follow prudential rules at the same time.[58] As the term calculated ambiguity suggests, it is by design.

Any form of capital consists of two components, 'an asset and the legal code', as Pistor explains.[59] The legal code determines property rights, collateral, contract rights, etc. specific to that asset. Offshore financial services are marked by a coding strategy that intentionally moves the underlying assets out of sight[60]—be it of the tax authorities, investors, creditors, or ex-spouses. Taken together, the non-resident principle, the lax tax and regulatory regime, and the intentional invisibility are necessary and collectively sufficient criteria to identify a specific cross-border financial transaction as an offshore financial service.

However, recently, some political economists studying cross-border financial flows have started to use the term 'offshore' as synonymous with all foreign

---

[54] Langbein 1997; Harrington 2016a; Knobel 2017.
[55] Zucman 2014; Harrington 2016a.
[56] Sharman 2010, 1.
[57] Sharman 2010.
[58] Ibid.
[59] Pistor 2020.
[60] Ibid.

currency flows outside the economic actor's country of residence. In these analyses, offshore finance has come to replace the term financial globalization.[61] Unfortunately, such a broad understanding undermines the goal to determine what is specific and influential about the empirical phenomenon of offshore finance. Using offshore finance and financial globalization synonymously mixes visible financial flows open to all economic actors with the invisible financial flows reserved for a set of exclusive actors: global banks, large multinational corporations, and high net-worth individuals. It obscures the specific nature of offshore finance and its potential impact on state power.

In this book, financial globalization is considered the container vessel that international political economy has long and insightfully studied,[62] while offshore finance is the vessel's machine room.[63] That machine room deserves more and more targeted attention. It is the subject of this book. The remainder of this chapter therefore discusses the nature and evolution of the two core pillars of offshore finance: offshore money creation and offshore tax planning.

## Offshore money creation

In the final years of World War II, the United States and Britain established the Bretton Woods System to regulate the international monetary system in conjunction with their domestic banking systems. The goal was to prevent another Great Depression. The resulting highly regulated financial systems limited the business of Britain's international banks which, up until the war, were the world's leading banks running sophisticated international financial transactions. The US American banking system, on the contrary, was still parochial and lagging its role as the provider of the world's new reserve currency, the US dollar.[64] Smelling an opportunity, British bankers in the 1950s came up with the idea to create US-dollar-denominated credit against their growing US dollar reserves from international clients.[65] The Bank of England made the trade in US dollars possible by accepting a new accounting technique. The City's merchant bankers, merging ring-fencing with little regulation, suggested that transactions where all parties were non-resident would be considered 'offshore'

[61] See Mehrling 2015; Murau, Rini, and Haas 2020.
[62] See Helleiner 1994; Kose et al. 2009; Schularick and Steger 2010.
[63] I take the metaphor of the machine room from interviews with practitioners who often referred to offshore financial services as the machine room or the plumbing of the international financial system.
[64] Helleiner 1994.
[65] Schenk 1998.

and not subject to national financial regulation. All other transactions would be onshore and regulated by the Bank of England.[66]

With this accounting technique, the term 'offshore' found its way into banking jargon. It described a new, specific form of cross-border financial transaction—namely one based on the non-resident principle, which was largely unregulated, barely taxed, and invisible to everyone outside the exclusive circle of partaking bankers and central bankers.[67] Trading US dollars outside the United States meant that transactions were outside the jurisdiction of the Federal Reserve and the US Treasury. Trading US dollars among non-resident banks in London meant they were outside the jurisdiction of Britain. The new technique allowed the circumvention of US American and British regulations at the same time.[68] Furthermore, as is the case for all interbank deposits, the interest paid on deposits or coupons in the Eurodollar markets is paid gross to the non-resident investor, who then choses to declare (or not) this income to their country of residency. If the financial instrument was a bond, they were issued as bearer bonds and hence the ultimate ownership was invisible.[69] Consequently, offshore dollar credit was cheaper and available in volumes not accessible through the highly regulated domestic banking systems.[70] The offshore dollar markets grew substantially and went from London further offshore to the Channel and Cayman Islands.[71] Participants called the London-based offshore US dollar markets Eurodollar markets to signify that these were US dollar transactions conducted in Europe. The term stayed even as the practice of creating offshore credit spread from the City of London to other offshore financial centres.

The emergence and significance of the Eurodollar market has been widely studied in international political economy and economic history.[72] It is only recently, however, that scholars identified the Eurodollar markets as the hallmark of the offshore financial system.[73]

At the outset, in the 1950s, classical banking was underpinning the nascent offshore dollar markets. Banks lent out US dollars against their US dollar deposits. They acted as intermediaries. There was one fundamental difference to classical banking though: there was no lender of last resort. Neither the

[66] O'Malley 2015.
[67] Burn 1999.
[68] Ibid.; Helleiner 1994; Green 2016.
[69] Norfield 2016.
[70] Helleiner 1994; He and McCauley 2010; Norfield 2016.
[71] Hampton 1996a, 1996b.
[72] Helleiner 1994; Schenk 1998; Burn 1999; Green 2016; Braun, Krampf, and Murau 2020.
[73] McCauley 2005; He and McCauley 2012; Ogle 2017.

Bank of England nor the Federal Reserve considered it their responsibility.[74] Nevertheless, the banks extended US dollar denominated credit at growing rates.

In the two decades following the Eurodollar's inception, next to the Eurocurrency market, two further elements of the offshore banking system developed: first in the 1960s the Eurobond market, a market for long-term securities. Eurobonds became the mainstay for all further financial innovation in the Eurodollar markets. To this day, no matter the financial instrument developed in offshore financial markets, the underlying security is the Eurobond.[75] The 1970s then saw the development of the Eurodollar loans market. Eurodollar loans were mostly extended to governments in the developing world, especially Latin America. Given the related volume and risks involved in Eurodollar loans, the lending banks started to work together as groups, so-called bank syndicates, to provide the funds for an individual borrower. The syndicates brought together European banks, first among them the Societé Générale, Crédit Lonnais, Deutsche Bank, Barclays, Midland, and Lloyds Bank. The Eurodollar loans market has been a catalyst for growing interdependence among internationally active banks through interlocking their balance sheets. With the advent of the syndicated Eurodollar loans market, risks became systemic.[76] The three pillars—Eurocurrency, Eurobond, and Euroloan markets—allowed European banks, even before the gold standard ended in 1971, to create fiat offshore US dollars.[77]

From the money view, we can acknowledge the historical importance of this moment. Since the seventeenth century, the power to create money has been shared between the state and *domestic* banks. Offshore money creation extended that power to *foreign* banks. Offshore banking 'bifurcates'[78] money issuance and money creation across borders. It has changed the nature of modern money.

The new power of European banks to create US dollars offshore did not go unnoticed. The Fed Chairman at the time, Arthur Burns, remarked that they had 'invented a new dollar creating mechanism of great power'.[79] Nevertheless, in the face of the 1973 oil shock, the United States, European governments, and their bureaucrats, consciously decided to let the system develop

---

[74] Burn 1999.

[75] O'Malley 2015.

[76] Altamura 2017.

[77] Friedman 1971; Goldfeld 1976.

[78] The metaphor of bifurcation goes back to Palan (2002), who used it to describe sovereignty in the context of offshore finance.

[79] Cited in Altamura 2017, 90.

unregulated.[80] The next decade was thus another decisive one for the development of offshore banking. Plagued by interest rate volatility, Eurodollar banks searched for hedges against the related risks. In 1981 they came up with three new derivatives for that purpose: currency swaps, interest rate swaps, and Eurodollar futures. All three derivatives are short-term credits. The three Eurodollar derivatives changed the participating banks' business model from a deposit-based approach to a liabilities-based approach because they made it possible, for the first time in banking history, to turn liabilities into profits.[81] The derivatives also became the market-based solution for addressing liquidity risks in a system without an institutional lender of last resort.

Despite the growing importance of the Eurodollar markets, the Federal Reserve and the US Treasury did not—and do not until this day—officially recognize their existence. To them, there is only a domestic US dollar.[82] According to this view, there is no structural difference between a US dollar created by US American banks in the United States and a US dollar created by global banks in offshore financial centres.

Yet, the money view reveals a structural difference between the two: the US dollar is a *public* liability of the Federal Reserve, the Eurodollar is a *private* liability of *foreign* banks. That is, once the US dollar was created and traded offshore, the top layer of the hierarchy of money was removed (see Figure 2.3).

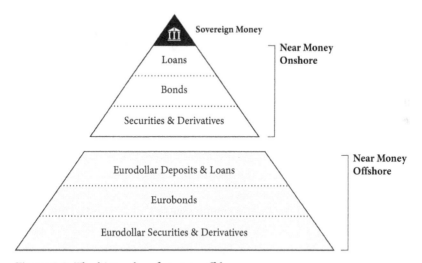

**Figure 2.3** The hierarchy of money offshore
*Source*: Own illustration.

[80] Altamura 2017; Braun, Krampf, and Murau 2020.
[81] O'Malley 2015.
[82] Mehrling 2016.

Since the Eurodollar is traded between non-residents, the Federal Reserve does not take the private promises to pay of non-resident banks onto its balance sheet. The Eurodollar, in other words, remains, at every stage in the hierarchy 'near money', which is denominated in US dollars. As a result, the Eurodollar system could expand US dollar credit *as if* it were transferable into sovereign money, although it was not—the signature of calculated ambiguity. In the words of an interviewee:

> The fundamental proposition of the Eurodollar market [is that] there is no dollars in it. So the things that banks are actually trading are promises to get dollars, which nobody ever wants. I mean no corporation that has a Eurodollar arrangement with a Eurodollar bank actually converts into physical Federal Reserve notes. This doesn't happen, nobody wants dollars. They just want to be able to transact these various forms of liabilities so that they all can claim that they have dollars, because that's what allows it to work. … The Eurodollar market is the furthest thing away from actual currency, because nobody wants the currency. They just want to have liabilities that they, if ever needed to, can convert to dollars somehow. What it really boils down to is the market saying, oh we don't have any dollars, but we are very certain that we can attain them if we ever needed to.[83]

In the absence of a lender of last resort, the transferability of near money from a lower to a higher level in the hierarchy was ensured by global banks. They transferred 'opaque, risky, long-term assets into money-like, short-term liabilities.'[84] Essentially, the Euromarkets were creating, in Hayek's sense, a denationalized money.[85] Eliminating the top layer of the hierarchy meant that, for the first time since the seventeenth century, money creation became ostensibly fully private, competitive, and removed from central banking.

However, we can deduce from the money view that in a system of near money, the trade-off between the risk of broken promises and the volume of money created increases in scale and scope (Figure 2.4). In other words, financial crises are intrinsic to offshore finance.[86]

Yet, between the 1950s and the early 2000s it seemed as if Hayek was right. The private denationalized Eurodollar markets appeared to perform well. They were growing. Already by the end of the 1980s, Eurodollar deposit

[83] Author's telephone interview with financial analyst, May 2017.
[84] Pozsar et al. 2010, 1.
[85] Hayek 1990.
[86] He and McCauley 2010.

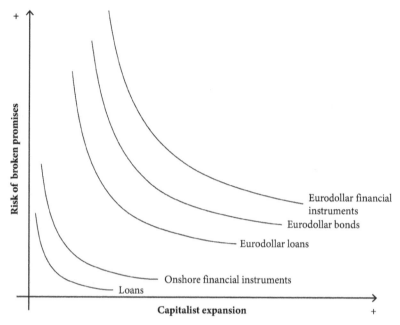

**Figure 2.4**  Risk and capitalist expansion offshore
*Source*: Own illustration.

markets alone outsized the domestic dollar deposit market.[87] Liquidity problems were solved through financial innovation in the form of derivatives
which allowed effectively matching surplus and deficit banks. Over time,
the Eurodollar became, according to an interviewee, 'the global currency'.[88]
With the help of globally active banks, offshore money creation expanded
dramatically.

The offshore banking system performed so well that by the end of the 1980s,
the arbitrage possibilities on both sides of the Atlantic led to an equalization of
interest rates. The London Interbank Offer Rate (LIBOR)—the interest rate at
which banks in London lend US dollars to each other—started to closely track
the Effective Federal Funds rate (EFFR)—the interest rate at which domestic
banks in the United States lend US dollars to each other.[89] The offshore dollar
market and the regular US dollar market appeared to have integrated into one
global US dollar market.[90] The Federal Reserve, the Bank of England, and the

---

[87] Windecker Jr. 1993.
[88] Author's telephone interview with financial analyst, May 2017.
[89] See https://fred.stlouisfed.org/graph/fredgraph.png?g=yfeV, Board of Governors of the Federal
Reserve System (US), Effective Federal Funds Rate [DFF], retrieved from FRED, Federal Reserve Bank
of St. Louis, 2 December 2020.
[90] O'Malley 2015.

BIS had initially traced the emergent Eurodollar system statistically. Yet, with the end of the interest rate differentials, they unwound their statistical efforts by merging the Eurodollar statistics with other debt statistics.[91] The Eurodollar was now also statistically invisible.

Expressed in the logic of the hierarchy of money, the disappearance of the interest rate differentials between the Eurodollar and the US dollar meant that market participants thought that credit denominated in each had the same risk of a broken promise to pay back; they seemed to be on the same level in the hierarchy. One appeared transferable into the other. Unlike its onshore twin, the Eurodollar was seen as functioning without an authority that guarantees its validity.

On 9 August 2007, however, the Eurodollar turned out to be no longer transferable into US dollars. On that day, the interest rates for LIBOR and the EFFR diverged.[92] It became clear that the pricing of the Eurodollar was fundamentally flawed. When the Federal Reserve had no intention to buy the 'promises to pay' by non-American Eurodollar banks to ensure their liquidity, the validity of the Eurodollar was called into question. Interbank lending froze. The hierarchy of money had broken down. The Eurodollar banks turned to their central banks for help. The European central banks' measures, however, proved insufficient to reignite interbank lending. Liquidity only came back once the Federal Reserve decided to monetize European banks' Eurodollar liabilities.[93] The tool the Fed chose for this were central bank liquidity swaps with selected foreign central banks, including the Bank of England, the European Central Bank, the Bank of Japan, and the Banco Central do Brasíl. The Fed acted indirectly as a lender of last resort to foreign commercial banks.[94] Roughly ten years on, the Fed used similar measures again in response to the COVID-19 pandemic market volatilities in March 2020. The Fed's decision to backstop the system is the latest decisive milestone in the evolution of the offshore banking system.[95] The Federal Reserve now engenders the possibility for offshore banks to turn their Eurodollar liabilities created outside US regulatory purview into sovereign money, US dollars backed by the United States. Seventy years in the making, a new global monetary system has been perfected.

[91] Gruic and Wooldridge 2012.
[92] Goldberg, Kennedy, and Miu 2010.
[93] Hardie and Thompson 2020.
[94] Mehrling 2011; McDowell 2017.
[95] Pape 2021.

## Offshore tax planning

Yet, from the money view, we can also deduce that this system could not work without the fiscal side. Cross-border financial flows require minimal transaction costs. Moreover, by creating money, liabilities are created and thus assets must show up on the other side of the balance sheet.

The systematic offering of tax planning services to non-residents took off in the 1960s and 1970s when small banking centres such as Switzerland or the Cayman Islands made these services a deliberate strategy for economic development.[96] Offshore tax planning works through four principal techniques: concealing ownership, shifting profits from high to low tax jurisdictions (or debt the other way around), keeping debt off a corporation's balance sheet, and facilitating round-tripping, that is, turning domestic into foreign direct investment.[97]

To achieve the maximum impact, different services are combined through different layers of corporate structures—creating affiliates in different locations, with the parent company having partial or indirect ownership in them. The resulting corporate structures are legally complex and make it difficult to account for and to tax resulting income across the entire corporate structure.[98] The British gas and oil company BP, for example, has nearly 1,200 affiliates in eighty-four countries across twelve layers, that is, affiliates of affiliates of affiliates and so on.[99] To navigate the murky offshore waters, individuals and corporations rely on the stewardship of international lawyers, accountants, and bankers versed in the laws and regulations of the client's home country and that of the respective offshore financial centre. Without them, offshore finance became impossible.[100]

For a long time, Switzerland was the most prominent example of a financial centre that also offers tax planning services. Up until the 1980s, Switzerland was the leading European tax haven. Then Luxembourg, Liechtenstein, Hong Kong, Singapore, the Bahamas, and others moved into the market, too. Subsequently, a network of complementary services between the different offshore financial centres developed. For instance, most bank accounts in Switzerland are held by intermediary shell companies incorporated in Liechtenstein, the

---

[96]  Genschel 2005; Palan, Murphy, and Chavagneux 2010; Ogle 2017. The historical roots of tax havenry often date back much further, see Guex 2021.

[97]  Sharman 2010.

[98]  Blouin and Robinson 2019.

[99]  Palan and Mangraviti 2016.

[100]  Sharman 2010; Pistor 2020.

British Virgin Islands, and the Cayman Islands.[101] Panama and the British Virgin Islands specialize in the setup of shell companies.[102] Luxembourg is one of the preferred locations for the incorporation of mutual funds, the Cayman Islands for hedge funds, and Ireland for money funds.[103] The practice of pooling the assets of wealthy individuals into collective funds and the use of shell companies has aligned the tax planning strategies of individuals with that of corporations. Advisors manage individual wealth or the treasury of a corporation channel investment through offshore centres which have—given the original place of the investment and the final intended location—the most advantageous set of bilateral tax treaties.[104] These bilateral tax treaties bring us to the origin of an international tax system that allowed offshore tax planning to develop.

By the 1920s most countries in Europe, Latin America, North America, but also Russia, Japan, and China had consolidated their tax systems based on a combination of taxes on labour and capital.[105] Increasing trade between these and other regions across the globe put national tax systems under pressure from two sides. In the absence of agreements between countries on how to tax corporate income generated through international trade, it would be taxed twice—once in the corporation's country of residence and once in the country where the income was sourced. This approach would impede international trade. Alternatively, to promote international trade, the corporate income could be taxed in neither the residence nor source country. This approach would deprive the state of a valuable source of income and threaten the tax consensus reached at home.[106] In the context of the League of Nations, a set of countries solved this predicament through a network of bilateral tax treaties which allocate taxing rights between residence and source country. The bilateral tax treaties were based on a so-called model agreement. However, from the outset gaps and mismatches in these bilateral treaties bore the potential for tax avoidance.[107] As the network of bilateral tax treaties grew—by the end of the twentieth century more than 3,000 such treaties had been concluded[108]—and so did the potential for exploiting gaps and mismatches. Four developments drove the incentive and possibility to minimize the tax

[101] Zucman 2013.
[102] Findley, Nielson, and Sharman 2014.
[103] Zucman 2013; Fichtner 2016.
[104] Author's interviews with various tax advisors.
[105] Seelkopf et al. 2021.
[106] Levi 1989.
[107] Rixen 2008; cf. Hearson 2021.
[108] Christensen and Hearson 2019.

burden via cross-border tax planning. First, in the decades after the World Wars a significant number of states saw a steep increase in wealth, inheritance, corporate and capital income taxes. In combination with decolonialization and the related repatriation of assets, wealth and income were extracted from these groups in unprecedented shares. Simultaneously, the development of the Eurodollar markets increased cross-border financial flows. Both developments created incentives for small economies to stay outside the network of bilateral tax treaties to attract foreign capital by offering non-residents low taxes, lax regulations, and a means to keep financial flows under the rug. Third, with the advance of globally integrated supply chains, corporate financing changed from national domestic currency loans to international debt denominated in US dollars, often issued in offshore financial centres. The resulting exorbitant growth of global financial transactions between the 1980s and the early 2000s compounded the fourth driver, the onset of the digital economy. Consequently, states engaged in fierce competition over attracting and taxing what was increasingly considered footloose capital. They also struggled with taxing an economy increasingly less linked to any specific geographical location. In short, by the 1990s at the latest, it became obvious that the international tax regime of the 1920s was no longer fit for purpose.[109] Nevertheless, change failed to materialize.

Despite mounting short-comings and challenges, the international tax regime defied change because it was still serving the interest of developed economies;[110] tax haven hosting small states resisted change summoning sovereignty;[111] and the invisible nature of offshore tax planning and the Organization for Economic Co-operation and Development (OECD)'s strategy to address the problems technically rather than politically, undermined pressure from civil society.[112]

The 2007–09 global financial crisis eroded these stabilizing dynamics at once. Faced with surging sovereign debt and corporate misconduct on an epic scale, G20 governments pledged to crack down on tax havens with little deference for smaller states' sovereignty. Unilateral and multilateral initiatives to protect the state's tax base emerged. First among them was the 2010 United States Foreign Account Tax Compliance Act (FATCA), which provided a blueprint for the OECD's so-called base erosion and profit shifting (BEPS)

[109] OECD 1998.
[110] Genschel and Rixen 2015.
[111] Sharman 2006.
[112] Christensen and Hearson 2019.

project.[113] Under the threat of sanctions, FATCA forced foreign banks to disclose financial information about their American customers to the Internal Revenue Service (IRS).[114] In addition, starting in 2013, a series of leaks from offshore tax havens uncovered the pervasiveness and brazenness of offshore tax planning by corporations and the well-to-do.[115] The revelations made the news amid a climate of austerity, induced by the response to the global financial crisis of 2007–09. Public pressure to stop the practice of aggressive tax planning gave a sense of urgency to the multilateral OECD BEPS.

The ensuing measures had mixed results. On the upside, FATCA played a crucial role in effectively ending bank secrecy.[116] The OECD BEPS project brought the international community country-by-country reporting of corporate income, and beneficial ownership registries. These initiatives became the stepping-stone for the automatic exchange of banking information and an international approach to taxing the digital economy, which now moves towards a global minimum tax.[117] The change to the international tax regime in the past fifteen years has been fundamental.[118] On the downside, the set of rules is again highly complex, creating new loopholes where old ones have been closed. The facilitators of offshore tax planning—the lawyers and accountants—have largely been left out the drive to clamp down on offshore tax planning.[119] The old separation between tax evasion, an illegal practice, and tax avoidance, an apparently legal practice, has survived the reforms. This division implies that one is 'bad', while the other is 'normal', when in fact all forms of offshore tax planning build on playing off one set of rules against another. Likewise, the trust—an old and central legal structure for offshoring wealth and corporate money—has outlasted the reforms. The effectiveness of the reforms may be ambivalent. The return of the state in international tax affairs is apparent.[120]

## 4  The encounter

State power, I contend, is the ability of the institutional association of rule (*Herrschaftsverband*) to mobilize and centralize resources to finance its political goals. It is a function of the state's ability to mediate successfully the

---

[113] OECD 2013.
[114] Hakelberg 2020.
[115] ICIJ 2016.
[116] Eccleston and Gray 2014; Emmenegger 2017.
[117] Giles, Chazan, and Keohane 2021.
[118] Christensen and Hearson 2019.
[119] Pistor 2020.
[120] Christensen and Hearson 2019.

bank and tax bargains. Offshore finance, on the other hand, is a much more circumscribed phenomenon. It is an instance of—but not the same as—financial globalization. It is a set of cross-border financial services marked by the non-resident principle, low or no taxation and regulation, and invisibility. Thanks to these services, global banks can create foreign money and wealthy economic actors—banks, large corporations, and the rich—can obfuscate it. Offshore finance can impact state power through both sides of the balance sheet: claims and liabilities, or debt and taxation.

As state power encounters offshore finance, an obvious proposition imposes itself: it obstructs the attempts of the institutional association of rule to finance its political goals via the bargains it struck with the financiers and taxpayers. Offshore finance undermines state power.

However, from the analysis of the nature of state power and offshore finance logically follows a second, less obvious proposition. Offshore finance provides access to international liquidity, a resource for the *Herrschaftsverband* outside of domestic bargains. It also allows the state to obscure the true distribution of costs and benefits of banking and taxation across different groups in society without creating political contestation. Offshore finance strengthens state power. I discuss each of these propositions in turn.

## Undermining state power

The instances that undermine state power are obvious: offshore finance limits the state's ability to finance its politics by cutting down its tax revenue. It also makes futile attempts to regulate banks' money creation thereby potentially pushing the costs of money creation onto the state's balance sheet.

Indeed, offshore tax planning creates substantial tax losses for the state.[121] These losses are, however, not equally distributed across countries.[122] The literature disagrees over why that is. One group of scholars explains the variance with structural factors: developed countries are said to lose less tax revenue than developing ones;[123] smaller countries less than larger ones;[124] closed economies less than open ones;[125] and countries at a distance to offshore financial centres less than those which are geographically close.[126] A second group

---

[121] OECD 2013; Zucman 2013, 2014.
[122] IMF 2014; Crivelli, De Mooij, and Keen 2015; Tørsløv, Wier, and Zucman 2018.
[123] Crivelli, De Mooij, and Keen 2015; Genschel and Seelkopf 2016; Cobham and Janský 2017.
[124] Genschel and Seelkopf 2016.
[125] Wibbels and Arce 2003.
[126] Zucman 2013; Blanco and Rogers 2014; Haberly and Wójcik 2015a; Tørsløv, Wier, and Zucman 2018.

argues that the effects of financial globalization on tax policies are conditioned by domestic politics and institutions, including regime type,[127] voter preferences,[128] veto players in the legislative process,[129] quality of governance,[130] and the level of public debt.[131]

Regardless of the source of variance, states appear to react in similar ways. To make up for the lost revenue, they increasingly tax labour over capital, especially but not exclusively through a shift from direct to indirect taxation. As a result, nominal corporate taxes across the globe fell from levels of around 40 per cent in the 1980s to about 25 per cent in 2013.[132] Zucman[133] argues that offshore tax planning has pushed the effective tax rates for corporations even lower than the nominal tax rates suggest. For the United States, he shows that in 2013 offshore tax planning pushed corporate taxes from the nominal rate of 33 per cent to the effective rate of 18 per cent.[134] However, given that corporate income taxes make up a small part of most countries' tax mix (in the OECD world about 9 per cent), on an aggregate level offshore finance did not deal a deathblow to the state's ability to finance its politics. It did, however, limit the state's ability to autonomously set its tax policies.[135]

The invisibility of offshore tax planning obscures the root causes and the extent of these systematic changes to the tax bargain. It distorts the distribution of the tax burden between capital and labour and within each of these groups. Offshore tax planning is a highly exclusive service available only to individuals in the highest income groupings and to corporations which are sufficiently large and internationalized. Consequently, offshore financial services may be used by individuals with high incomes from labour and may exclude those with small incomes from capital ownership. For individuals and corporations alike, offshore tax planning creates rents through lower tax rates which are not available onshore. It advantages economic actors with a high net-worth over all others. As long as this advantage remains invisible, it is unlikely to fuel the conflict over sharing the tax burden.

Regarding offshore money creation, there is a clear trade-off between capitalist expansion—liquidity—and the risk of broken promises—financial instability leading to crises. The more we get from one, the higher the likelihood of

[127] Genschel, Lierse, and Seelkopf 2016.
[128] Meltzer and Richard 1981.
[129] Basinger and Hallerberg 2004.
[130] Genschel and Seelkopf 2016.
[131] Swank 2016.
[132] IMF 2014.
[133] Zucman 2014.
[134] Ibid., 133.
[135] Genschel 2005.

the other. In the same vein, the empirical literature found that the Eurodollar markets can destabilize the international financial system potentially forcing the state to foot the bill for bailouts.[136] Offshore finance is inherently unstable.

Finally, historical studies document that, while developed with the knowledge and even support of the state, offshore banking happens largely outside the state's regulatory purview.[137] As discussed, in the onshore economy, the struggle over money creation has never been answered in favour of either the state or the banks. Instead, they share that power. Offshore, the power to create money is extended across borders from domestic banks to non-resident banks in foreign jurisdictions. There, outside times of global crises, money creation has become fully private, competitive, and removed from central banking. The non-resident principle in combination with low taxation and regulation and invisibility, allows banks to operate almost unregulated. Via weakening a central bank's regulatory oversight, offshore money creation tilts the power balance between the state and banks in favour of the latter. Banks can do more at a higher risk with higher expectations for profits than in the onshore economy. Unsurprisingly, global banks continued to engage in offshore banking long after the regulations that gave rise to the Eurodollar markets—capital controls, reserve requirements and withholding taxes—had been abandoned by the United States and other major economies between the 1970s and 1990s. The power to create US-dollar-denominated money was incentive enough to maintain the system. As in the case of tax planning, offshore banking advantages a small set of actors—large internationally active banks—over all other financiers. Additionally, it raises the question who has to pay in case any of these large banks has liquidity issues. Nevertheless, the invisibility of the structural advantage and the potential systemic risk prevents these issues entering into the bargain over how to distribute the costs and benefits of money creation.

## Strengthening state power

The instances where offshore finance strengthens state power are more subtle. But they are no less impactful. Offshore finance offers the state two principal advantages: it provides preferential liquidity and offers the possibility of a politics of the invisible.

---

[136] He and McCauley 2010; Calomiris and Haber 2014; Altamura 2017; Tooze 2018.
[137] Burn 1999; He and McCauley 2012; O'Malley 2015.

Offshore dollar markets are among the most liquid markets in the world. Many governments are borrowing in the Eurodollar markets, especially (but not exclusively) Latin American ones. Offshore markets provide liquidity not available onshore—at better conditions. Issuing debt offshore is usually cheaper than onshore, rates are lower and so are transaction costs and taxation.[138] Moreover, offshore dollar markets are attractive for sovereign borrowers because they make it possible to be indebted in US dollars—the world's leading currency, without being indebted to the United States, a US bank, or even under US law. Most offshore financial centres—from the City of London to the Cayman Islands—run under British common law. Given its age, British common law creates a high level of legal certainty in case of dispute. It is also less punishing on the debtor compared to US law.[139] Consequently, offshore finance can provide borrowing countries with broader access to the desired foreign currency, while retaining, especially in times of financial distress, a better negotiating position than in the onshore economy.[140] Better still, from the perspective of the state, given that offshore markets offer the world's leading currencies, they can also help to finance a state's political programme where the domestic cycle of money, tax, and debt is dysfunctional. Offshore banking can strengthen a state's power when contested domestic creditor–debtor relationships constrain it. It offers a new set of debtor–creditor relationships.

As for governments, offshore finance provides preferential liquidity for large firms with enough financial weight and legal sophistication to issue debt offshore. Historically, this feature of the Eurodollar markets was a key motivation for US governments not to regulate them: they provided cheap access to credit for US corporations at times when regulations made the domestic banking system expensive and shallow.[141]

The possibility for a politics of the invisible means that the state uses the obscure nature of offshore financial services to pursue contradictory economic policies simultaneously without being called out on it. It is the state's trump card in the offshore game. Offshore banking allows the state to regulate its domestic banking system while allowing loose financial conditions offshore. It allows the state to support capital accumulation by deregulating financial markets offshore while maintaining the welfare state onshore. Offshore tax

---

[138] Black and Munro 2010.
[139] Author's telephone interview with investment banker, May 2017; with tax lawyer, London, June 2017; with tax lawyer, Mexico City, November 2015.
[140] Binder 2022.
[141] Helleiner 1994.

planning allows the state to relieve corporations and the wealthy from their tax burden, while continuing to extract taxes from labour and the lower income classes. Providing corporations with tax saving opportunities offshore makes them less prone to attack welfare policies at home. In other words, the state sustains its tax revenues from labour through obscuring the fact that corporations may not pay their share and by delivering on its promises of material returns for the tax payments by upholding the welfare state despite pressures to consolidate public budgets. The invisibility of offshore financial services relieves the state from having to mediate conflict over the distribution of the costs and benefits of taxation and money creation. It allows the terms of the bank and tax bargain to be altered in favour of a small group of economic actors without creating political contestation. Offshore finance can strengthen state power via the politics of the invisible.

In short, offshore finance and state power are linked through money. From a theoretical perspective, the resulting relationship is not straightforward. There are instances that undermine the state's ability to finance its politics and instances where this ability is strengthened. Which forces prevail and under which conditions, must be determined empirically.

## 5  Studying state power in the age of offshore finance

At this point, we meet our second challenge: empirically studying the relationship between state power and offshore finance. Thus far, scholars have a fragmentary empirical understanding of the offshore phenomenon. For instance, estimates about the size of the offshore world cover only specific elements. Gabriel Zucman[142] estimates how much global individual wealth is offshore. The United Nations and the International Monetary Fund (IMF) provide an assessment of how much foreign direct investment is channelled through offshore financial centres[143] while the BIS offers insights into specific segments of the offshore dollar markets such as offshore corporate bond issuance.[144] As we have seen, this patchy empirical basis results from the nature of offshore finance itself.

The empirical assessment in the following chapters therefore focuses on crucial cases—cases where the effects of offshore finance on state power are likely

---

[142] Zucman 2015.
[143] UNCTAD 2015; Damgaard, Elkjaer, and Johannesen 2019.
[144] McCauley, McGuire, and Sushko 2015.

to present themselves in such a way that it is possible to detect them.[145] Europe and Latin America are among the regions most affected by offshore financial services.[146] Within Europe, I contrast Britain, the inventor of offshore finance with Germany, the quintessential tax state. Within Latin America, I contrast Brazil, the world's second largest issuer of offshore dollar debt, with Mexico, a country that has moved from a very high to a negligible level of exposure to offshore financial services.

Beginning in the nineteenth century, the case studies consider the specific nature of each state from the money view and how it changes over time; the evolving nature of money creation and taxation; and the distribution of the related costs and benefits across different groups of society. It determines the contemporary exposure to offshore financial services by presenting a rough estimate of the scale and pattern of the uses and abuses of offshore financial services. It then explains empirically what happens when state power encounters offshore finance—does it limit or strengthen state power? And what are the underlying mechanisms?

As discussed, offshore finance's invisibility comes in different shapes and forms. The most famous examples include banking secrecy, trusts and fiduciary accounts, or bearer bonds. The most important strategies to make offshore financial services invisible are more elusive, though. For instance, complex ownership structures across borders and legal forms disguises the beneficial owner of a financial transaction. Or take the Eurodollar as another example. It appears on paper like a regular US dollar. Yet it is, unlike its onshore twin, not backed by a lender of last resort (at least not outside of global crises). To distinguish the two, it has become customary among practitioners on Wall Street to refer to a green dollar—one created in the US and a red dollar—one created through credit offshore.[147] That difference between a green and a red US dollar escapes our macroeconomic statistics just as much as the difference between a substantial greenfield investment and one into an empty shell company.[148]

The statistical invisibility of offshore banking and offshore tax planning is the result of a web of conscious decisions, though it is not necessarily strategically knit. With limited regulation comes limited documentation. Likewise, a legal code skilfully walking the tightrope between two sets of rules

[145] Gerring 2009.
[146] Tørsløv, Wier, and Zucman 2018.
[147] Snider and Gromen 2019.
[148] Damgaard, Elkjaer, and Johannesen 2019.

leaves limited traces in official statistics. Or data, once set up to trace offshore banking, is merged with onshore statistics as is the case with BIS bond data. In the late 1990s, the BIS lumped together three different types of bonds— Eurobonds, foreign bonds, and domestic bonds—into one common database, thereby obscuring the difference between the three.[149]

Finally, policymakers, by ignorance or intent, may not request offshore-specific data. For a long time, for instance, the banking secrecy in Switzerland was tolerated by other countries, until, in 2010, the Obama administration decided to request information about bank accounts held by US citizens in Switzerland. The related information now shows up, if not in official statistics, at least in those of the IRS. What is and is not counted in macroeconomic statistics reflects and, once acted upon by policymakers and economic actors, shapes the international economy. Statistics are 'political artefacts' to quote Mügge.[150]

Consequently, debates run high among scholars over how best to measure a phenomenon whose distinct nature is to be out of sight. Many researchers work with best 'guesstimates' arguing that a rough estimate about the phenomenon across countries is better than none.[151] Others are weary of the politics of numbers. Once out, they are quoted and acted upon long after their correctness might have been questioned.[152] These researchers caution against rough estimates and quantitative cross-country comparisons.[153]

The book exists within this tension. It takes a cautious approach towards using quantitative data but uses or produces best guesstimates where they enlighten the analysis. The quantitative analysis presented in the book exclusively serves one purpose: to build a rough idea about the size of the phenomenon in comparative perspective. The estimates do not and cannot contribute to the debate about how best to quantify the demand for offshore financial services.[154] All quantitative data is triangulated with data from qualitative interviews with practitioners of offshore finance conducted during research stays in Britain, Germany, Brazil, and Mexico. For those inclined, more details on data and methods are presented in the appendix.

---

[149] Gruic and Wooldridge 2012.
[150] Mügge 2020.
[151] Zucman 2015; Tørsløv, Wier, and Zucman 2018; Alstadsæter, Johannesen, and Zucman 2019.
[152] Andreas 2008.
[153] Blouin and Robinson 2019.
[154] SeeHenry 2012; Zucman 2013; Crivelli, De Mooij, and Keen 2015; Alstadsæter, Johannesen, and Zucman 2018; Tørsløv, Wier, and Zucman 2018.

Overall, the book's approach prioritizes empirical depth over theoretical parsimony and the identification of larger patterns over forensic detail. It explains the relationship between offshore finance and state power in historical rather than law-like terms.[155] In that spirit the subsequent four chapters bring to centre stage the empirical assessment of state power and offshore finance in Britain, Germany, Brazil, and Mexico.

---

[155] Sil and Katzenstein 2010.

# 3

# Britain

## Heartland of offshore finance

Britain holds a special place in the offshore world. Unlike any other country, it is at once a high tax country,[1] a large economy, and an offshore banking centre. In the City of London, the financial sector offers offshore banking services to foreign economic actors. In turn, the country's corporate and wealthy citizens use offshore financial services abroad. Britain's central and unique role in the offshore world makes an analysis of how offshore finance affects state power particularly intricate. Unlike in Germany, Brazil, or Mexico, the British state is not structured around a domestic cycle of money, tax, and debt which then encounters the external offshore world. Rather, having invented offshore banking, offshore finance has become simultaneously external and internal to the British state.

The following historical empirical analysis of that intricate relationship reveals that from the inception of the Eurodollar in the 1950s to the onset of the global financial crisis in 2007, offshore finance strengthened British state power. The politics of the invisible helped to keep domestic capital engaged in financing the state despite the expansion of mass democracy and the welfare state. At the same time, it obscured the structural privileging of large economic actors over everyone else. The centrality of the City of London in the Eurodollar system also afforded the British state international influence beyond its actual political and economic weight.[2]

However, when in 2007–09 the global financial crisis—rooted to a significant extent in the offshore dollar markets—hit the country with full force, the relationship turned destructive and undermined state power. The crisis laid bare the fragility of offshore money creation and the politics of the invisible. British state power became simultaneously contested from within and by foreign governments. This contestation put in motion Britain's decade of crisis—culminating in Brexit. In the case of Britain, offshore money creation

---

[1] A high tax country in the sense of tax revenue as a share of GDP.
[2] Green 2020.

*Offshore Finance and State Power.* Andrea Binder, Oxford University Press. © Andrea Binder (2023).
DOI: 10.1093/oso/9780192870124.003.0003

has been more consequential for state power than offshore tax planning and money laundering.

The analysis in this chapter traces the changing nature of the British state and its ability to finance its political goals; the exposure to offshore finance; and the effect when the latter meets the former across three critical historical junctures: (1) the 1688 Glorious Revolution, the starting point for the first successful cycle of money, tax, and debt, (2) the beginning of mass democracy in 1918 altering Britain's longstanding tax and bank bargains, and (3) Margaret Thatcher's 'Big Bang' in 1986, which opened up the institutional association of rule towards foreign economic elites.

## 1   British state power from the money view

The seventeenth-century Financial Revolution is a good place to begin an analysis of the nature and development of the British state and its sources of power from the money view.[3] With the introduction of the land tax in 1692, the landed classes tolerated for the first time a direct tax on their wealth as a contribution to financing the Crown's war efforts. Two years on, in 1694, with the foundation of the Bank of England, the English government was able to establish permanent public debt. With the merger of the kingdoms of England and Scotland in 1707, the pound sterling became the common currency of Great Britain. In short, by the time the dust of the 1688 Glorious Revolution had settled, an initial cycle of money, tax, and debt was running smoothly. Britain was the first European state to successfully raise revenue from a combination of tax and debt. It had established modern money.[4]

The combination of two institutional innovations made this development possible: the Bill of Rights (1689), limiting the power of the monarch by ascribing to Parliament the right to make laws and levy taxes, and the Bank of England (1694), the first private bank to create sovereign credit-money. The intertwined nature of British parliamentarism and capitalism lead to a *Herrschaftsverband* (institutional association of rule) shaped by a relationship between the king-in-parliament and the moneyed classes so close that it was difficult to meaningfully distinguish between a political and an economic elite.[5]

The Bank of England, established as a private bank, initially mobilized the financial resources of about 1,300 financiers to lend to the government of King

---

[3] Dickson 1993; Desan 2014.
[4] Dickson 1993; Bonney 1999; Desan 2014.
[5] Cain and Hopkins 2015, ch. 1.

William III and Queen Mary II. The Crown had borrowed from these same financiers before the foundation of the Bank of England, but individually and under a legal framework that the monarch, before the Bill of Rights, could change at will. The Crown could default on a creditor and then turn to another to borrow again. Once sovereign lending became—through the Bill of Rights and the Bank of England—collective and governed by legal statutes, the risk of default decreased significantly. For the same people who were members of Parliament were also among the 1,300 financiers of the Bank of England, creating 'a virtual identity of borrower and lender'[6] as Macdonald observes. The financiers as parliamentarians could ensure that the government repaid its debt because they made the decisions about government spending and servicing of the national debt. The lower classes, excluded from the franchise and democratic decision-making, had to pay for the servicing of the debt via excise duties and other indirect taxes. Lending to the government had become a safe bet. The financiers were now willing to make government debt permanent by lending to service the debt.

By the early nineteenth century, however, the Napoleonic wars had become so expensive that financing them through borrowing alone was unsustainable. Now the wealthy had to contribute to the war effort via direct taxation too. Yet, the principle for direct taxation remained the same as that for government debt: the franchise restricted by property led to the identity of the taxpayer and the taxman. This way, the moneyed classes could ensure their taxes were spent in their interest, that is, on defence, imperial expansion, and debt service. They could also ensure that once the war was fought, debt would be repaid and direct taxes on the wealthy lowered.[7] This system of public finance reached its peak with Britain's triumph over Napoleon in 1815. In the late seventeenth up to the mid-nineteenth century, the institutional association of rule consisted of the king-in-parliament and the moneyed classes creating the identities of borrower and lender, taxman and taxpayer, political and economic elites.

The development of British capitalism, however, created structural tensions within the economic elites. The British capitalist enterprise started out as agrarian capitalism and its related landed wealth, followed by commercial and financial capitalism, and then with the Industrial Revolution, industrial capitalism.[8] It was the culture and values of the landed elite that dominated the rise of all subsequently emerging economic elites. Landownership became the single most important signifier of belonging to the institutional association

---

[6] Macdonald 2003, 371.
[7] Ibid., chs 6 and 8.
[8] Cain and Hopkins 2015.

of rule.[9] The respective capital owners often had contradictory economic and foreign policy interests.[10] For instance, the landed elite preferred isolationist international policies, being reluctant to finance the state's wars and imperial expansion. The financial, commercial, and industrialist capitalists were interested in imperial expansion and therefore willing to contribute to financing the state.

Another dividing line within the economic elites ran between 'gentlemanly and industrial capital', to put it in Cain and Hopkin's terms.[11] Gentleman capitalists derived their wealth from rents, not from hard work. As members of the leisure class, they had time for politics in London. They served as government ministers and occupied leading positions at the Bank of England. They considered their privileges to be a legitimate return for their service to the country.[12] Gentleman capitalists were closer to power—personally and geographically— than their industrialist counterparts in the north. The industrialists thus became part of the association of rule at arm's length.[13]

From the mid-nineteenth century onwards the idea of universal suffrage took hold in Britain. Electoral reforms between 1832 and 1918 successively extended the franchise to the entire adult population. As in the past, the economic elites' strategy to mitigate the effects of a substantially more inclusive institutional association of rule was to co-opt contenders into their value system.

Take the Labour party leadership as an example. In the first post-war decades, the Labour leadership was made up of people from outside the moneyed classes. Yet, by the time of the Blair government in 1997, this was no longer the case. The Labour prime minster had been recruited from the moneyed elite. Although his successor, Gordon Brown, had a different background, he accepted the centrality of the City's interests as a constraint to his policy proposals. In the timeframe of half a century, the traditional core of the institutional association of rule successfully conveyed their values to the former contenders from the Labour Party. To a considerable degree the notion of privilege in return for public service and the pre-eminence of the interests of the City within the larger set of national political interests weathered the change.[14]

Nevertheless, mass democracy severed the identity of the taxpayer with the taxman and changed the identity of lender and borrower. That is, the previous

---

[9] Scott 1991.
[10] Macdonald 2003; Daunton 2007.
[11] Cain and Hopkins 2015, 41.
[12] Scott 1991, ch. 3.
[13] Scott 1991; Macdonald 2003; Cain and Hopkins 2015.
[14] Scott 1991; Cain and Hopkins 2015.

near identity between economic and political elites was weakened. As a result, the 200-year-old formula for financing the British state through debt, indirect taxes, and an occasional direct contribution by the wealthy in case of war was altered. Mass democracy forced the old economic elites to negotiate with the broadened political elite over how to finance the state and how to spend the revenue. It heralded the age of the welfare state.

Against the background of a broadening institutional association of rule and a loosening of close ties between economic and political elites, the subsequent sections in this chapter assess the related conflict over money creation and taxation in more detail.

## Bank bargain

The bank bargain is the institutionalized response to distributional conflicts over the benefits and costs of money creation. Two elements of Britain's Financial Revolution gave birth to that bargain: the recoinage of 1696 and the foundation of the Bank of England two years earlier. The recoinage of 1696 embedded into the emerging bank bargain John Locke's vision of money as an expression of an external, fixed value (that of the metal from which the coin was minted) naturally arising from private exchange. This notion of money strengthened the creditors' claim to repayment of exactly the value they had lent. It also took money out of the state's sphere and out of politics.[15] At the same time, Parliament legislated tax laws that accepted paper notes issued by the Bank of England—founded as a government bank—as tax payments. This practice gave paper money (which obviously has no fixed natural value) a value at par with the gold coins that served as the unit of account. The value of money arose out of sovereign authority.[16] It firmly rooted money within the state's sphere and politics. The Bank of England tied these two practices together, creating a site of shared power between the British state and its private financiers to create money.

The Bank of England turned out to be a smooth mechanism for the institutional association of rule to centralize and mobilize resources. The state used those resources to finance war and imperial expansion. *En passant*, it also further increased the riches of the bank's wealthy stockholders.

Yet, the coalescence between the government and its financiers was not all peace and harmony. Its hybrid nature as a public institution and a joint-stock

---

[15] Desan 2014, 11–21; Eich 2020.
[16] Ingham 2004; Desan 2014.

company inevitably created tensions between the interests of the state and that of the financiers. For instance, as a public institution, the Bank of England was supposed to be responsive to the government's financing needs. Yet, as a joint stock company, the Bank of England was accountable to its stockholders only.[17] One reason that the coalition between the state and its financiers held nonetheless, was their agreement to spend the money on imperial expansion.[18] Another was the close personal relationships between them.[19]

For a long time, the Bank of England was a government's bank without being a central bank. By 1833 the Bank of England had become the sole issuer of the pound sterling as legal tender. But it did not bind together the individual small goldsmith banks in London and the country banks in rural England into a banking system. It also did not maintain financial stability and ensure liquidity in the money markets. As a result, British banks other than the Bank of England were unstable and inefficient. Moreover, the Bank of England's function as a government's bank meant that all the available credit went to the government, starving the productive sector of financing. The Bank of England ensured the country's enormous success in outspending France during the Napoleonic wars. Yet, the Industrial Revolution happened despite, not because of the it.[20] The Bank of England and its shareholders reaped the benefits of creating money without bearing the costs.

It was the industrialists' growing influence throughout the nineteenth century that finally pushed the Bank of England to transform itself through a series of reforms from a government's bank into a modern central bank—although still fully under private ownership. Importantly, in 1847, it became the lender of last resort to the entire domestic banking system.[21] The reforms allowed sterling to become the world's reserve currency. The small banks consolidated or disappeared and by 1870, the British banking system was more stable and provided more liquidity to the productive sectors than ever before.[22] The benefits of money creation where now more widely spread.

Yet, the smooth sailing did not last for long. In 1873, a financial crisis hit Britain. It emanated from the outside and revealed that the pound's international role had a domestic price. The conundrum was to ensure convertibility of the pound into gold while avoiding acting as a lender of last resort to the sterling indebted world—a responsibility not aligned with the interests of the

[17] Vogl 2015, ch. 4.
[18] Calomiris and Haber 2014, ch. 4.
[19] Cain and Hopkins 2015, ch. 1.
[20] Calomiris and Haber 2014, ch. 5.
[21] Collins 1988; Mehrling 2011.
[22] Calomiris and Haber 2014, ch. 5.

bank's stockholders.[23] For the first part of the conundrum, the answer was logically easy, although politically potentially expensive. Given that the Bank of England cannot increase the volume of gold, the only way to ensure convertibility was to limit the money supply domestically through limited government spending and through tight control of the currency by the Bank of England.[24] In other words, the costs of money creation that served domestic and international economic actors had to be borne by industrial capital and wider society. For the second part of the conundrum, how to lend to the world without acting as a lender of last resort, even Bagehot was shy of an answer.[25] This second part of the conundrum remained unsolved.

Nevertheless, in the late nineteenth century, the future of the pound sterling appeared bright. As the City was at once small and outward looking, it was well placed to connect the wealthy's fortunes with international banking. One reflection of this development was the professionalization of trusts as a means for estate planning. The trust was a popular instrument to keep the diversifying estate together over generations. It also made ownership invisible, a welcome instrument to keep assets safe in face of the extension of the franchise and the related growing distance between taxman and taxpayers. Landowners had been using trusts to manage and pass on their fortunes since the Middle Ages, yet the system was informal and based on kinship between the settlor and the trustees.[26] Institutionalizing trusts in the second half of the nineteenth century made private banking a growing business for the financiers. Better still, it allowed them to mobilize resources for their banks without having to employ their own means. This manner of asset mobilization gave London-based banks an important competitive advantage over the provincial joint-stock banks. The provincial banks served the banking needs of the population and industry. The City amassed the fortunes of the country's well-to-do to finance sovereign debt and the international distribution of manufactured goods.[27] Now, the Bank of England was no longer the sole big wig in town. Rather, the whole banking sector in London and beyond worked smoothly and was consistent with the interests of the institutional association of rule. Banking, commerce, and related services—insurance, accounting, legal advice, entrepôt services, etc.—grew and served Britain's international ambitions, colonial and otherwise. The growing financial and service sector created what Cain and Hopkins

---

[23] Mehrling 2011, 22–23.
[24] Cain and Hopkins 2015.
[25] Mehrling 2011, ch. 1.
[26] Harrington 2012; Harrington 2016b, chs 1 and 4.
[27] Calomiris and Haber 2014, ch. 5; Cain and Hopkins 2015, ch. 1.

term 'invisible earnings'.[28] Unlike manufacturing and trade, the products and processes generated by the financial sector were largely invisible to those outside of it. The resulting invisible influence and income was a good match with gentlemanly culture. Invisibility soothed the financiers' growing discomfort with the industrialists' class warfare and the extension of the franchise.[29]

In sum, three characteristics marked the British bank bargain in the long nineteenth century: division, invisibility, and dominance. The division ran between banks in London and outside of it. It reflected the conflict between financial and industrial capital, the former interested in conditions that furthered empire and international trade, the latter in conditions that furthered industrial production. The invisibility of the products, processes, and incomes generated in the financial service sector was the financial capitalists' trump card. They could enjoy their liquid wealth discretely, and their seeming detachment from the class warfare that was poisoning the relationship between workers and entrepreneurs made them seem fit for public office and acting in the national interest. Finally, the political dominance of finance capital within the association of rule ensured the state's commitment to sterling as a world reserve currency and hence a commitment to convertibility. The Bank of England—as a private institution with a public mandate—acted as the custodian of these interests transforming them into a perceived national interest.[30]

Yet, with the early twentieth century, change was coming. Although Britain was victorious in the wars, the empire was coming apart; its public finances were in shambles; and the United States had successfully contested Britain's international and monetary leadership. Moreover, the surprise win for the Labour Party in the general election in 1945 flushed into Parliament and government positions people who had thus far been outside the institutional association of rule. The extended role of the state in politics and the economy during the wars had tilted the power relationship within the association of rule in favour of the new political elites. Again, the fates and fortunes of the Bank of England reflect the shift: in 1946, Clement Attlee's Labour government nationalized the central bank.

In hindsight, the nationalization of the Bank of England can be dismissed as symbolic.[31] Nevertheless, at the time, finance capitalists read the nationalization of the Bank of England as a signal of the shifting power balance within the

---

[28] Cain and Hopkins 2015, 501.
[29] Ibid., chs 5 and 18.
[30] Burn 1999; Cain and Hopkins 2015, ch. 4.
[31] Burn 1999; Dellepiane-Avellaneda 2013.

state.[32] Just as much as its operational independence under Tony Blair fifty-one years later was signalling the Labour Party's reconciliation with finance capital.

Yet back in 1957 the influence of the financial elite seemed precarious. When the pound sterling again came under pressure, the conservative government aimed to stabilize the currency as in the past. Yet, this time, the measures were not limited to spending cuts. They also included a restriction on the use of sterling to finance trade outside the sterling area, credit limitations, and other measures. For the first time since the foundation of the Bank of England, the costs of money creation had also to be borne by the financiers. The restrictions cut off the funding sources of London's merchant and overseas banks.[33] The financiers could no longer be sure about their dominance in the institutional association of rule. To preserve their business, influence, and wealth, they needed a plan B.

Well connected with the upper classes at home and in the colonies, bankers knew that since the 1920s, the wealthy had begun to incorporate trusts in Jersey.[34] This trend gathered momentum with the onset of decolonization in the 1950s. Former colonists decided to settle in Jersey rather than to move back to the homeland.[35] Jersey had everything the wealthy elite historically considered its privilege: sterling, low taxes, gentlemanly discreteness, and a smack of empire. By the late 1950s to early 1960s, 70 per cent of bank deposits in Jersey belonged to non-residents. To collect those assets, London's merchant and overseas banks opened branches on the island. In the decade between 1950 and 1960, the number of banks there increased from seven to thirty.[36] Once there, the banks were able to create money against these assets. They could then lend this money on to their headquarters back in London because the credit restrictions did not apply in Jersey.[37] The permissive tax environment made that business profitable.[38] The merchant and overseas banks had discovered the beauty of offshore.

Next to offshore private banking and intra-bank financing, the banks that had moved offshore came across a third new line of business. As the financiers registered the increasing price for and decreasing success of maintaining sterling convertibility, it became clear that if the City of London were to have a

---

[32] Macdonald 2003, ch. 9.

[33] Burn 1999; Calomiris and Haber 2014, ch. 5.

[34] This development was not limited to Jersey; it took place in a similar fashion in other Channel Islands. However, as the data in section two demonstrates, today Jersey is Britain's most important offshore centre and hence the discussion here focuses on it.

[35] Author's telephone interview with offshore expert, October 2018.

[36] Hampton 1996b.

[37] Hampton 1996a.

[38] Author's telephone interview with offshore expert, October 2018.

future as an international banking centre, this future lay in the US dollar. The financiers now aimed to decouple, as much as possible, the fate of the City of London from that of sterling.[39] In the 1950s, the amount of US dollars flowing into London was at a historical high. The merchant and overseas banks, and later the joined-stock banks, seized the opportunity of taking non-resident US dollar deposits and lending against those deposits to international business partners.[40]

The Bank of England, interested in restoring the international role of the City, did what it could to support that business. For instance, it allowed the banks to keep two separate books, one 'onshore' book for its domestic activities and one 'offshore' book for its non-resident services.[41] This accounting technique turned the nineteenth-century invisible nature of banking into an explicit policy. It also reinforced the traditional division between domestic and international banking. Onshore banking remained under national and international restrictions, while offshore banking was, thanks to being among non-residents and denominated in a foreign currency, largely unregulated. The banks could now create money offshore.

Ahead of the end of dollar–gold convertibility in 1971, offshore money creation was free from the restraints of convertibility. That is, offshore banks could create fiat money—a privilege that had been, since 1694, exclusively that of the central banks. Consequently, the Eurodollar market grew and developed offshoots into other markets and places.

Nevertheless, the Bank of England remained, as Green puts it, the 'epistemic authority' of the Euromarkets.[42] From the beginning, the transactions between non-residents in a foreign currency involved technical details that the participating banks had to clear with the Bank of England. In addition, despite nationalization, the revolving door between the City banks and the Bank of England kept turning. Therefore, the Bank of England now had two potentially contradictory goals: ensuring financial stability while preserving the banking sector's freedom from government interference.[43] One expression of this double-faced mission was that the Bank of England guarded its Eurodollar knowledge, keeping the Treasury and the government in the dark about the newly developing markets.[44] Another expression was that the Bank was not concerned about the Euromarkets' potential contradictions with government policy. The Bank was only concerned about a potential call on its dollar

---

[39] Burn 1999.
[40] Helleiner 1994, ch. 4.
[41] Palan 1998; O'Malley 2015.
[42] Green 2016, 444.
[43] Burn 1999; O'Malley 2015.
[44] Burn 1999.

reserves as American banks, attracted by the Eurodollar business, began to move into London. The Bank of England faced its nineteenth-century conundrum again: how to lend to the world without acting as a lender of last resort. Only this time, it was about a foreign currency.

The Bank's answer was to not impose reserve requirements on the banks participating in the Euromarkets. The reasoning went that reserve requirements indicated the possibility for a bailout in case the Eurodollar business should go awry—an impression that the Bank of England was, just as in Bagehot's days, adamant to avoid. Offshore finance internationalized the creation of the US dollar, but not the Bank of England's role as lender of last resort.[45] The offshore credit markets worked so smoothly that by the end of the 1960s and early 1970s, even British public sector agencies started to borrow offshore.[46] The interests of the financiers and the government merged again. Financial capitalists regained within the association of rule some of the dominance that they had enjoyed vis-à-vis industrial capital and the government prior to 1918. Yet, the British financiers were now dealing in US dollars. Their influence now was, even if tacitly, at the discretion of American banks and the US government.[47]

## Tax bargain

The sharing of power between the British state and the financiers could not have developed the way it did, were it not for taxation.[48] Beyond the 1692 land tax, the Crown was unsuccessful, for a long time, in coaxing the moneyed classes into paying direct taxes. The wealthy understood that a meaningful income tax would enhance the Crown's power. Moreover, a direct form of tax would have meant valuing the wealth they owned. The propertied classes preferred to keep that value private. If they were to contribute to financing the state, they would do so, as discussed above, by extending credit. Yet, financing the state via debt would have been impossible without anything showing up on the asset side of the government's balance sheet. Luckily for the Crown, in the late seventeenth century, England's international trade was flourishing, not least because of preferential terms of trade through colonialization. Indirect taxation of the traded goods through tariffs and excise duties raised sufficient revenue to make the government a credible borrower.[49]

---

[45] Ibid.; Green 2016.
[46] Green 2016.
[47] Ibid.
[48] Bonney 1999.
[49] O'Brien and Hunt 1999.

Yet, by the end of the eighteenth century, with the French revolution and the Napoleonic wars, this approach to financing the state had reached its limits. If the institutional association of rule was to defend its political freedom domestically and internationally, the propertied classes had to contribute to the government's revenue in a direct manner. Therefore, in 1799, Prime Minister Pitt the Younger was the first political leader in Europe to introduce an income tax. However, he did not do it lightly.

Pitt found the tax 'repugnant',[50] echoing the sentiment of his well-to-do peers. In their view, the tax broke their natural privilege to go untaxed and to keep the value of their property private.[51] What made the tax acceptable, though, was the identity between the taxman and the taxed. Against this background, Pitt's promise to repeal the tax after the war was credible. The wealthy considered the tax a temporary nuisance and most of them paid. By the end of the war the government had mobilized thirty-six times more revenue than in the previous two centuries.[52] Nevertheless, Pitt kept his word and Parliament repealed the tax after the victory against France. The state was to be financed once again by debt and indirect taxes.

By the mid-nineteenth century, the division between landed and commercial wealth that marked banking in Britain also became visible in tax matters. The financial and commercial elite (this time siding with the industrialists) promoted free trade to expand Britain's role in international trade. It advocated for a reduction of tariffs and excise duties—aware that this meant the government needed another source of income. As in banking matters, the financial and commercial elites proved to be dominant. By the 1880s, the government reduced tariffs and duties while reintroducing income tax, this time for good. Yet, William Gladstone, then Prime Minister, was aware that the design of the tax would matter to make it legitimate with all parts of the propertied classes. He set out to negotiate what would become known as the Gladstonian fiscal constitution.[53]

The main purpose of the fiscal constitution was to remove the conflict over taxation from parliamentarian politics. Gladstone's formula for compromise rested on three principles: consent, balance, and neutrality. Consent between the moneyed classes was reached by aligning the right to vote with the threshold for income tax; by ensuring that every group had to contribute to the tax, irrespective of the source of their income; by spending the resulting revenue

---

[50] cit. in Brooks 2014, 34.
[51] Ibid., ch. 2; Macdonald 2003, ch. 7.
[52] O'Brien and Hunt 1999.
[53] Daunton 2007.

on the goals of all taxed classes—defence, serving interest payments, free trade, and imperial expansion; and by a collaborative process between the tax administration and the taxpayer, even at the expense of tax evasion.[54] To uphold that consensus, a balanced and general budget was important. That is, revenue was not allocated to a predetermined policy. Rather, the Treasury secretly determined how the revenue should be spent and revealed the budget to Parliament only shortly before the vote to avoid undue influence of one group of taxpayers at the expense of another.[55] The Gladstonian fiscal constitution successfully patched up the division within the moneyed classes over taxation. It also successfully ratcheted up the government's coffers. By 1906 revenue from direct taxation surpassed that from indirect taxes.[56]

While the wealthy classes were divided over the usefulness of an income tax, they were united in their attempt to avoid it. Gladstone's emphasis on consensus meant that rather than establishing a high number of general rules that Parliament needed to deliberate, in case of conflict the tax administration would challenge individual taxpayers in the courts. As a result, tax law became highly specific and fragmented.[57] This legal setup in turn provided the breeding ground for the politics of the invisible: using loopholes in the law, the wealthy transferred their income abroad, where it was outside the tax net. This was particularly easy for those capitalists whose income was invisible. Despite the possibilities, however, cross-border tax avoidance was still rare. Tax rates were too low to arrange systematically a person's wealth with a view on the tax bill.[58] Gladstone's fiscal constitution was by and large solid. Yet, by the late nineteenth, early twentieth century, three developments began to merge that would fundamentally displace Gladstonian finance: mass democracy, mass warfare, and mass welfare.

By 1918 suffrage had become universal. Yet, the expansion of the franchise did not immediately change the institutional association of rule. It took until the Labour Party's victory in 1945 for the change in the electoral system to translate into a parliamentary majority that recruited its members from outside the traditional institutional association of rule. Nevertheless, the extension of suffrage in the late nineteenth century towards a larger proportion of the male population, did change the government's discourse about public spending. From the 1890s onwards, unions and the Labour Party advocated for a

---

[54] Daunton 2002, ch. 1.
[55] Ibid.
[56] Brooks 2014, ch. 2.
[57] Daunton 2002, ch. 1.
[58] Brooks 2014, ch. 2; Daunton 2002, ch. 1.

redistribution of wealth via taxation and for easing the plight of the working classes via the establishment of a welfare state. The welfare state, Labour advocated, should be financed from tax, not contributory insurance schemes, which the party considered regressive. Two decades later, in the run up to World War I, the discourse about taxation changed further, as the government intended to shift to progressive taxation. The intended reforms were partially an expression of a drive towards more equality. It was, however, also an expression of the drive to cast a wider tax net: progression allows for taxing more people. Rhetorically, the government stuck to Gladstone's ideal of a consensual, balanced, and neutral income tax system, binding politicians to a certain degree to follow words with deeds.[59]

With these fundamental changes in discourse and policies, a new dividing line emerged. This time it ran between the moneyed and the working classes. The wealthy elites continued to favour state spending on defence, imperial expansion, and debt service. The lower classes envisioned a larger role for the state, one that provided education, health, transportation, and other public services.[60] Given economic growth, the lower classes also had more to contribute to the state's revenue than in the past. Although mitigated through progression, they paid income tax and—as in the past—even more through indirect taxes. The new dividing line between capital and labour reinforced the existing one between the moneyed classes in London and the industrialists in the provinces. Unlike the finance capitalists, the industrialists often supported the workers' call for a welfare state. Industrialists saw it as a means to ease their conflicts with an increasingly organized working class. Lloyd George's 'People's budget' in 1906, then, included a hitherto unheard-of level of spending on social welfare financed by increased taxes on the wealthy.[61] It signalled to the financial capitalists that mass democracy meant a tectonic shift in British tax politics.

As the years 1914 to 1918 went on to prove, the same held true for mass warfare. The cost of war led to a doubling of income tax revenue in 1914 compared to the previous years.[62] By the end of the war in 1918, the standard income tax rate reached 30 per cent and the surcharge for the very wealthy stood at 22.5 per cent. In addition, the government levied an excess profit duty of 80 per cent.[63] The wealthy paid, assuming that, as in the past, this level of direct taxation was

---

[59] Daunton 2002, chs 1 and 14.
[60] Macdonald 2003, ch. 8.
[61] Daunton 2002, ch. 1.
[62] Ibid.
[63] Brooks 2014, ch. 2.

a momentary nuisance to finance the war. Yet, the extension of the franchise had dissolved the eighteenth- and nineteenth-century quasi-identity between the taxman and the taxpayer. When the war was over, the size of the national debt was enormous, and the economy was in a depression. Unexpectedly, the government did not bring down the tax rates for the wealthy. On the contrary, the 40 per cent of tax revenue that the government spent to service the war debt held by the country's most wealthy, triggered a debate questioning the legitimacy of the rentier class.[64] It became clear that, concerning taxation, after World War I, the moneyed classes had lost their complete dominance in the institutional association of rule. The consequences were noticeable. The share of national income owned by the wealthy decreased, that of wage earners increased proportionally.[65] Yet, the well-to-do did not meekly forgo their wealth and influence. Instead, they resorted to the politics of the invisible and went offshore. They set out to recreate their pre-1914 world.

The politics of the invisible was noticed, however. In the 1920s, the Labour politician Hugh Dalton complained in the House of Commons that the 'rich are not only getting richer, but ... some of them have gone to Jersey'.[66] Indeed, the channel island emerged as a tax haven for British wealthy individuals during that time.

Unlike the British mainland, Jersey had no personal income tax until 1928 and even then, its rates were substantially lower than Britain's. Income tax rates in Jersey reached their peak at 20 per cent in 1948, compared to the 45 per cent collected on the mainland. Jersey also did not levy taxes on corporate income, capital gains, and gifts. Most importantly, it had no estate duty tax.[67] The latter made the island particularly attractive as a location for trusts holding private wealth set up to manage inheritance.[68]

Nevertheless, then Chancellor Winston Churchill shrugged off Dalton's complaints adjudging that a man is free 'to arrange his affairs as not to attract taxes enforced by the Crown as far as he can legitimately do so within the law'.[69] The wealthy had discovered offshore as a means to preserve their wealth and keep it invisible, obscuring the true scope of inequality in a country whose citizenry grew impatient with the privileges of the well-to-do.[70] The genie was out of the bottle.

---

[64] Daunton 2002, ch. 2.
[65] Ibid.; Macdonald 2003, ch. 9.
[66] Cited in Sabine 2006, 183.
[67] Hampton 1996b.
[68] Author's telephone interview with tax expert, October 2018.
[69] Cited in Sabine 2006, 183.
[70] Cummins 2022.

Yet, it was not only individuals moving their wealth offshore; corporations did so too. By the 1930s tax avoidance reached such proportions that the government passed its first anti-avoidance laws.[71]

From the perspective of tax, World War II and its aftermath replayed the same motives, only starting from a higher level: increase tax rates during the war, keep them up afterwards, and spend an important amount of the post-war tax revenue on debt service. Yet, the landslide victory of the Labour Party under Clement Attlee in 1945 changed the game. At least rhetorically, the government aimed for the rentier through taxation and the nationalization of key industries.[72] Besides setting tax rates on income of up to 80 per cent,[73] Attlee's Chancellor of the Exchequer, Hugh Gaitskell, also created a set of defensive laws protecting Britain's corporate tax base against abuse. The Tory governments following Attlee in the 1950s upheld these defensive measures.[74] Likewise, they were committed to the welfare state, including high tax rates and spending on public services.[75]

At close inspection, this so-called 'post-war consensus', however, turned out to be a party consensus more than a consensus within the institutional association of rule. The use of offshore trusts and other means of tax avoidance accelerated during the 1950s and 1970s. These assets made up such a substantial amount that it was worthwhile for Britain's banks to move offshore too and collect the deposits.[76] Offshore financial services were here to stay.

## 2  Contemporary exposure to offshore finance

The historical development and use of offshore financial services in Britain is well documented. The country's contemporary exposure to offshore finance remains, however, largely invisible. There are no national statistics tracing either offshore money creation or offshore tax planning. For instance, her Majesty's Revenue and Customs (HMRC), the British tax authorities, publish annual data on the gap between the theoretically possible and the actual amount of tax collected.[77] Yet, by neglect or intent, the chosen estimation method for the tax gap largely misses out on the loss related to offshore tax

[71] Brooks 2014, ch. 2.
[72] Daunton 2002, ch. 7.
[73] The effective rates were never this high as the allowances were generous.
[74] Brooks 2014, ch. 2.
[75] Cain and Hopkins 2015, ch. 26.
[76] Hampton 1996b.
[77] HMRC 2018.

planning.[78] It remains invisible. This section makes some of the statistically invisible visible based on data from BIS locational banking statistics and interview results. It covers the time from the Big Bang in 1986, the third critical juncture in the development of Britain's institutional association of rule, until 2020.

The quantitative data have to be taken with a grain of salt as they cannot create a full picture of the offshore world. Likewise, the assumptions I make to extrapolate money creation and tax planning from the BIS locational banking statistics strongly simplify a complex world. Appendix 1 describes the methodological details of the rough estimate, including its limitations. Unlike Germany, Brazil, and Mexico, Britain is simultaneously using and providing offshore financial services. Therefore, the quantitative analysis covers British economic actors' uses of offshore financial services in other offshore financial centres and the provision of offshore money creation in the City of London to the rest of the world.

## The uses and abuses of offshore financial services

From the perspective of the British state's ability to mobilize resources, relevant offshore financial flows are those between Britain and the entirety of offshore financial centres. In these flows, offshore claims represent assets held by British economic actors (i.e. central government, financial firms, corporations, and households) in offshore financial centres and liabilities represent debt they issued there.

Figure 3.1 depicts these flows between 1977, the beginning of the locational banking statistics, and 2019. Offshore assets and debt affect state power differently, but collectively. Offshore assets and debt influence the government's finances through fiscal and monetary channels. Offshore assets may go untaxed and therefore may lead to a loss in tax revenue. Offshore debt, on the other hand, may transmit volatilities from the offshore markets into the domestic economy. The graph therefore depicts offshore claims and liabilities separately and as a sum. It is the sum that represents a country's exposure to offshore finance. Figure 3.1 presents it in absolute numbers and as a percentage of GDP.

British offshore exposure developed from 43 per cent of GDP (or US$101 billion) in 1977 to its peak of 158 per cent (US$5.1 trillion) in 2007. It sank

---

[78] Brooks 2014, ch. 1; CIOT 2018.

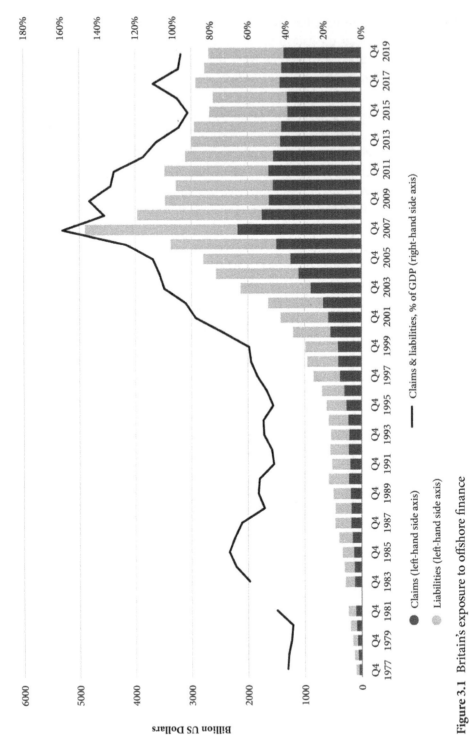

**Figure 3.1** Britain's exposure to offshore finance

*Source:* BIS locational banking statistics, World Bank, own calculations.

from there to 95 per cent of GDP (or US$2.7 trillion) in 2019. Exposure to offshore financial services experienced the strongest growth between 1998 and 2008. In that decade, offshore exposure relative to GDP grew by almost 170 per cent. Between 2007 and 2019, Britain's offshore exposure decreased by 40 per cent. Nevertheless, Britain's exposure to offshore financial services today is still higher than at any time prior to 2006. Throughout the entire timespan, we can see that liabilities outweigh claims. Britain is a net-borrower in the offshore markets—economic actors use money created by banks in offshore financial centres to finance their own operations.

As discussed in Chapter 2, offshore money creation is the act whereby banks lend money to non-residents in a currency foreign to the jurisdiction in which the transaction takes place. Theoretically, every internationally traded currency in the world can be created in these offshore markets. In practice, it is mostly US dollars that are so created.[79] Unlike the other three cases discussed in this book, however, British economic actors deposit and borrow offshore in a set of foreign currencies as Figure 3.2 shows.

Disaggregating Britain's offshore exposure by currency denomination, I find that since 1998, roughly 80 per cent of the overall offshore exposure has taken place in the offshore US dollar and offshore euro markets.

The offshore assets in particular that British economic actors hold offshore can be used for tax planning purposes. According to an interviewee, offshoring in Britain is driven by taxes on capital and banks' balance sheet management: 'The wealthy put their wealth into trusts offshore to avoid ... tax. It is also the banks who book assets offshore to back up their offshore debt'.[80]

Assuming that all offshore assets are undeclared and, if onshore, were taxed at the full applicable rate, we can develop a simple, rough estimate of the upper bound of lost tax revenue due to offshoring pictured in Figure 3.3.[81]

The maximum tax loss ranges between 12 per cent of GDP in 2000 and 15 per cent in 2019. It peaked at 25 per cent of GDP in 2010, decreasing from then onwards in line with overall offshore exposure. These numbers are staggering but must be seen in context.

First, given that Britain also provides offshore financial services, offshore assets are a means of banks' balance sheet management. It cannot be determined based on BIS data to what extent it constitutes taxable income. In addition, it is unlikely that—as assumed in our estimate—all offshore assets go untaxed and would be taxed if onshore. At the same time, British banks, in the

[79] He and McCauley 2012.
[80] Author's telephone interview with offshore expert, October 2018.
[81] Details of this approach, including its limitations, are discussed in Appendix 1.

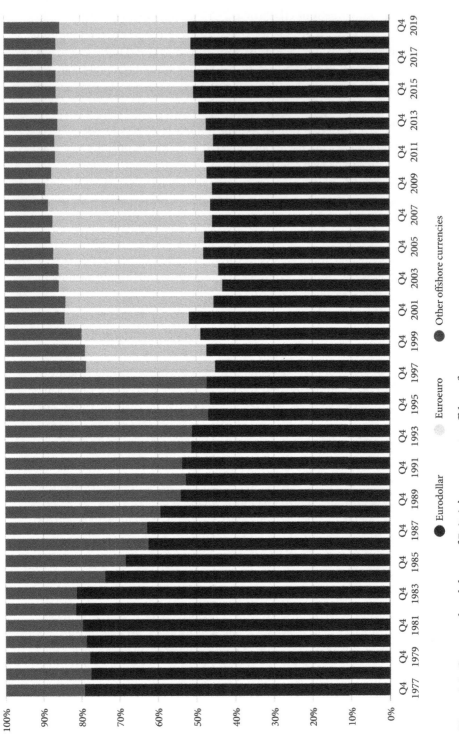

**Figure 3.2** Currency breakdown of Britain's exposure to offshore finance

*Source:* BIS locational banking statistics, own calculation.

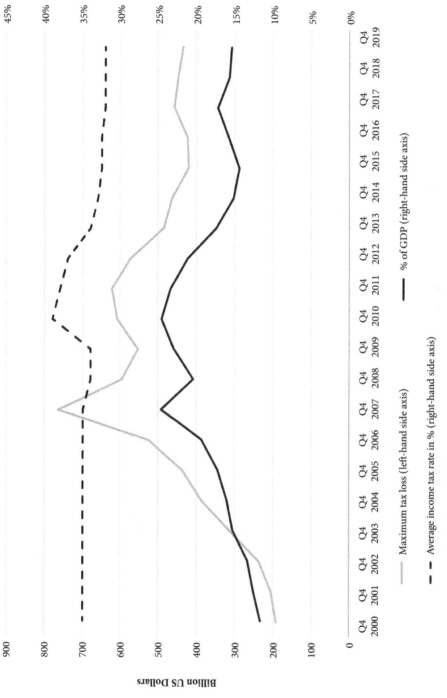

**Figure 3.3** Britain's estimated maximum tax loss

*Source:* BIS locational banking statistics, World Bank, OECD, own calculations.

same way as other corporations, do use offshore financial sectors to plan their taxes.[82] Not least because the New Labour governments (1997–2010) dismantled the defensive measures that Labour Prime Minister Clement Attlee and his successors had built around the British corporate tax base in the early post-war years. As a result, industrial-scale tax planning for multinational corporations became commonplace in Britain.

Second, the Thatcher (1979–90) and Major (1990–97) governments had already initiated a shift from direct to indirect taxation.[83] In terms of financing the state, other taxpayers picked up the loss caused by a drop of corporate and high-income tax rates. The same government that dismantled defensive measures against offshore tax evasion demonstrated that the British state is nonetheless able to finance its political programme via taxation and even, if so desired, in a progressive manner. The New Labour governments' tax and benefit reforms let to a net increase of revenue of £7.1 billion while 'significantly reducing the incomes of richer households and increasing those of poorer ones.'[84] In short, offshore tax planning may lead to significant tax losses in Britain. Yet, it has not limited the British state's ability to mobilize resources to finance its political programme.

As with tax planning, the financial flows depicted in Figure 3.1 can also be used for money laundering by British economic actors. However, there is remarkably little evidence of British public or private actors using offshore financial centres to launder money. This ostensible restraint stands out in comparison to the other three case studies. Indeed, according to Transparency International's corruption perception index, Britain is among the world's ten least corrupt countries.[85] Where the predicate crime is limited, there is a limited need to launder money offshore. Yet, interviewees pointed out that for offshore money laundering from tax evasion, the empirical data are less clear. It is impossible to determine how much of the above-discussed offshore tax planning is illegal, and how much is legal. It is known, however, that it is usually individuals, not firms that evade taxes. Corporations have the necessary legal and accountancy advice to keep tax planning activities legal.[86] It stands to reason that in Britain, offshore financial services play a limited role in money laundering.

[82] Aubry and Dauphin 2017.
[83] Daunton 2002, ch. 1.
[84] Browne and Phillips 2010, 1.
[85] Transparency International 2017.
[86] Author's interview with corporate tax lawyer, London, September 2017 and with tax lawyer, London, September 2017.

Finally, if we disaggregate the data by counterparty country, we can see the most prominent offshore financial centres used by British economic actors. In line with the historical development of offshore finance in Britain, the top five offshore financial centres are, in declining order, Jersey, Switzerland, the Netherlands, the Cayman Islands, and Luxembourg. Except for the Cayman Islands, British economic actors use offshore financial services in Europe.

## The provision of offshore financial services

The scale and pattern of the offshore financial services that the City of London provides to the world cannot be quantified with existing data. The BIS data cannot be disaggregated by sector. It is therefore impossible to differentiate between Britain's onshore and offshore economy (see Appendix 1 for details). The following analysis thus draws on qualitative data and secondary sources.

In their study on the nature of offshore financial centres, Bernardo Garcia and colleagues identify Britain as a 'conduit' offshore centre.[87] Conduit offshore centres are intermediary centres between the location of the investor and the final recipient of the investment. Investments are routed through conduit offshore centres for tax purposes.[88] Next to tax, however, there are other reasons to route investments through Britain. Most importantly, these reasons include the British legal system, which counts as the world's most developed legal framework to deal with international trade and investment issues, as well as the size and internationalization of Britain's banks.[89] Especially large and complex financial instruments can only be issued in New York or London.[90]

In the contemporary period, the City's traditional offshore banking business grew, aided by two important government policy choices.

First, Margaret Thatcher's 1986 'Big Bang' which intended to keep the City competitive as, in the late 1970s and early 1980s, deregulation gave US American financial firms an edge over their British competitors. The new regulations made it possible for foreign banks to own British brokers. International financiers swiftly started to buy traditional British banks.[91] Prominent examples include S.G. Warburg, which was bought by Swiss Bank and Morgan Grenfell, acquired by Deutsche Bank. Deutsche had long tried to increase its initial 5 per cent share in Morgan Grenfell to tap into British know-how

---

[87] Garcia-Bernardo et al. 2017, 1.
[88] Garcia-Bernardo et al. 2017; Damgaard, Elkjaer, and Johannesen 2019.
[89] Author's interview with tax lawyer, London, July 2017.
[90] Author's interview with lawyer specializing in British banking law, Mexico City, November 2015.
[91] Tooze 2018, ch. 3.

of investment banking. Yet, to no avail. Morgan Grenfell's majority shareholders rejected the offer. The situation only changed, as one participant in the takeover remembers, 'when, in the wake of deregulation, the [British] banks ... were exposed to free market forces'.[92] The American banks, however, moved into London most forcefully. Morgan Stanley, Goldman Sachs, Citibank, and others were all buying British banks. By the early 2000s, none of the largest ten merchant banks pre-Big Bang was still British owned. The City became foreign-owned and British-staffed.[93] This process of opening the institutional association of rule towards foreign financiers culminated in 2013 with the appointment of the Canadian Mark Carney as the first foreigner to lead the Bank of England.

Second, Blair's New Labour government coming into office in 1997; the introduction of the euro in eleven continental European countries in 1998; and China's growing hunger for Eurodollars, gave offshore money creation in London another boost. The New Labour government signalled its support through further financial liberalization and by transferring the right to set interest rates from the Treasury back to the Bank of England. In combination with previous reforms, these measures made financial transactions possible in the City of London that made bankers on Wall Street burst with envy.[94]

The steadily growing offshore business from the late 1990s onwards is striking for two reasons.

First, it falls into a time when the US Federal Reserve aimed to tighten the US dollar money supply. Between 2004 and 2006, the US central bank raised the federal funds rate from 1 to 5.4 per cent.[95] Yet, British offshore financial institutions continued to expand the Eurodollar supply undisturbed by US monetary policy.

Furthermore, the emergence of the City of London as a centre for the offshore euro came as a surprise to eurozone members. It moved London to the core of the European financial system despite Britain's reluctance to fully commit to the European Union as a political project.[96] Both effects support the argument that offshore and onshore currencies follow separate logics and have different implications. Although denoted in the same way, offshore and onshore currencies are indeed two separate monies (see Chapter 2).

Opening the City of London to little regulated international financial flows also had consequences for money laundering. As the overall inflow of money

---

[92] Historische Gesellschaft der Deutschen Bank 2017, 59.
[93] Augar 2008.
[94] Tooze 2018, ch. 3.
[95] Snider 2018 PodCast to Townsend.
[96] Thompson 2017.

increased, the amount of illicit money grew too. There is a long list of money laundering scandals involving the City of London. For kleptocrats, Russian oligarchs, or Pakistani and Chinese fleeing capital, London's financial and real estate markets have been the destination of choice.[97]

In a report from 2018, Britain's National Crime Agency (NCA) observes that 'given the volume of financial transactions transiting the UK, there is a realistic possibility the scale of money laundering impacting the UK annually is in the hundreds of billions of pounds'.[98] The large scandals in recent years were all part of banks' business with non-residents and US-dollar-denominated. They were part of London's Eurodollar business. For example, the 'Russian Laundromat', a global money laundering scheme uncovered in 2014 by a consortium of investigative journalists, helped wealthy Russians move US$20.8 billion out of Russia.[99] The scheme involved ninety-six countries, but London was central to it. Most shell companies used for the fraud were registered there.[100]

Indeed, the NCA finds that British companies and trusts are 'used extensively to launder money', because they are easy to open and appear to be legitimate businesses.[101] In addition, the report finds that 'a small number' of corrupt lawyers, accountants, bankers as well as trust and company providers help laundering money through London's financial sector. Foreign exchange markets are particularly vulnerable.[102] In short, money laundering in Britain relates to non-residents and the transactions are often denominated in US dollars. Apparently, an increase in offshore dollar business comes with an increase in offshore money laundering.

The government and the financial sector (including the Bank of England) largely took the approach of see no evil, hear no evil, speak no evil. The predicate crime was committed in foreign lands and hence did not appear to be Britain's problem. Especially as the foreigners' wealth stored in London was a welcome asset for the credit-creating machinery in the City of London. Over time, with the rise of the international anti-kleptocracy regime in the early 2000s, the illicit sources of funds became more politically contested. Successive governments passed laws to root out 'dirty' money, but the implementation of these laws was wanting.[103]

---

[97] Sharman 2017, ch. 4; NCA 2018.
[98] NCA 2018, 23.
[99] OCCRP 2014.
[100] Harding 2017; Milne 2018.
[101] NCA 2018, 39.
[102] Ibid., 23–39.
[103] Sharman 2017, ch. 4.

In sum, the contemporary exposure to and provision of offshore financial services in Britain leave little doubt that offshore finance plays an important role for the British political economy. It tells us little, though, about how it affects the power of the British state. The next section turns to this question.

## 3 The encounter

The previous two sections established the specific nature and development of the British state and its sources of power as well as the country's exposure to offshore financial services from the money view.

The British institutional association of rule was, for a long time, marked by a near-identity between economic and political elites, between the state and its financiers, the taxman and the taxpayer. As that tight elite started to broaden—first to include industrial capitalists, then to lower classes through the advent of mass democracy, and finally to foreign financiers through the liberalization of bank ownership—the interests within the *Herrschaftsverband* started to conflict with each other. These conflicts were initially mitigated through the country's tax and bank bargains. In both bargains depoliticizing the controversy—money creation and taxation—played an important role.

Entrenching a (random but fixed) content of metal into coins, as suggested by John Locke in 1695, purported the perception of money as something natural (and thus politically indisputable) rather than social (and thus politically contested). It also embedded, via the desirability of 'sound money', creditor protection into the bank bargain.[104] The depoliticization of money systematically strengthened the hand of financiers over government. Likewise, around two hundred years later, the Gladstonian fiscal constitution aimed to remove taxation from parliamentary politics to achieve consent between the elites that made up the British state.[105]

However, as the institutional association of rule expanded once more, this time through mass democracy, the conflicting interests between the different elites were hard to overcome. Incapable of forming the bank and tax bargains in their favour, gentleman capitalists moved offshore to recreate their pre-1914 world; a world of small, tight economic and political elites that exclusively determine the rules for money creation and taxation and their resulting contribution to financing the state.

---

[104] Eich 2020.
[105] Daunton 2007.

By the 1990s, the New Labour governments' embrace of offshore banking brought offshore finance back into the domestic bank and tax bargains—via the politics of the invisible. The country's exposure to offshore finance grew exponentially. Along came a growing influence of foreign financiers within the institutional association of rule. Consequently, todays' offshore finance is both external and internal to the British state.

How did these developments affect the power of the British state to finance its political goals? This question entails, as discussed in Chapter 1, an element that asks about the mechanism of the effect—how does it work?—and one that asks about the quality of the effect—is it enhancing or limiting state power?

Given the cycle of money, tax, and debt it is taxation and money creation that are the key potential mechanisms through which offshore finance can affect state power. Despite the significant revenue loss related to offshore tax planning, the British state could mobilize—through a redistribution of the tax burden to those taxpayers who do or cannot go offshore—enough resources to finance its political goals. In the case of Britain, the central mechanism of how offshore finance affects state power is offshore banking. Invented and maintained by financial elites in the City of London, offshore finance is an extension of and fundamental threat to British state power as the subsequent analysis demonstrates.

## Strengthening state power

The invention of offshore financial services allowed the City of London to extend its banking model—connecting private wealth management with providing credit—across borders. From the 1950s onwards, offshore money creation had thus become a part of the British cycle of money, tax, and debt.

Offshore money creation has had two fundamental advantages. For one, offshore money creation has allowed Britain to provide liquidity to the international economy. Britain thus could co-share the role of the banker to the world with the United States, and put itself at the centre of the European financial system without joining the common currency. Better still, it allowed Britain to do so without paying the domestic political price attached to maintaining the pound's international role. Thanks to offshore money creation, Britain could retain its monetary autonomy and profit from creating the two leading global currencies, the US dollar and the euro.[106] Partaking in the power to create US

---

[106] Thompson 2017; Hardie and Thompson 2020.

dollars and euro extended Britain's international influence beyond the country's actual political and economic weight.[107] Offshore money creation allowed Britain to co-constitute global financial capitalism.[108]

Nevertheless, the City's ability to create US dollars was possible only because the US government did not contest offshore money creation.[109] Its ability to create euro, in turn, hinged on a lack of anticipation by the eurozone governments about the importance of Britain in internationalizing the euro without being part of the single currency.[110] Despite the resulting interdependence, offshore banking helped the City, as intended, to maintain its historically important role in international finance.

Second, offshore money creation and tax planning offered the government political space via the politics of the invisible. British post-war Tory governments, especially under Churchill and Margaret Thatcher, ensured the City's continuous success. Yet, none of them supported offshore finance as much as the Blair and Brown governments did.[111] Through avid deregulation, New Labour responded to the demands from the City to further extend the possibilities for offshore money creation and tax planning, framing these services as a means of efficiency. If the activities in the Euromarkets and the related tax planning were not ruled to be illegal, the politics of the invisible was now presentable within the economic and political elites. This is exemplified by the fact that the British government rents public buildings from private companies which are incorporated in Jersey, Bermuda, and elsewhere in the offshore world.[112] The Labour governments' new attitude towards offshoring recalibrated the power between the government, financiers, and taxpayers once more. The financiers, free to use offshore within a legally welcoming context, could profit personally and professionally from tax-reduced offshore transactions. Moreover, the offshore practices that were once an exit of the propertied classes from a tax system that no longer aligned with their interests had become an intrinsic part of that order again. The gain in power for the financiers, however, was not at the detriment of that of the state. The state had intentionally established a legal framework that allowed for corporate offshore tax and regulatory arbitrage.[113] Economic growth and other taxpayers picked up the slack caused by offshore tax planning. The New Labour policies resulted

[107] Burn 1999; Green 2016.
[108] Green 2020.
[109] Helleiner 1994; Altamura 2017.
[110] Thompson 2017.
[111] Ibid.
[112] Brooks 2014, ch. 9.
[113] Author's interview with tax lawyer, London, June 2017.

in a redistribution of power within the group of taxpayers from those using offshore financial services to those who could, or did, not.

The degree to which the state sided with those groups of financiers and taxpayers that used offshore financial services over everyone else remained invisible. The logic underlying offshore finance was to extend the invisible earnings of gentlemanly capitalism to the offshore world and—with the agreement of the Bank of England—off the regular balance sheet. Invisibility was a welcome instrument of gentlemanly capitalism to keep assets safe in face of the extension of the franchise and regulations.

It was also an instrument for governments, especially labour-led ones, to lessen the tension between serving old and new constituencies, Blue and New Labour. London was the world's leading supplier of global liquidity. The City's offshore business contributed to the government's tax revenue, and created large incomes for the workforce in the City. At least a share of these top incomes went untaxed. For instance, the bonus payments of top bankers were paid right into offshore bank accounts.[114] In return, the New Labour governments could implement progressive tax policies and spending that led to a perceivable drop in child and pensioner poverty. The politics of the invisible allowed Labour to oversee a drop in poverty and an increase in income inequality driven by the rise of top incomes at the same time.[115]

Besides its obscure nature, offshore banking and tax planning were invisible because the system simply worked. Indeed, in the late 1990s, early 2000s offshore banking worked so well that it made 'everything look shiny and wonderful, rainbows and unicorns', to quote a hedge fund manager.[116] Offshore money creation and tax planning remained uncontested in the larger public. In short, Britain provided preferential liquidity to the world, earning international influence in return. At the same time, the politics of the invisible was an excellent tool to uphold the old order, keeping the City of London and the financial elite at the centre of the international financial system and the national interest—despite the rise of the US dollar and of mass democracy.

## Undermining state power

The ever-expanding offshore markets worked for Britain—until they no longer did. When the global financial crisis brought the international financial system

[114] Brooks 2014, chap. 6.
[115] Joyce and Sibieta 2013.
[116] Snider to Townsend 2018, pt. 7.

to its knees, the Eurodollar markets played a significant role in the melt-down.[117] In the heydays of offshore banking—the decade between 1997 and 2007—the Eurodollar exposure of European banks grew to about half of their overall foreign currency exposure. Banks from Britain, the European Union, and Switzerland accumulated a collective on-balance sheet exposure of more than US$8 trillion. They refinanced about three-quarters of that exposure through inter-bank lending and the rest through a combination of money market funds, central bank funding, and foreign exchange swaps. That is to say, European banks created US dollars, the vast majority of it in London, but they lacked, contrary to the early days of the Eurodollar, a corresponding source of retail US dollar deposits.[118] Dependent on funding sources from the wholesale market, the European Eurobanks quickly ran dry when these markets suddenly froze in 2008. The banks lost their ability to create fiat offshore money almost overnight.[119]

Now a lender of last resort would have been useful. Yet, throughout the development of the Eurodollar system, the Bank of England and the Federal Reserve had both declined that role. Bagehot's decedents on both sides of the Atlantic were still lacking a solution of how to lend to the world without acting as a lender of last resort. The second-best option, then, appeared to be a central bank currency swap between the Federal Reserve and European central banks in combination with a decade of quantitative easing. These measures established the Fed—and through the swaps also the Bank of England—as money dealers, activities usually done by commercial banks.[120] These measures stabilized British offshore money creation at the level of 2006 in terms of GDP.[121] The subsequent low interest rate environment in combination with renewed regulations structurally changed the Eurodollar markets.[122] However, the lack of any sustained growth in Eurodollar credit beyond the level of 2006 in over a decade left the City of London struggling with its offshore banking business. It threatened the City's role as offshore banker to the world. The struggle was further compounded by the eurozone crisis and the political crisis of Brexit. Relinquishing membership in the European Union was the first far-reaching political decision taken against the interests of the City of London.[123] The City subsequently lost significant portions of the share market, especially

---

[117] Tooze 2018, chap. 3.
[118] Goldberg, Kennedy, and Miu 2010, 4.
[119] Snider 2018 podcast to Townsend, pt. 6.
[120] Mehrling 2011.
[121] See Figure 3.1 above.
[122] Interview with banker, London, July 2019.
[123] Thompson 2017.

to Amsterdam. In early 2021, the Dutch city surpassed London as Europe's largest share trading centre. However, more important from the perspective of offshore finance is London's loss of euro-denominated interest rate swaps, one of the core elements of offshore money creation.[124] Although there are no data relating to other elements of London's euro market such as bonds and loans, the loss of derivatives trading is an indication that London's pre-eminent role as an offshore centre for the euro may come to an end.[125]

The triple crisis was not one for the City of London alone. Thanks to the size and centrality of offshore banking in the British economy, British taxpayers were ultimately going to be responsible for bailing out the banks post-2008. It was an expensive affair. By 2010, the total amount taxpayers had to shoulder was £124 billion, their theoretical exposure (should all banks in government possession fail) £512 billion.[126] The bailout and the subsequent policies of austerity became a long-term liability to the state's ability to finance its welfare state politics. Presented with the choice of continuing to finance the welfare state at post-war levels or to service debt, the British state prioritized the latter and used quantitative easing to prop-up the former. This choice left 20 per cent of Britain's population struggling with poverty.[127] As in the early days of gentlemanly capitalism, the London-based banks (and by extension the state) had reaped the benefits of money creation, and the costs were distributed widely.

In the end, it was offshore tax planning that ignited the public's contestation. The issue became one of national interest in 2013 with the House of Commons' public hearing of senior managers of Starbucks, Amazon, and Google regarding their offshore tax planning strategies.[128] The hearing was followed by public protests against 'tax dodging' multinationals in 2014.[129] Yet, as different interviewees pointed out, HMRC has never brought the legal structures underlying offshore tax planning to the courts. Instead, HMRC opens criminal investigations into individuals and if these investigations reach the conclusion of tax evasion, the authorities reach a deal about the level of the fine and the repayment of taxes with them.[130] Interviewees had different assessments why HMRC is reluctant to bring the offshore schemes to the courts. One saw it as the result of a policy focusing on maximizing the tax revenue in

---

[124] See Chapter 2.
[125] Smith-Meyer and Busquets Guàrdia 2021.
[126] National Audit Office 2010.
[127] Alston 2018.
[128] Committee of Public Accounts 2013; Hodge 2016.
[129] Rawlinson 2014.
[130] Author's interview with corporate tax lawyer, London, October 2017; author's interview with tax lawyer, London, September 2017; author's telephone interview with employee of civil society organization, October 2017.

the short term by recovering payments and at the same time avoiding lengthy litigation processes.[131] Another saw it as the result of a deliberate strategy of HMRC to maintain a situation where offshore tax planning structures are neither clearly legal nor illegal.[132] The global financial crisis exposed what the politics of the invisible had obscured. The British state sided with the exclusive set of actors who can and do go offshore over those who do not or cannot. Once the invisible became visible, it started to undermine British state power.

## No straightforward relationship

Britain is the heartland of offshore finance. It invented it. The state and the Bank of England created a permissive environment for offshore finance to prosper. Contrary to Germany, Brazil, and Mexico, Britain provides preferential liquidity via offshore money creation to other states. It has used and developed its legal code to serve that purpose. It also uses offshore financial services to extend the financial elite's time-tested politics of the invisible across borders.

The economic actors who use and provide offshore financial services were and still are to a significant extent identical or very close to the political elites legislating on offshore finance. The *Panama Papers* and *Paradise Papers* leaks revealed that public figures, including the former Prime Minister David Cameron, Queen Elisabeth II, and prominent party donors, especially of the Tory Party and the United Kingdom Independence Party (UKIP), hold (mostly legal) offshore accounts.[133]

Consequently, over the course of the past seventy years, offshore finance has altered the nature of the British state. Starting out as a phenomenon serving the interests of the institutional association of rule, offshore finance became a part of it. Offshore finance extended gentlemanly capitalism's politics of the invisible across national borders. The old financial elites, coming under pressure in the post-war years, from the outside through the rise of the US dollar and from the inside through mass democracy, reached for a time-tested approach to defend their position. They co-opted contenders into the institutional association of rule and the politics of the invisible. Especially the co-optation of international financiers in the late 1990s was consequential. It preserved the preeminent role of the City of London's interests within a larger set of national

---

[131] Author's interview with corporate tax lawyer, London, October 2017.
[132] Author's telephone interview with employee of civil society organization, October 2017.
[133] The Guardian 2016, 2017.

interests. But it also led to a certain extent to a denationalization of the British state. The relationship between financial and political elites loosened relative to the past. The Bank of England, initially a site of shared power between the royal government and its financiers, started to represent the shared interests of domestic and international financiers. Government and Parliament remained dominated by the moneyed classes. Now an internationalized financial capitalist class negotiated with the British moneyed classes, and the taxpayers over how to finance the British state. That bargain led to an ever-expanding power of financiers to create US dollars and euro. Offshore money creation, thus, has been more consequential for state power than offshore tax planning. The related significant revenue loss was balanced through a redistribution of the tax burden to those taxpayers who do not or cannot go offshore.

The resulting relationship between offshore finance and state power in Britain is not straightforward. It enhances and limits state power. In addition, offshore money laundering even left the power of the state to finance its politics untouched. It brought the revenues from foreign economic and political crime into Britain (and with it at times the related political conflict), yet it did not affect the state's ability to finance its political goals.

From its beginnings in the 1950s to the global financial crisis, offshore finance was a strategy of the British state to patch up class warfare domestically and maintain political influence internationally. It changed the distributional conflict of money creation and taxation in favour of London-based and international financiers maintaining privileges offshore once mass democracy had shrunk them onshore. In the case of Britain, mass democracy engendered offshore finance.

Thanks to offshore finance, British governments—especially Labour-led ones—could pursue contradictory economic and social policies without being interrogated about it. Offshore banking strengthened the British state's power because it was a direct and indirect source of funding. More important still, it was a means to keep the financial sector competitive. Given the shared power of money creation between the state and banks, the City of London's success in creating US dollars and euro conferred political competitiveness to the British state.

Once the Euromarkets faltered and the politics of the invisible had been laid bare, offshore finance developed destructive forces. The United States and eurozone member states instantaneously contested the City of London's offshore money creation.[134] Likewise, Parliament and the public contested

---

[134] Thompson 2017.

large-scale offshore tax planning strategies used by large corporations and the well-to-do[135] and the pre-eminence of finance in the British economy more broadly.[136]

The money view on state power and offshore finance highlights that the financial crisis and the following eurozone crisis were not external shocks to Britain. They were the result of London-based banking, of offshore money creation without a lender of last resort. They were the result of the importance of the financial elites within the institutional association of rule.

The inclusiveness towards foreign financiers was also an element in how Brexit played out for the City. Dominated by international financiers, the financial elite took it for granted that the age-old understanding of the City's interests as a national interest would hold in the referendum. They underestimated that the electorate's woes with European Union membership lay elsewhere, not least in migration policies.[137]

That is, offshore finance did not undermine the British state's ability to finance its politics because of tax loss and the inability to regulate money creation. These policies have been driven by an institutional association of rule in which the financial elite historically has had a dominant role. Offshore finance undermined the British state's power because the system became transparent once it turned dysfunctional. As the true nature of the bargain over money creation and taxation in Britain became apparent, it was contested domestically and internationally.

Brexit is the current critical juncture for the relationship between offshore finance and state power in Britain. At the writing of this book, the direction of travel—enhancing or limiting state power—is still open. The British state may aim once more to salvage its international standing through offshore finance. It may preserve its US dollar business and turn from Europe to Asia.[138]

---

[135] Shaxson 2012; House of Lords 2013; Hodge 2016.
[136] Christensen, Shaxson, and Wigan 2016.
[137] Thompson 2017.
[138] Green and Gruin 2020.

# 4

# Germany

## The tax state and its adversaries

If Britain is the inventor of offshore finance, Germany is its catalyst. This assessment runs counter to conventional wisdom, which has Germany as one of offshore finance's prime victims. Germany is a classic high tax country, a large and open economy that shares a border with three globally important offshore financial centres: Switzerland, the Netherlands, and Luxembourg. Indeed, private individuals and firms make substantial use of these tax havens. However, Germany is not exclusively at the receiving end of offshore financial services. Rather, from the early days of the Eurodollar markets, offshore money creation was a lucrative but risky business for a select number of German banks. Driven by the export-orientation of the German economy and the related US dollar overhang, Germany played an enabling role in the development of the Eurodollar markets in the 1960s and 1970s.

However, unlike in Britain, offshore money creation did not become a substantial part of Germany's cycle of money, tax, and debt. Germany is the classic example of a state where that domestic cycle encounters the external offshore world.

The historical empirical analysis in this chapter demonstrates that, in line with the arguments made in Chapter 2, the mechanism whereby offshore finance affects state power can be seen on both sides of the balance sheet: taxation and money creation. Yet, in contemporary Germany—as in Britain— offshore banking has been more consequential for state power than offshore tax planning.

Contrary to conventional wisdom, however, the analysis also reveals that offshore finance enhances state power. Via the politics of the invisible, it has allowed successive German governments to pursue contradictory economic policies without being questioned. It also provided the state with access to preferential liquidity when there were insufficient domestic means to cover the costs of reunification. Yet, as in the British case, these power-enhancing effects where limited to the good times.

*Offshore Finance and State Power.* Andrea Binder, Oxford University Press. © Andrea Binder (2023). DOI: 10.1093/oso/9780192870124.003.0004

During the constitutional crisis of the Weimar Republic, the scale of hiding money offshore did undermine the state's ability to finance its political goals at a moment when state finances were in tatters. Then again, with the global financial crisis—rooted to a significant extent in offshore money markets—offshore finance unfolded destructive forces. However, in a marked difference to the Weimar Republic and to the British experience, contemporary Germany had built domestic institutions mitigating these power-undermining effects. The state found means to reap the benefits of offshore finance for domestic politics, while keeping the costs externally.

This chapter analyses the counter-intuitive relationship between offshore finance and state power in Germany through three phases: (1) the rise and fall of imperial Germany—starting with the foundation of the German Customs Union (*Zollverein*) in 1833 and ending with the advent of World War I; (2) the long interregnum of the Weimar Republic and Nazi Germany; and (3) the contemporary period starting with post-war Germany, including unification and the introduction of the euro in 1998. In contrast to Britain, the critical junctures are not central momentes of change in a continuously evolving polity, but transitions between five radically different political regimes: the German Empire (1870/71–1918), the Weimar Republic (1918–33), National Socialist Germany (1933–45), the Bonn Republic (1949–91), and the Berlin Republic (1991 to today).

## 1  German state power from the money view

Unsurprisingly, then, the formation and evolution of Germany's institutional association of rule and its strategies to finance its political goals are markedly different from the British experience (see Chapter 3). In the early eighteenth century, when England, Wales, and Scotland had a shared cycle of money, tax, and debt, the twenty-five small states that would one day merge into the German Empire ran on six different currencies with 119 different coins and 117 different sorts of paper money.[1] It was only in the nineteenth century with the foundation of three successive institutions—the *Zollverein*[2] in 1833, the German Empire in 1870/71, and the *Reichsbank*, Germany's central bank, in 1876—that the country developed a cycle of money, tax, and debt comparable to that of Britain. Consequently, the analysis of the institutional association of

---

[1] Ullmann 2005.
[2] The *Zollverein* was a customs union between the different states that were to become the German Empire, but—unlike the Empire—also included Luxembourg.

rule and its struggles over how to finance the state starts in the late nineteenth century, about two hundred years later than in Britain.

The foundation of the German Empire in January 1871 was the unification of twenty-five previously independent states. These small states had already developed elements of modern statehood, in particular tax systems and a small but functioning cycle of money, tax, and debt.

With unification into a federal nation state, the tax systems at the state level were complemented by tax rules on the federal level.[3] On the monetary side, the development was more centralized. Five years after the empire's foundation, the thirty-three state-level 'banks of issue' (*Notenbanken*) were merged into one central bank, the *Reichsbank*, now issuing the new single currency, the mark. The Reichsbank, from its beginnings, was a classic central bank concerned with currency issue, integrating individual banks into a national banking system, and acting as a lender of last resort. That is, unlike the Bank of England, the *Reichsbank* was more a bureaucratic institution than an institutional reflection of the relationship between the imperial government and its financiers.

Instead, it was the establishment of three commercial banks—Deutsche Bank (1870), Commerzbank (1870), and Dresdner Bank (1872)—that fundamentally shaped the institutional association of rule in the empire's early years. It was the development of modern banking that unified, from the mid-nineteenth century onwards, corporate and financial capital into a money elite. Given the late arrival of parliamentarism in Germany—compared to Britain anyway—Germany's political class consisted of functionaries more than of politicians: government representatives, high rank civil servants, judges, scholars, clerics, and functionaries of other important institutions.[4] Together, they built Germany's so-called *Funktionselite*, an elite of functionaries. The money elite remained separate from but built close relationships with the *Funktionselite*.

The history of Deutsche Bank is an exemplar of that constellation. The purpose of establishing the bank in 1870 was to finance industrialization and, with the idea of imperial expansion in mind, foreign trade previously handled by international banks.[5]

The relationship between Deutsche Bank and the government was strategically closely knit from the beginning. Georg Siemens, one of the bank's founders, went to great lengths to establish a relationship with the emperor.

[3] Ullmann 2005.
[4] Rebenstorf 1995; Kaina 2004.
[5] Gall 1995.

He managed to meet William II personally on a trip to the Middle East in 1898. Three years later, Siemens was considered as a candidate for Minister of Finance. Although Siemens declined, he maintained close ties with the emperor. Besides politics, Georg Siemens also had close personal ties with Germany's industrializing enterprises. He was the second cousin of Walter von Siemens, founder of the electrical company of the same name. After initially focusing Deutsche Bank's business on commercial banking, it was Georg Siemens who moved the bank into universal banking and with it into the large-scale financing of industrial enterprises. Siemens and other electrical companies were among the earliest recipients of credit from Deutsche Bank.[6] They were soon joined by other industrializing sectors such as coal and steel mining. As part of its financing of industry, Deutsche Bank became a shareholder in its client companies. In turn, important clients became members of the bank's supervisory board. The inter-locking boards of commercial banks and large corporations became a hallmark of German banking. The industrialization process and the development of universal banking in Germany mutually reinforced the strengthening of cartelized industries and big banks.[7]

This money elite has been unwavering across time and regimes. The same business-owning families dominate the wealthy classes today as in 1871, and the same banks still dominate the German banking system.[8] The *Funktionselite*, on the other hand, was not stable across time. Its members have largely been replaced with each regime change.[9] Moreover, it expanded over time to also include parliamentarians, union leaders, and leading figures from the media.[10] Together, the money elite and the *Funktionselite* make up Germany's institutional association of rule. Across the three phases, the interplay between a stable money elite anchored in German industrialism and a regularly displaced elite of functionaries shaped the German state and its struggle over how to finance its political goals. This struggle is institutionalized in Germany's bargains over money creation and taxation.

## Bank bargain

The shared power of money creation between the state and banks is entrenched in Germany's three-pillared banking system. The founding of Deutsche Bank, Commerzbank, and Dresdner Bank in the early 1870s

[6] Ibid.
[7] Ibid.; Gerschenkron 1979.
[8] Bartels 2017; Berghoff and Köhler 2007.
[9] Schäfers 2004.
[10] Kaina 2004.

complemented the pre-existing two pillars: the savings and cooperative banks at the local level, and the *Landesbanken* at the regional level. These two pillars had developed in the states preceding and then constituting the German Empire.

Savings and cooperative banks emerged in the early to mid-nineteenth century. They were a local response to rural poverty caused, among other events, by a lack of access to credit for farmers and craftsmen. Around 1830, the public *Landesbanken* developed to settle the accounts between the savings banks and to provide finance to the state governments through issuing bonds. *Landesbanken* were comparable to central banks, only on a smaller scale.

These three pillars were tied together into a national banking system with the foundation of the Reichsbank in 1875. This newly created central bank on the federal level was a reincarnation of the Prussian state bank and directly subordinate to the Chancellor.

The three-pillared banking system determined how money was created in the empire: local savings and cooperative banks created the money for financing small businesses, farmers, and craftsman. Regional *Landesbanken* backed up the local money creation and provided funding for state governments. Large private banks created money for industrial corporations. The *Reichsbank* backed up the *Landesbanken* and the big commercial banks. The imperial banking system created competition between the locally and regionally organized savings and cooperative banks as well as between the large commercial banks. As a result, during the early days of empire, access to credit was affordable for most economic actors ranging from private individuals, over farmers, to small firms, big corporations, and the state governments. In addition, the banking system stabilized the financial system along ownership structures. In times of crisis, the publicly owned savings banks and *Landesbanken* were to be bailed out by the taxpayer. The privately owned commercial and cooperative banks had no such guarantees but could rely on the publicly owned *Reichsbank*, as a lender of last resort. The bargain distributed the costs and benefits of money creation across different groups of society. It was not an exclusive one.

However, very different to the role of the Bank of England, the *Reichsbank* was not established to finance the government. Reparations from France, defeated in the Franco-Prussian war in 1870/71, were used to repay the debt of the empire's predecessor states. At its foundation, the German Empire was debt free.[11]

---

[11] Ullmann 2005.

Also, the federal government's spending needs were still limited. Thanks to French gold, the war chest in Berlin-Spandau was full.[12] Spending on civilian causes—including much of Chancellor Bismarck's foundations of the welfare state—fell mostly upon the states.[13] Reflecting the interests of the money elite, the *Reichsbank's* raison d'être was to act as a currency watchdog and a bankers' bank. It did not act as a government's bank.

So, the question of how to finance the federal state only became crucial with World War I. The Industrial Revolution had brought with it the possibility of industrial-scale warfare. If the scale of human suffering surpassed the imagination of contemporaries, so did the actual economic costs of modern warfare. Germany's war chest in Berlin-Spandau proved to be full by the standards of the old times only. In the new times, the gold in Spandau was good for financing a mere two days of fighting.[14] The German Empire urgently needed to mobilize resources.

Excluded from international financial markets after the outbreak of the war, the only possible source was domestic borrowing. Issuing eight war bonds between 1914 and 1918, William II raised US$27 billion from small savers, wealthy individuals, and corporations.[15] The financiers saw the war and its expansionary goals as being aligned with their own interests to expand beyond the confines of the empire. However, given the risks, they preferred lending over financing the war via tax. William II was so adamant not to tax the money elite that tax receipts actually declined during the war. As a result, Germany paid the costs of war 100 per cent out of money creation unsecured by tax income. It paid for the war with debt and inflation.

By the end of the war, the money supply had multiplied by six and the *Reichsbank* directly held a fifth of the government's debt.[16] Germany turned into a quintessential debt state.

Faced with defeat abroad in September and a revolution at home in November 1918, William II abdicated and fled into exile. The November Revolution was the preliminary climax of a class struggle between the growing working class and the money class over the distribution of the wealth created throughout the Industrial Revolution and the burden of World War I. It cumulated in the proclamation of the Weimar Republic (1918–33) simultaneously by a social democrat and a socialist.

[12] Wagner 1902.
[13] Ullmann 2005.
[14] Macdonald 2003, 414.
[15] Ibid., 407.
[16] Ibid., ch. 9.

During the Weimar Republic, the question of how to finance the state arose again with renewed vigour because of a combination of costs to the government: domestic debt accumulated during the war, the social costs of a growing welfare state, and—although less than often claimed in German public discourse—war reparations. Despite this accumulation of public costs, the money elite remained unwilling to contribute to the state via taxation, not least because it disliked the young republic. So, the government, in cooperation with the *Reichsbank*, chose to inflate the debt away and to submit the public finances to a course of austerity. Between 1918 and 1925 German debt decreased from 179 billion to 6.8 billion mark.[17] The chosen policies hit the working class badly. The small savers, who had invested their savings into government war bonds, lost their savings and felt the consequences of cuts in welfare programmes at the same time. Worse still, with the inflation and banking crisis of the 1920s, the cycle of money, tax, and debt broke down entirely. The money elite, on the other hand, owned much of their wealth in the form of land and real estate and were hence less affected by inflation. The cash that they still held was transferred abroad.[18] The German public only regained trust in an official tender currency when, in the reform of 1923/24, the mark was replaced with the *Reichsmark* (RM), which was pegged to the US dollar at a fixed rate.[19] The US dollar became central to the re-establishment of a domestic cycle of money, tax, and debt.

The National Socialist dictatorship (1933–45) found yet another answer to the question of how to finance central government and its belligerent ambitions. It turned Germany into a tax, debt, and predator state. To begin with, the banks and corporations were largely in line with the Hitler government's economic policies—not least because the government-funded recovery and remilitarization flushed money into the pockets of the large industrial conglomerates. The close relationship between the government and its corporate creditors found its expression in the *Mefo-Wechsel*, bills of exchange between the government, the large banks, and business conglomerates. The *Mefo-Wechsel* allowed the National Socialist government to debt-finance arms production.[20]

Yet, there was also suspicion between Hitler's *Funktionselite* and the money elite. The banks and corporations watched warily as the state's role in the economy grew. Motivated by anti-Semitism, the National Socialists, for their part,

---

[17] Macdonald 2003.
[18] Ibid.; Winkler 2005.
[19] Deutsche Bundesbank 2016.
[20] Ibid.

took issue in the concentration of power in the hands of private banks which were often staffed or owned by Jews. Too dependent on corporate creditors, though, the National Socialists did not manage to break up the big banks.[21] The government's dependency on corporate creditors was rooted in the fact that the general population was in no mood to extend credit to the state. The memories of being duped by the government over its war lending after 1918 were still fresh. Resorting to a politics of the invisible onshore, the government placed government bills directly with the publicly owned savings banks that had been forced into line. The small saver became, without knowing it, a creditor again. Finally, the National Socialist dictatorship financed an important amount of its war of aggression through forced extraction: occupied territories in eastern Europe had to supply raw materials and slave labour, western countries were taxed, forced to use overvalued paper money or, like Greece, to provide forced credits.[22] Instead of domestic taxation, the forced extraction of foreign wealth securitized the government's borrowing. The cost of money creation had been extended to social groups outside the state's borders.

When Germany lost the war in May 1945, it did so again with a large volume of public debt. Much of Europe was destroyed and Germany, too, was in tatters. Again, money creation without corresponding taxation had broken the circle of money, tax, and debt. People resorted to barter. The bargain over money creation had collapsed. In addition, growing tensions between the capitalist Western Allies and the socialist Soviet Union over the terms of occupation stoked the fire of class warfare.

Under military rule, in June 1948, the Western occupying forces, the United States, Britain, and France, introduced the *Deutsche Mark* (D-Mark). This currency reform wiped out West Germany's public debt and re-established the circle of money, tax, and debt—again through pegging the new currency to the US dollar. A few months earlier, in March 1948, the Allies had already established West Germany's new central bank. A new constitution, founding the Bonn Republic (1949–89), was passed about a year later, on 8 May 1949. Note the chronology: the Western Allies introduced a currency and a central bank, before a new German state was founded. Recognizing the priority of the Allies to establish the bank before the state led Vogl to term the Bonn Republic an 'economic society',[23] in which the liberalized economy was not supposed to limit the power of the state, but to legitimate it in the first place.

---

[21] James 2004.
[22] Macdonald 2003.
[23] Vogl 2015.

The local savings banks and the *Landesbanken* emerged from the upheaval largely untouched. The big banks and Germany's newly independent central bank, the *Bundesbank*, were back in business by 1957. Simultaneously, the question of how to finance the state sprang up again. This time, the question was posed against the background of a state that was physically destroyed, morally and financially bankrupt, and that faced mounting regime competition between the capitalist western powers and the socialist Soviet Union. The competition between capitalism and socialism mirrored the unsolved class conflict within German society. As a result, social spending rose and with it government debt, particularly in the years between 1969 and 1982.[24] During the 1980s, social spending and sovereign debt slowed down, but the expansionary policies of the 1960s and 1970s had provided an old answer to the recurrent question of how to finance the state: public debt. Yet, throughout the Bonn Republic and until the end of the 1990s, the powerful and independent *Bundesbank* managed public debt in a conservative manner, focusing on long-term bonds.[25]

That conservative outlook did not, however, apply when providing credit to others. With the economic recovery of the country, the *Bundesbank*, awash in US dollars, pursued, in the words of Röper, a 'rigorous money exporting policy'.[26] This policy included the direct participation of the *Bundesbank* in the Euromarkets by placing parts of its US dollar reserves there. Moreover, the *Bundesbank* subsidised the roughly forty German banks participating in that market by providing them with currency swaps at below market rates.[27] Led by Deutsche Bank, German banks set up or used their existing subsidiaries in Luxembourg. Deutsche Bank was determined to make Luxembourg the main centre for the Euro-D-Mark market, the way London was the uncontested centre for Eurodollar business.[28] In the same way as British banks, German banks created money in offshore financial centres.

By the mid-1960s, this policy had turned Germany into the principal provider of Eurodollars to US banks. The large US banks borrowed US dollars from German banks and lent them on to US corporations to import goods from Germany. The lending and borrowing between German and US banks in Eurodollars created a recycling mechanism for the abundance of US dollars

[24] Ullmann 2017.
[25] Trampusch 2015.
[26] Röper 1970, 456.
[27] Röper 1970.
[28] Büschgen 1995.

circulating in the international economy. This, in turn, was said to reduce the US balance-of-payments deficit[29]—an effect welcomed in Washington.[30]

Furthermore, in 1964, the German government introduced a 25 per cent coupon tax. The tax would not apply, however, to income from bonds denominated in D-Mark issued by non-residents. As a result, by the mid-1960s a Euro-D-Mark market had developed which adhered to the same principles as the Eurodollar market in all respects except that the issues were denominated in D-Mark. The first Euro-D-Mark bond issue was an offering for Argentina, with Deutsche Bank as the lead manager. Deutsche Bank soon developed into Germany's largest Eurodollar bank. Other banks that competed to lead syndicated Euro-D-Mark bond issuances were Dresdner Bank, Commerzbank, and Westdeutsche, the *Landesbank* of North Rhine-Westphalia.[31] From the beginnings of German engagement in the Euromarkets, some of the state-owned *Landesbanken* were involved in offshore money creation too.

In the 1990s, the combination of growing government expenses and political discontent led to an unlikely combination of forces that would allow Deutsche Bank and some *Landesbanken* to get a hitherto unseen exposure to the Euromarkets. After initial euphoria about German reunification, by the mid-1990s public debt ballooned in tandem with unemployment rates. The costs of unification surpassed even the estimates of pessimist observers.[32] The conservative–liberal coalition had to go on a borrowing spree, while the *Bundesbank* and the money elite, watching worrisome inflation indicators, pushed for austerity measures. Cutbacks in social spending were severe and by the end of the 1990s, West Germans feared for their welfare state, whilst East Germans were still waiting for the 'blooming scenery' Chancellor Kohl had promised.[33] The costs of unemployment benefits accruing mainly at the state level and the exposure of the *Landesbanken* on the Euromarkets helped to find funding there.

Yet, throughout the Bonn Republic, offshore finance was not only a matter of legitimate banking. A 2017 investigation by the magazine *Der Spiegel*[34] and public broadcaster *Das Erste*[35] revealed how offshore structures also played a

---

[29] Balance of payment statistics provide net flows only. Based on these net flows, it is impossible to determine if Eurodollar flows indeed finance the US current account deficit. Analysing gross and net flows separately Borio and Disyatat (2011) find that they do not. There is no comparable analysis for the early decades of the Eurodollar markets.

[30] Dickens 2005.

[31] O'Malley 2015, ch. 1.

[32] Burret, Feld, and Köhler 2013.

[33] Kohl 1990.

[34] Dettmer and Röbel 2017.

[35] Lamby and Koch 2017.

central role in the illegal party donation system that had financed Kohl's ascendance to power.[36] The slush funds had initially been set up by Germany's first post-war Chancellor Konrad Adenauer and his supporters from the country's largest corporations.

In 1954, Adenauer and industrial magnates set up an association, the *Staatsbürgerliche Vereinigung* (civic union), which pooled donations from these magnates and then acted as the official donor of that money to the conservative Christian Democratic Union (CDU) and the liberal Free Democratic Party (FDP). That same year, parliament passed a law that made donations to parties and charities tax deductible. Through pooling the money at the *Staatsbürgerliche Vereinigung*, the actual donors could remain anonymous, while still receiving tax deductions. However, four years later, in 1958, the constitutional court outlawed this practice, because it undermined the constitutional rule of transparent accountability of party finances. In response to this ruling, the *Staatsbürgerliche Vereinigung* set up, over the coming decades, a sophisticated offshore structure to ensure the anonymity of donors and avoid having to declare the funds. This structure included research institutions with the legal form of a foundation headquartered in Liechtenstein with bank accounts in Switzerland. The *Staatsbürgerliche Vereinigung* made payments for fake research projects to these institutions in Liechtenstein into their Swiss bank accounts. From there the money would be transferred in cash to an anonymous bank account in Switzerland owned initially by two members of the CDU's treasury and close aides of Helmut Kohl. From this bank account, the money would be transferred to a trust account in a Luxembourg subsidiary of a German private bank. The bank transferred the money internally to its German bank account and from there, Kohl's aides would withdraw the money in cash and deposit it in the CDU's official bank account. All related documentation was stored in an anonymous safe in Switzerland.[37]

For their part the industrialist donors had come up with a money-laundering-cum-tax-fraud system. They would donate large sums to a catholic missionary congregation in Sankt Augustin near Bonn. The congregation would provide receipts for these large sums to the firms who could deduce it from their tax liabilities. Subsequently the congregation would pay back the larger share of the money to the firms and donate the smaller share to the

[36] Parts of the slush fund system was revealed in the 1980s under the parliamentary and judiciary investigation of the Flick affair (Kilz and Preuss 1983). Another part of the system was revealed in the late 1990s as part of the CDU party donation scandal (see von Arnim 2000). The new investigations now show that the two scandals were part of one system that was built around Helmut Kohl's raise to power.

[37] Dettmer and Röbel 2017.

*Staatsbürgerliche Vereinigung.*[38] When the corporate tax fraud scheme raised the suspicion of the tax authorities in the late 1970s, Kohl's aides in the party treasury got nervous. To obscure all traces to the CDU and to them personally, the aides set up another foundation in Liechtenstein, called Norfolk, which now became the owner of a new bank account in Switzerland and the lease holder of the safe with all the documentation. They also made sure that from 1980 onwards the *Staatsbürgerliche Vereinigung* would no longer donate to the party. The association was liquidated ten years later, and its remaining money was channelled into the offshore system which was by now mainly operated by Helmut Kohl's two aides.[39]

In 1971, Helmut Kohl had lost out to his opponent Rainer Barzel in the competition for the party chairmanship. Two years later, Barzel was politically damaged after he lost the general election. The slush funds sweetened his decision not to run for the chairmanship again with payments amounting to DM1.7 million. The slush funds allowed Kohl and his supporters to fund campaigns and create loyalists in the party's often financially strained state chapters. There is no evidence that the industrialists' donations were related to direct favours for the companies. Yet, it is unlikely they came for free.

Two details emerged from an investigation into a part of the slush fund system in the 1980s. After having paid out Barzel, one of the donors, Kurt Biedenkopf, at that time the chief executive officer of the large chemicals firm Henkel, became general secretary of the CDU once Kohl had become the chairman. The other donor, Flick, a coal and steel magnate at the very core of the slush fund system, requested a tax exemption from the ministry of finance when he sold his shares of the car company Daimler to Deutsche Bank. The exemption was granted.[40]

In 1999, the whole system finally came apart. Kohl's two aides who ran the offshore system were identified in relation to an illegal cash donation by an arms dealer. Kohl publicly admitted having known about illegal donations of DM3 million but claimed to be ignorant of the slush fund system. According to the investigation, between 1973 and 1998, the slush funds had provided him with over DM200 million in addition to the party's official finances.[41]

In the long view, Germany's bank bargain has been characterized by its three-pillar system. To a significant extent that system insulated banking for farmers, craftsman, and small and medium-sized companies from banking

[38] Lamby and Koch 2017.
[39] Dettmer and Röbel 2017.
[40] Kilz and Preuss 1983; Historische Gesellschaft der Deutschen Bank 2017.
[41] Dettmer and Röbel 2017; Lamby and Koch 2017.

for the wealthy and industrial conglomerates. The bank bargain has also been marked by the close but separate relationship between a stable money elite and a constantly changing *Funktionselite*. Against the background of being duped of repayment after both world wars, the bank bargain is influenced by a money elite suspicious of a political elite that mobilizes resources through borrowing. In this context, offshore banking became a tool in the institutional association's strategy to finance its political goals, especially on the state level. Moreover, offshore banking has been a means for the money elite to strengthen the conservative forces within the *Funktionselite* by financing the CDU's slush fund system.

## Tax bargain

As with banking, taxation has been marked by the stability of the money elite and the changing nature of the *Funktionselite*. With the notable exception of the Weimar Republic, the money elite has had a basic willingness to contribute to the state via taxation if that meant safeguarding its own privileged position within it.

The founding moment of this basic willingness to contribute was Germany's aborted March Revolution of 1848. Just as its French forerunner in 1789, the revolution started as a tax revolt. Siding with the revolutionaries, the Prussian national assembly decided on a tax boycott to bring down the monarchy. Yet, the boycott found little support among the bourgeoisie. The wealthy would rather pay taxes than risk a revolution.[42]

Class warfare started with industrialization in the mid-nineteenth century, shaped the Weimar Republic, and peaked with the Cold War. The class struggle expressed itself in the demands of the working classes to participate politically and economically in the institutional association of rule. The money elite was willing to pay for some of the socio-economic demands to keep the political ones at bay.[43] The inclination to pay tax rather than to share power contributed to the stability of the money elite over time.

Importantly, the German tax state emerged from the level of the individual states. In 1820, a new law on government debt was passed in Prussia, obliging the otherwise absolutist monarch to convene a national assembly should it wish to issue debt. In response, William III of Prussia went to great

---

[42] Ullmann 2005.
[43] Schmidt 2012.

lengths to avoid sovereign debt. William ruled by the principle of the frugal state, avoiding expenses where possible. The resources he did need were raised through state-owned railroad companies and indirect taxation.

However, even in absolutist Prussia, policymakers and scholars criticized the regressive nature of indirect taxation. Weighing frugality against tax justice, the Prussian elite created a consensus around the notion of a 'principle of performance' (*Leistungsfähigkeitsprizip*) informing tax policy. The principle of performance meant that those who have more should contribute more to state revenue and should get more in return for their payments. The principle linked the mobilization and centralization of resources with how they would be spent. It stands in contrast to the idea of the distribution of the tax burden being exclusively based on the ability to pay, with the government free to spend the revenue in line with its political goals. The principle of performance would come to inform the federal tax system of the German Empire.[44] The money elite made sure that if it paid, it also had a say in the spending. As a notion of tax justice, the principle of performance informs tax policies of the institutional association of rule to this day.

In the 1870s Saxony was the first state to introduce a progressive general income tax. Prussia followed suit in 1893.[45] However, decisions about how to respond to mounting pressures from the working classes to participate in the growing wealth came from the federal level. Between 1876 and 1914, Chancellor Otto von Bismarck initiated—in response to the increasing influence of social democracy—a health, occupational accident, and old age insurance system.[46] This system also embraced the 'principle of performance': the higher the income, the higher the contributions, and the higher the benefits in the case of insurance. Furthermore, the old age insurance established the sharing of contributions between employer and employee. The principle of shared contributions was later extended to all pillars of the social insurance system. Shared contributions are a hallmark of the conflict over how to distribute the costs and benefits of taxation. They reflect the basic willingness of the money elite to contribute to the welfare state. Yet, it also means that the pacification of class warfare became a corporate cost. It did not directly reduce the money elite's private wealth via taxation.

Alongside the social security system, income taxation continued to develop too. By 1914, the income tax systems of the different states had converged, and the tax became the most important source of state revenue. Yet, as income tax

[44] Ullmann 2005.
[45] Ibid.
[46] Schmidt 2012.

spread, so did resistance towards it. State revenue became more vulnerable to tax evasion. In response, Saxony and some of the southern states developed strong tax enforcement capacities. Prussia, on the other hand, staying true to its leitmotif of the frugal state, considered a specialized tax administration to be too expensive. It opted for strong laws in combination with weak law enforcement, an emphasis on the privacy of individual taxpayers, and general leniency towards the mistakes laymen might make in their tax declarations. In other words, Prussia became complicit in tax evasion.

On the eve of World War I, taxes made up 64 per cent of public revenue, fees 27 per cent, and debt 8 per cent.[47] As discussed above, anxious not to further alienate the money elite, the emperor decided to finance the war via debt.

Following the defeat of the German Empire in 1918, the Weimar Republic therefore had broken public finances from the outset. Unemployment and the impoverishment of large parts of the population, caused by the war and the reneging of government debt, gave class warfare a hitherto unknown fierceness.[48] Yet, the strained financial situation during the early Weimar years provided little leeway to extend social welfare programmes. The new *Funktionselite*, broader than the old imperial elite because of the introduction of universal suffrage and the unionization of the working class, tried to put the young republic on financially solid ground.

The first finance minister, Matthias Erzberger, a centrist, centralized tax administration and legislation at the federal level to reform it. This reform included top rates of 65 per cent on income and wealth and strict capital controls. The new tax system would prove to be more durable than the Weimar Republic itself.

The high tax rates on the wealthy were short-lived though. They did not survive the resistance of the money elite, which expressed itself in capital flight and tax evasion justified as opposition against an unpopular democratic and, in its early days, a left-leaning republic.[49] German capital was deposited in significant amounts in neighbouring tax havens, especially the Netherlands and Switzerland. In the inter-war period, Switzerland had already been an offshore financial centre catering to clients from all over the world. Amsterdam, on the other hand, became an offshore financial centre largely focused on hosting German wealth. Wealth management was handled, in part, by German banks, including Deutsche Bank, who set up foreign subsidiaries in the Netherlands for that purpose. The reasons for going offshore ranged from tax avoidance to

---

[47] Ullmann 2005.
[48] Schmidt 2012.
[49] Ullmann 2005.

regulatory arbitrage, to seeking a safe haven in foreign currencies at a time of political and monetary instability.[50] Despite the wealthy's rampant offshoring, the tax revenue generated through Erzberger's reform and the relative economic recovery between 1924–28 allowed the conservative government to pacify the class struggle by introducing unemployment insurance. After that short respite, however, renewed economic recession led the government on to a course of austerity. The gains made by the working classes throughout the Weimar Republic were largely lost again.[51]

The following social, political, and economic upheaval in the years of National Socialist Germany (1933–45) left the tax and social security systems largely unchanged. The social insurance system provided little opportunity for political exploitation and the new National Socialist *Funktionselite* recognized early on that the money elite was—as during the German Empire and the Weimar Republic—unwilling to fund an expansion of the state via taxation. However, the National Socialist government tried to improve the tax morale of the population by framing tax payments as a form of devotion to the German nation. Moreover, in line with the regime's anti-Semitic ideology, the Hitler government systematically looted the Jews. In the fiscal year 1938/39 alone, 5 per cent of the regime's revenue came from forcedly extracted resources. The expropriation of the Jews had been made possible, among other factors, by Erzberger's centralization of the tax administration.[52] During the occupation, the United States was therefore adamant that Germany be returned to a federalized tax system. Tax administrations were again fragmented and are— to this day—accountable to the state, not to the federal level. Consequently, states must finance the tax administration and law enforcement. However, they must also pass on much of the recovered revenue to the central government. State governments thus have an incentive for strong laws combined with weak enforcement[53]—a strategy already well known to the Prussians.

After World War II, taxation and the class struggle in the Bonn Republic (1949–91) represented the regime competition between the capitalist western and the socialist eastern blocks. The money elite in West Germany was wary of socialism across the border. The threat of an economic system that might jeopardize their property rights motivated the money elite to contribute to the West German state via tax payments and social security contributions. True to the

---

[50] Farquet 2019.
[51] Schmidt 2012.
[52] Ullmann 2005.
[53] Tax Justice Network 2018a.

principle of performance, their contribution was associated with an expectation of economic state support. The 1950s to mid-1970s were hence marked by an unprecedented expansion of the state and its expenses. During these years, the principal willingness of the money elite to contribute to the state, the legacy of the National Socialist notion of taxation as a contribution to the nation, and the constitutional setup of West Germany as an economic society merged. The notion of the tax state became part of Germany's post-war national identity.[54] However, with the oil shocks in the mid-1970s, expansionary policies came under pressure. Therefore, starting in the 1980s and picking up speed with the end of regime competition in 1989, the 1990s and early 2000s saw a gradual, but significant change in the tax system of the Berlin Republic (1991 until today). Offshore finance played its role in that change (in Section 2).

Taking a long view, the German tax bargain was marked by the federal nature of the state and the willingness of the money elite to pay rather than to risk upheaval. Principles and ideas about taxation developed in the different states merged at the federal level. These principles and ideas included the notion of a frugal state as a means to stay independent from the money elite; the principle of performance as a tool of big taxpayers to influence expenditure; and social security as a means to mitigate class warfare without diminishing personal wealth. Offshore finance entered the tax bargain mainly as a means for the money elite to distance their wealth from the governments of the interregnum phase, which it considered untrustworthy.

## 2  Contemporary exposure to offshore finance

In contemporary Germany, the Prussian emphasis on tax secrecy and other forms of guarding financial privacy lives on. This attitude has earned the country a spot among the world's ten most secretive jurisdictions.[55] There is thus, as in the case of Britain, little publicly available information on the scale and pattern of the contemporary uses and abuses of offshore financial services in Germany. As in Britain, offshore finance is largely invisible. The following analysis reconstructs some of what is obscured based on data from BIS locational banking statistics, interview results, and historical analysis. The resulting rough estimate must be taken with a pinch of salt. It cannot show the full picture and rests on assumptions which simplify a complex world.

[54] Author's interview with civil society organization, Berlin, March 2017, with tax expert, Berlin, February 2015.
[55] Tax Justice Network 2018b.

The methodological details of the approach—including its limitations—are discussed in detail in Appendix 1.

## The uses and abuses of offshore financial services

Seen from the money view, the relevant financial flows are those between Germany and the entirety of offshore financial centres. They constitute the scale and pattern of Germany's exposure to offshore finance. Claims represent money held in offshore financial centres, liabilities debt issued there.

Figure 4.1 shows the claims and liabilities of German economic actors towards offshore financial centres between 1977 and 2019. Offshore assets and debt affect state power differently, but jointly. Simply put, offshore assets may go untaxed, while offshore debt may transmit volatilities from the offshore markets into the domestic economy. The graph therefore depicts offshore claims and liabilities separately and as a sum. It is the sum that represents a country's overall exposure to offshore finance. Figure 4.1 presents it in absolute numbers and as a percentage of GDP.

From the start of BIS reporting, offshore claims and liabilities together grew from 3 per cent of GDP (or US$17 billion) in 1977 to about 24 per cent of GDP (or US$953 billion) in 2019. Offshoring peaked in 2007 at about 42 per cent of GDP (or US$1.4 trillion). From 2009 onwards, offshoring declined. Germany's offshore exposure grew continuously from the beginning. Yet, growth rates strongly accelerated between the early 1990s and early 2000s. In this decade, offshore exposure grew on average 3 per cent annually. In comparison, Germany's economic growth was at an average rate of 1.6 per cent per year during that time.[56] After the global financial crisis, offshore exposure declined but, as in Britain, at a lower rate than it had grown before. As a share of GDP, offshore exposure in 2019 is at the level of 1999.

Analysing the two sides of the balance sheet separately, we can see that until 1990, claims and liabilities are roughly balanced. Liabilities then started to out-grow claims and Germany became, for a decade, a net borrower in the offshore markets. The position of net borrower coincided with Germany's increased funding needs in relation to unification.

In 1998, Germans voted Chancellor Kohl out and a coalition of the Social Democratic Party (SPD) and the Green Party came into government. With the first progressive government in power since the end of the war, the old question

---

[56] World Bank 2018.

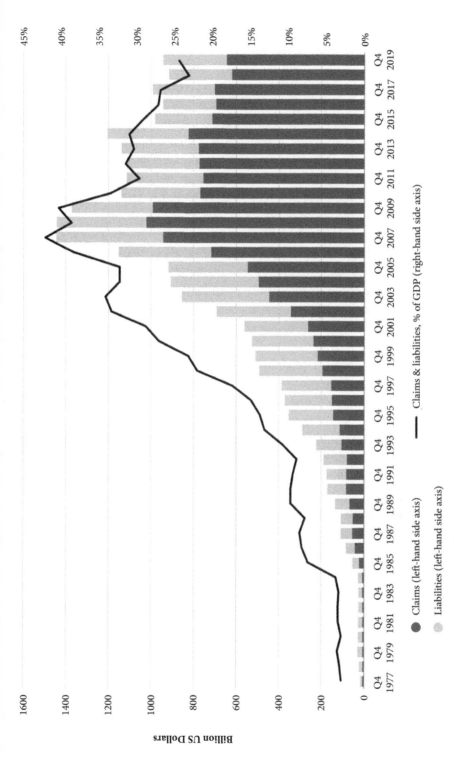

**Figure 4.1** Germany's exposure to offshore finance

*Source:* BIS locational banking statistics, World Bank, own calculations.

of how to finance the state returned urgently. The context of the question was radically different from when it was last posed in the 1950s.

First, with German unification the problem of systems' competition had come to an end, but the subsequent economic repression and ballooning unemployment had severely strained the public coffers. Furthermore, in 1999, Germany was a founding member of the euro, a single currency of eleven, later nineteen, European states. A year before the euro became the official means of payment, the ECB was established in Frankfurt as the watchdog of the new euro currency. The introduction of the euro and the founding of the ECB had weakened the *Bundesbank*'s power. Hans Eichel, the new German finance minister, seized the opportunity to weaken the central bank further with regards to managing public debt. The new government needed money to implement the policy changes they envisaged and the *Bundesbank*'s traditional conservatism towards short-term debt was unhelpful in this regard. The law governing the role of the *Bundesbank*, written by the Allies in 1948, put the German central bank outside the control of the legislative and the executive. Trying to influence the central bank's policy was therefore not an option for Eichel.

Instead, the government established a publicly owned private liability company that would henceforth replace the *Bundesbank* as the manager of sovereign debt. The new Federal Finance Agency (BaFin) immediately moved to substitute the *Bundesbank*'s conservative debt strategy with a market-based funding approach, including short-term debt and the use of instruments such as interest rate swaps and other derivatives.[57] As Figure 4.1 shows, the financial de-regulation and the introduction of the euro grew German banks' offshore business to hitherto unseen heights. Deutsche Bank used the monetary union to position itself as the world's largest foreign exchange trader, which provided the means to engage fully in the Euromarkets. Deutsche Bank thus became one of the world's most successful and influential banks. The *Bundesbank* was aware of these developments. It did not blink.[58]

Additionally, the municipalities and states, which had to bear the brunt of the costs of unemployment benefits accruing in the years after reunification, were severely stripped of revenue. Refinancing themselves in the money markets was a welcome tap into liquidity.[59]

---

[57] Trampusch 2015.
[58] Author's interview with banker, Munich, November 2018; with offshore finance expert, August 2018.
[59] Trampusch and Spies 2015.

The *Landesbanken* were happy to issue debt on their states' and communes' behalf. Their domestic business model was not particularly profitable, and the state guarantees allowed them to refinance themselves on the international markets under favourable conditions.[60] The big commercial banks, however, did not like the *Landesbanken* on their turf. They saw the state guarantees as an unfair advantage and initiated proceedings against them with the European Commission. The Commission decided in favour of the commercial banks. To help the *Landesbanken* adapt to the new competitive framework, the federal government allowed them an adjustment period of three years. Knowing that they would soon have to refinance themselves on worse terms, the *Landesbanken* leveraged up, especially in the Euromarkets. The funds were invested on into foreign assets. This business was mainly done through Ireland.[61] That is, next to Deutsche Bank, the *Landesbanken* also accounted for the steep increase in offshore exposure in the late 1990s.[62]

Nevertheless, from 2001 onwards, the trend reversed, and Germany became, by far, a net lender in the offshore markets and has maintained in that position up to 2019. Next to economic actors depositing money offshore, German banks actively engage in offshore money creation.[63]

As discussed in Chapter 2, offshore money creation is the act whereby offshore banks lend money to non-residents in a currency foreign to the jurisdiction in which the transaction takes place. Disaggregating Germany's offshore exposure by currency denomination, Figure 4.2 shows that between 1977 and 2019, the share of the Eurodollar in all offshore exposure oscillated between 65 and 75 per cent. Exceptions are the years 1995–1997, where the Eurodollar share in claims and liabilities dropped below 50 per cent. Clearly, Eurodollar banking is a substantial part of Germany's offshore activity, but other foreign currencies, such as the Swiss Franc, also play a role.

Unlike Eurodollar banking, offshore tax planning—both illegal and legal— was very much at the forefront of the interviewees' minds. Despite the apparent size of the phenomenon, the German Finance Ministry never attempted to quantify the amount of taxes lost due to offshore tax planning.[64] However, as established in Chapter 2, offshore tax planning presupposes offshore money flows as presented in Figure 4.1. Assuming that all offshore claims are undeclared and untaxed, and applying an average income tax rate, the German state

---

[60] Author's interview with banker, Berlin, February 2017.
[61] Author's telephone interview with offshore expert, August 2018.
[62] Author's interview with banker, Munich, November 2018.
[63] Author's interview with banker, Munich, November 2018.
[64] Author's interview with employee of the ministry of finance, March 2018.

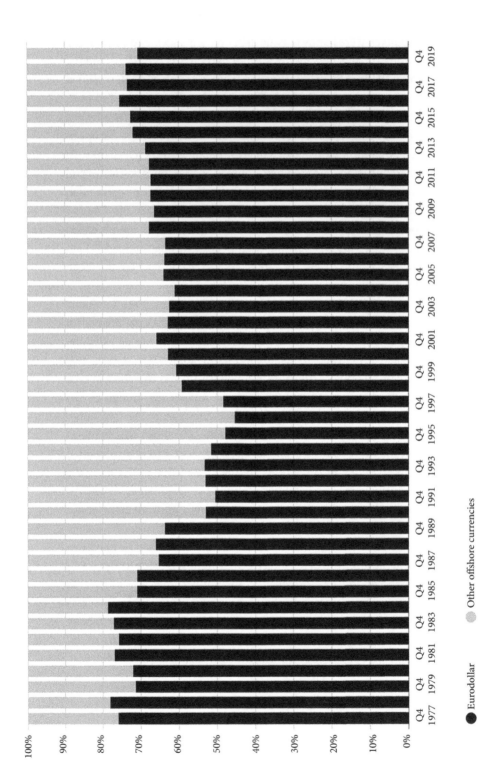

**Figure 4.2** Currency breakdown of Germany's offshore exposure
*Source:* BIS locational banking statistics, own calculations.

lost between 2000 and 2019 about 5–7 per cent of GDP per year, as Figure 4.3 depicts. Revenue loss peaked with overall offshore exposure in 2007 at 10 per cent of GDP (or US$348 billion). As in the case of Britain, this rough upper bound estimate has its constraints; details are discussed in Appendix 1.

Compared to Britain, the tax loss related to offshore finance is much lower, despite Germany's larger economy. This finding echoes the claim of interviewees that compared to international standards, German tax advisers and firms exercise a certain restraint with regards to the aggressiveness of their tax planning structures.[65] It reflects the willingness of the money classes to pay as long as tax policies reflect their interests.

The tax reforms under the Schröder government are a case in point. They separated the corporate and capital income tax assessment from the personal one. Corporate and capital income tax changed from a progressive to a flat rate tax with lower rates than in the past.[66] Therefore, the money elite could hold their private wealth as corporate wealth and be taxed at lower rates than wage earners.[67] This group was also successful in avoiding wealth and inheritance taxes by arguing that these taxes would threaten the survival of family-owned businesses, the backbone of Germany's economy.[68] Compared to the post-war years, the proportion of corporate tax as a percentage of GDP almost halved.[69] The government's revenue is now mostly funded by social security contributions (38 per cent), followed by taxes from personal income, profits, and gains (27 per cent). Consumption taxes are the third most important source of tax revenue (28 per cent). Taxes on corporate income contribute only 5 per cent.[70]

However, the tax reforms did little to relieve the pressure of progressive personal income taxation on those with high incomes in the middle classes. Unable to break the public consensus that all classes are supposed to contribute according to their means, the conservative governments, inheriting Schröder's tax reforms, provided their upper middle income and wealthy voters with a backdoor: the politics of the invisible.[71] Starting in the 1950s and well into the early 2000s, different conservative governments, in Prussian fashion, actively

---

[65] Author's interview with member of parliament, Berlin, January 2017; with tax expert, Berlin, February 2017; with civil society organization, Berlin, March 2017.
[66] Bach 2016, 201; Ullmann 2017.
[67] Bach 2016.
[68] Author's interview with member of parliament, Berlin, January 2017; with tax expert, Berlin, February 2017; with civil society organization, Berlin, March 2017.
[69] Author's interview with civil society organization, Berlin, March 2017.
[70] OECD 2017a.
[71] Author's interview with civil society organization, Berlin, March 2017; with tax lawyer, Berlin, January 2017.

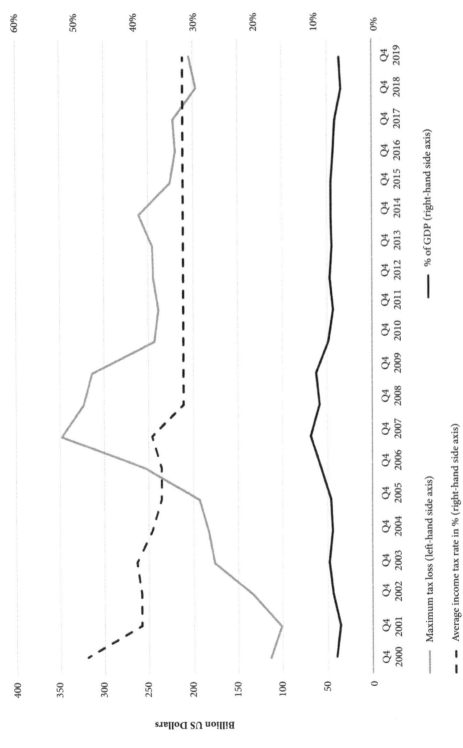

**Figure 4.3** Germany's estimated maximum tax loss

*Source:* BIS locational banking statistics, World Bank, OECD.

turned a blind eye to individual tax evasion via offshoring. In the words of one interviewee:

> Using offshore finance for minimising personal taxes was a mass phenomenon and at least the conservative parties did not want to alienate their voters by outlawing offshore financial services. The motivation to address the issue was probably also chocked off by the fact that the CDU used the offshore system itself to hide their illegal party finances.[72]

Maintaining the identity of Germany as a tax state, on the individual level resistance to personal income tax was high. The change to that state of affairs came—as has been the case historically—from the state level.

In 2006, the tax administration of North-Rhine Westphalia actively started to work against the federal level's politics of the invisible. It bought leaked data from banks in Liechtenstein, Switzerland, and Luxembourg to investigate individual tax evasion. These so-called CD-purchases (the first leaked data sets were stored on a compact disc) revealed the identities of tax-cheating wealthy Germans. The CD-purchases were soon followed by public leaks, including the *Panama Papers*. Together, the CD-purchases and leaks applied pressure to the offshore banks and their tax-evading clients to come clean. The leaks delegitimized the large-scale mass tax evasion via offshoring.[73] A wave of voluntary self-declarations ensued, resulting in over 4 billion euro washing into the state's coffers between 2010 and 2014.[74]

In addition, the government started to tighten the laws around voluntary self-declarations and financial transparency.[75] At the same time, the money elite entered a generational transition. The large fortunes accumulated after World War II were now being handed to the next generation. In the process of inheritance, offshore structures complicate matters. As one wealth manager put it:

> The heirs just don't want to bother with the offshore accounts. They fear waking up in the morning, learning from the newspaper that their money is involved in some illegal structure. They don't want to worry. They just want to get rid of all the structures.[76]

---

[72] Author's interview with tax lawyer, Berlin, January 2017.
[73] Author's interview with tax lawyer, Berlin, January 2017.
[74] Seibel 2014.
[75] Interview with civil society organization, Berlin, March 2017; with tax lawyer, Berlin, January 2017, with staff at the finance ministry, Berlin, March 2017.
[76] Author's telephone interview wealth manager, January 2017.

A tax lawyer confirms: 'It is mostly elderly people who come to us, hoping to fix their tax affairs so that they can handover clean money to the next generation.'[77] Indeed, between 2007 and 2015, deposits in Switzerland dropped from US$6.6 billion to about US$800 million.[78] Likewise, an employee of a Swiss investment fund claimed

> If there is a +49 on my display, I don't even pick up the phone anymore. Serving German clients is to have one foot in prison [laughs]. I mean, we rather serve clients in Latin America or Asia.[79]

Alstadsæter and colleagues argue that the drop could be related to a shifting of assets to other offshore centres.[80] However, the interviewees did not mention any offshore centres that were replacing private deposits in Switzerland. For Germany, the drop in Swiss offshore assets appears to be genuine. Next to the law enforcement measures taken by German state and federal governments between 2006 and today, the global financial crisis may also explain the drop in private tax planning. The crisis led wealthy Germans to seek financial safety at home. They repatriated some of their internationally mobile capital. For instance, the savings bank of Hamburg, the largest of Germany's savings banks, had an increase of deposits of €500 million in the four weeks between September and October 2008 alone.[81] In combination, the public scandals, legal changes, the inheritance question, and volatility in offshore markets have led to a paradigm shift with regards to offshore tax evasion in Germany.

When it comes to corporate tax planning, Tørsløv and colleagues estimate that in Germany profit-shifting brought the corporate tax rate down from a nominal rate of 30 per cent to an effective ralte of 11 per cent.[82] This number, however, obscures the fact that the effective tax rate did not drop equally for all kinds of corporations. Since profit-shifting is mainly done by multinational corporations, most local firms still pay the 30 per cent corporate tax rate while the multinationals' pay well below 11 per cent. As in the British case, tolerating offshore tax planning means that the state sides with those corporations who do have access to offshore financial services at the expense of everyone else.

The *Panama Papers*, leaked secret records of 214,000 offshore companies set up with the help of the Panamanian law firm Mossack Fonseca, revealed

---

[77] Author's interview with tax lawyer, Berlin, January 2017.
[78] Swiss National Bank 2017.
[79] Author's telephone interview with employee at Swiss investment fund, March 2017. +49 is the German country code.
[80] Alstadsæter, Johannesen, and Zucman 2018.
[81] Seifert 2008.
[82] Tørsløv, Wier, and Zucman 2018.

how German economic and political actors abuse offshore financial services. The leaked data exposed that the assets held offshore by Germans were not there because of the wealthy's sheer cleverness. It was offshore because German banks systematically advised their rich clients to put it there.[83] The leaked internal communication of Mossack Fonseca employees suggests that German banks did not always know or regularly check who was the beneficial owner of a specific shell company—breaching anti-money laundering law. The data further suggest that larger German banks acted as correspondent banks for smaller financial institutions that were allegedly involved in money laundering. According to the data, more than twenty German banks did business with Mossack Fonseca, among them Germany's largest commercial banks such as Deutsche Bank and Commerzbank, but also several *Landesbanken*. *Landesbanken*, publicly owned banks, helped their clients to evade taxes in Germany.[84]

Or take the 2006–09 Siemens corruption scandal as another example, it was the largest publicly prosecuted corporate corruption scandal in Germany before the payments company Wirecard in 2019 set new records for criminal corporate behaviour in post-war Germany. Siemens has been, from its foundation in the mid-nineteenth century, a fundamental element of Germany's money elite. It is a large electrical engineering firm and a central part of the German industrial landscape. The scandal erupted after the public prosecutor in Munich, where Siemens's headquarters are based, received an anonymous letter accusing the corporation of running a large system of slush funds for bribing foreign officials. In the course of the ensuing investigation, Siemens was suspected to have paid, between 2001 and 2007, bribes to foreign officials totalling US$1.4 billion. In a plea bargain, Siemens admitted to only five breaches of US law, but not to the allegation of bribery. Nevertheless, the corporation agreed to a record fine of US$1.6 billion. Due to the plea bargain, many of the corrupt payments were never fully investigated and the actual mechanics behind them remained hidden from public sight.[85]

The leaked Mossack Fonseca files shed some light onto the bribery practices of Siemens subsidiaries in Latin America. The CEOs of different regional and national offices would siphon off money from official Siemens accounts and pooled them in the accounts of a shell company, Gillard Management, setup by Mossack Fonseca. The shell company held accounts in Switzerland, Singapore, and Panama, into which the pooled slush funds were paid. From these

---

[83] Also, author's interviews with tax expert, Berlin, February 2016; with employee of the Ministry of Finance, Berlin, March 2017.

[84] Obermayer and Obermaier 2016.

[85] Berghoff 2018.

accounts the managers of the different Latin American branches of Siemens could make payments, usually to 'advisors' and other middlemen who would then hand the money to the foreign officials.[86] These practices were standard in different divisions of Siemens during the 1980s and 1990s. In those years, none of this was illegal in Germany. Rather, until 1999 companies could deduct bribes from their taxes if paid to foreign officials and until 2002 if paid to foreign businessmen. Yet, between 1998 and 2002 foreign corruption was successively outlawed, whilst Siemens's practices changed little and slowly.[87] When the prosecutions finally started in 2006, the managers in Latin America became nervous, first restructuring and then dissolving the shell companies they held with Mossack Fonseca and the related bank accounts.[88] To what extent this put a definitive end to Siemens using offshore illegal activities is impossible to determine. Reliable data on offshore money laundering simply does not exist. It is impossible to tell what proportion of the financial flows depicted in Figure 4.1 is of illegal origin. In addition, in Germany court sentences and fines related to money laundering are not published, neither is the amount of frozen assets. Germany's financial regulator, the Federal Financial Supervisory Authority (BaFin), has little in-house resources. Auditing and monitoring anti-money laundering provisions are largely outsourced to private firms.[89]

Finally, disaggregating the data on overall offshore exposure by counterparty country, we can identify where the offshore lending and borrowing by German economic actors takes place.

The top five offshore financial centres, measured by median stock of offshore claims and liabilities between 1977 and 2019, are Luxembourg, the Netherlands, Switzerland, Ireland, and the Cayman Islands. The quantitative data echo interview results and the literature, arguing that economic actors prefer geographically near offshore centres.[90] Two observations stand out.

First, the importance of Luxembourg—far beyond the Netherlands and Switzerland. Comparable to Britain's historical relationship with Jersey as the go-to next-door offshore financial centre, Luxembourg plays that role for Germany. A member of the German imperial customs union from 1834 to 1919, the Grand Duchy of Luxembourg has long had strong ties with Germany. However, after being occupied by Germany during World War I, Luxembourg turned to Belgium. The two countries entered a monetary union in 1922.

---

[86] Obermayer and Obermaier 2016.
[87] Berghoff 2018.
[88] Obermayer and Obermaier 2016.
[89] Tax Justice Network 2018a.
[90] Blanco and Rogers 2014; Haberly and Wójcik 2015a; Alstadsæter, Johannesen, and Zucman 2018.

As an effect of that union, Luxembourg had no central bank between 1922 and the introduction of the euro in 1998. This meant that, unlike in Germany, there were no reserve requirements for banks in Luxembourg. Hence many German banks, first among them Deutsche Bank, opened subsidiaries in the tiny neighbouring country to circumvent German banking regulation. In 1963, Deutsche Bank was also central in bringing the first ever issue of a Eurobond to Luxembourg. Having successfully handled this issue, the Grand Duchy became, after the City of London, one of the prime locations for listing Eurobonds.[91]

Second, the Cayman Islands is the only non-European offshore financial centre among the top five. The Cayman Islands is the American equivalent to Luxembourg. Operating under British common law, the Cayman Islands is an important financial centre mediating financial flows between the United States and the rest of the world, in particular the United Kingdom. It has developed into an important hub for the US American investment fund industry and multinational corporations.[92] That is, in the selection of the top five offshore financial centres used by German actors, Luxembourg and the Cayman Islands are offshore centres acting mainly as banking hubs, while Switzerland, the Netherlands,[93] and Ireland are more classic tax havens.[94] The analysis of the most popular offshore financial centres emphasizes again the importance of offshore banking in relation to offshore tax planning. What these findings mean for how offshore finance affects the power of the German state to finance its politics is the subject of the following section.

## 3 The encounter

In Chapter 2, I argue with Skinner and Weber that the state, the institutional association of rule, is unique and can only be conceived of in its genealogy.[95] The preceding analysis indeed has exposed the fundamental differences between the German and British states and their strategies to finance their political goals.

In Britain, we can observe a traditional homogeneity between the economic and the political elites and a dominance of financiers as opposed to entrepreneurs within the economic elite. As mass democracy arrives and

---

[91] Röper 1970; Roulot 2013; O'Malley 2015.
[92] Haberly and Wójcik 2015b; Fichtner 2016.
[93] For a more detailed description of the Netherlands as offshore tax haven, see Chapter 6.
[94] Zucman 2015; Fichtner 2016;.
[95] Weber 1999; Skinner 2009.

markets become internationalized, the British institutional association of rule broadens to include lower classes and foreign financiers. As financiers lose their exclusive position within the institutional association of rule, the development of offshore financial services becomes a means for the monied classes to retain their privileges.

In Germany, on the contrary, we observe a separation between the economic elite—a rather homogenous money class with wealth rooted in industrial enterprise—and the political *Funktionselite*. The members of the *Funktionselite* are replaced with each regime change the country goes through. It is also the *Funktionselite* that broadens with the arrival of mass democracy in Germany, while the money elite remains exclusive. The question of how to finance the state is thus renegotiated regularly between a stable money elite and a changing *Funktionselite*. The resulting bargains follow the 'principle of performance', that is, the logic that the wealthy's contribution to the state's finances grants them state spending that is aligned with their interests.

Against this background, offshore financial services have been a means for the money elite to distance its wealth from the *Funktionselite* in times of constitutional crisis. The money elite also used offshore finance to strengthen conservative forces within the institutional association of rule. The *Funktionselite* in turn used offshore finance to extend the money elites' privileges without renegotiating with the electorat the bargain over money creation and taxation. Moreover, governments, particularly at the state level, also used it to access liquidity. Offshore finance is used to invisibly sweeten the deal for an exclusive set of economic actors via a politics of the invisible.

Take money creation as an example. In the contemporary period the *Bundesbank* has had a conservative approach to money creation. Consequently, the costs or risks of money creation are limited, but so are the possibilities for banks to benefit from it. Offshore finance provides the opportunity for a select number of German banks to reap the benefits of money creation, while attempting to keep the costs outside the German banking system. Similarly, offshore tax planning makes the bargain over the tax burden a better one for those wealthy individuals and large corporations that can access offshore financial services. In line with the theory in Chapter 2, the key mechanisms through which offshore finance can affect state power in Germany are thus money creation and taxation.

Having identified the mechanism through which offshore finance affects state power in Germany, I now turn to the quality of that relationship—is it enhancing or limiting state power?

## Strengthening state power

Contrary to common arguments, we can observe that offshore finance strengthened state power. In post-war Germany, offshore finance proved a useful tool to lessen tensions within the institutional association of rule. It was a means for the money elite to support the stronghold of a conservative *Funktionselite* in a democratic context via party financing. It was also a means for labour-led governments to keep the money elite committed to financing a growing welfare state whilst keeping class warfare in check as the real terms of the deal remained obscure. It allowed the state to pursue contradictory policies without being questioned.

Germany could be a high tax country at home and allow an exclusive set of actors to reduce its tax burden offshore. It allowed the financiers to create money offshore, contributing to the provision of preferential liquidity, especially in London and Luxembourg. In this way, the financiers could reap the benefits—profitable banking—whilst keeping the risks and costs outside the domestic banking system. This bifurcation of benefits and risks was possible because corporate financing, true to its nineteenth-century roots, remained largely based on either own (family) resources or traditional bank borrowing.[96]

The German banks' offshore borrowers came from elsewhere. In 1982, the *Bundesbank* and Germany's big banks came, in Büschgen's words, to a 'gentlemen's agreement' that Eurodollar instruments could only be traded in US dollars.[97] Deutsche Bank then became the largest lender for supranational issues and the second largest for lending related to public investment projects.[98] Likewise, the bank became active in the Eurodollar derivatives market geared towards corporate lenders in Latin America, Africa, and also in the United States. With such exposure, the Latin American debt crisis in the early 1980s and the breakdown of the Eastern bloc at the end of the decade were fully felt on Deutsche's balance sheet. It did not affect the German state though. The risks and costs of borrowing in the Eurodollar market were largely born by the foreign borrowers (see Chapters 5 and 6).

Although Deutsche Bank was the biggest, it was not the only German bank operating in the Eurodollar markets. Publicly owned *Landesbanken* were also lead managers of Eurodollar loans. That is, the state itself participated in offshore money creation, and also reaping the benefits. At the level of individual

---

[96] Büschgen 1995; Bundesbank 1997.
[97] Büschgen 1995, 684.
[98] Büschgen 1995.

states, offshore finance became a source of funding. State governments and communes appreciated access to preferential international liquidity, when not enough was available domestically to stem the financing of reunification. In addition, offshore money creation helped export-oriented German firms to manage exchange rate risks. Moreover, these corporations gained a competitive edge by reducing their tax burden via tax planning. That is, offshore finance strengthened the state's ability to finance its politics in direct and indirect ways. Directly, it provided a source of rents and financing for the state and its financiers. Indirectly, it strengthened the state's ability to finance its politics by easing, via the politics of the invisible, distributional conflict over the costs and benefits of money creation and taxation across different groups in society.

## Undermining state power

It is also true that Germany's tax losses due to offshore finance have been significant. However, unlike during the Weimar Republic, contemporary offshore tax planning does not threaten state power. The difference between the Weimar Republic and today is that the German state started to actively shape its relationship with offshore finance. In the post-war period, the institutional association of rule laid the foundation for offshore money creation by German banks and, for a long time, allowed offshore tax planning to flourish. The relationship between offshore finance and the German state is no longer an antagonistic one. Nevertheless, there are instances in the contemporary period, too, that undermine state power. They are just not related to taxation. It is offshore banking that—at least temporarily—threatened German state power.

In 2007, when the Eurodollar markets froze abruptly, it became obvious that offshore money creation benefited the banks in good times but became a risky business for the state in bad times. The German Eurodollar banks transmitted international fragilities into the otherwise conservative and stable German domestic banking system and brought the entire system to the brink. To be able to respond effectively, the German state was dependent on the Federal Reserve's support in the form of central bank swaps (see Chapter 2).

The foreign investments of the *Landesbanken* turned into toxic assets and were downgraded during the global financial crisis. The leverage of the *Landesbanken* became untenable. In consequence, the federal government merged two *Landesbanken* and bailed out three others. Subsequently, the *Landesbanken* retreated from the Euromarkets. Post-2007, Deutsche Bank, historically the German leader in the Euromarkets, sustained its Eurodollar business throughout the global financial crisis, yet its engagement became largely limited to on-balance sheet transactions.[99]

Bailing out the banks cost roughly a quarter of German GDP.[100] As well as these economic costs, the state had to put up a significant amount of political capital to retain its control over offshore finance. Tensions between the *Funktionselite* and the money elite mounted. Yet, as Deutsche Bank remains important to finance the export industry's international business in Eurodollars and in the absence of alternatives, Germany did not come off the Eurodollar system after the crisis. The benefits of creating money offshore for the banks has shrunk compared to its heyday in the late 1990s to early 2000s. The risks and potential costs for the power of the state remain.

## Resilience

As in the British case, offshore banking was more relevant for state power than offshore tax planning. And, again in a similar fashion to Britain, offshore banking strengthened state power until the inbuilt tendency for crisis made offshore banking costly for state power.

However, the stark contrast to Britain is that for Germany offshore finance did not alter the nature of the state. Instead, the institutional association of rule found a way to tap into offshore financial services while mitigating its effects on domestic politics.

From the German Empire through to today, the German banking system was able to create the money needed to finance capitalist expansion. Credit has been affordable for most economic actors throughout most of Germany's regimes. The shared power of the state and banks to create money is reflected in a banking system that is organized along ownership structures.

Publicly owned savings banks and *Landesbanken* were primarily established to serve domestic economic actors and state governments. In times of crises, they were to be bailed out by the taxpayer. The privately owned commercial and cooperative banks in turn could rely on the central bank as a lender of last resort. The large commercial banks especially served large domestic firms and were involved in the international banking business. In these basic features, the German banking system changed little between the

---

[99] Author's interview with banker, Munich, November 2018.
[100] Hüfner 2010.

1870s and the 1960s. The stable and regulated nature of the banking system limited the ability of banks to expand their business.

It was with the arrival of offshore money creation in the 1960s that this state of affairs changed. Following the lead of Deutsche Bank, large commercial banks and some *Landesbanken* became players in the Eurodollar markets. Their participation in offshore money creation was facilitated by the decision of the *Bundesbank* to recycle its US dollar overhang in the Eurodollar markets. The *Bundesbank* regulated the offshore activities such that the Eurodollar and Euro-Deutschmark exposure would not undermine its monetary policy. Part of the regulations ensured that all Euro-D-Mark bond issues would have to be done with a German lead manager, thereby allowing the *Bundesbank* to keep control over the currency. These regulations were also in the interest of the German banks as it kept foreign competitors at bay.[101] However, as inflation rose in the USA in the late 1960s, the German government became concerned that recycling US dollars would mean recycling US inflation too. In addition, German corporations had started to borrow in the Eurodollar markets, which reinforced the influx of US dollars into the German financial system, putting the fixed exchange rate under pressure. In response to these developments, the government started to advocate for regulation of the Euromarkets. The *Bundesbank* urged their US counterparts to set up reserve requirements for US banks borrowing in the Euromarkets. Additionally, Germany promoted capital controls on corporate borrowing in the Euromarkets and a floating of the D-Mark against the US dollar.[102] Likewise, throughout the 1970s and 1980s, the *Bundesbank* maintained a conservative outlook on short-term debt instruments such as credit derivatives or floating rate notes, many of which were pioneered in the Euromarkets. The *Bundesbank* regulated these instruments more strongly than its US American and British counterparts.[103] As a result of these measures, the Eurodollar market lost its anchor in the official dollar reserves of Germany.[104] Despite the regulations, the German banks could continue to partake in the Euromarkets. Yet, the power of the state to finance its politics was protected from undue risks building up in the Eurodollar markets.

Offshore money creation was aligned with the state's interests. From the perspective of the institutional association of rule, offshore money creation became a means to keep liberalization and internationalization outside the German banking system, while still catering to the interests of Germany's big

[101] Moore 2004.
[102] Farnsworth 1971.
[103] Moore 2004.
[104] Dickens 2005.

banks and export industry. The *Landesbanken* were the weak spot, though. They transferred the risks of offshore money creation into the domestic banking system which was financing state governments and small and middle-sized companies. The *Landesbanken* together with a handful of large commercial banks created a big—but temporary—hit to German state power with the financial crisis in 2007–09. The German state weathered the storm. It ensured the *Landesbanken* would henceforth refrain from offshore money creation.

Turning to offshore tax planning and the resilience of the German state towards it, we must consider that, historically, the German state found various ways to finance itself. The money elite was willing to pay tax to preserve the existing order. Yet, it was much less willing, particularly compared to their British counterparts, to pay tax to wage war. War had to be paid for by other means. Therefore, the German Empire and National Socialist Germany were to a considerable extent predator states, forcibly extracting resources from other countries through invasion and from their own population through repression and terror. In addition, modern Germany has, from the late nineteenth century until today, been a social security state. The state owns most elements of the social insurance system and contributions, directly deduced at source, are by law shared between employers and employees. Social security contributions are often lumped together with general tax payments, in the public discourse as much as in economic statistics. However, from the money view, the differences are profound. For the government social security contributions mean that revenue is earmarked for specific expenses. Social security contributions limit the discretionary spending power of the state. For the money elite, shared social security contributions are a means to pacify the class struggle in the form of corporate expenses, not in form of a direct reduction of their personal wealth. The success of this model of public finance is reflected in the fact that today income inequality is at the level of 1913, while the intensity of class warfare is not.[105] In relation to Germany's GDP, social security contributions almost doubled between the 1950s and today, while tax revenue remained unchanged.[106] As social security contributions are difficult to evade offshore, the government fenced off one important source of its income from offshoring.

Additionally, since the early days of the Bonn Republic, offshore tax planning, individual and corporate, has been an expression of how the *Funktionselite* did—or did not—accommodate the money elite's interest to lower its

[105] Bartels 2017.
[106] Bach 2019.

tax burden. Between the beginning of the Bonn Republic and the late 1990s, the state implicitly allowed them to minimize taxes offshore. This leniency was an expression of the close relationship between the money elite and the conservative *Funktionselite* in the early post-war years and from 1982 until 1998. In addition, it is likely that the *Funktionselite* under the Adenauer and Kohl governments had no interest in regulating offshore financial services as it was using it for its own corrupt purposes. Offshore accounts, as discussed above, played an important part in hiding and laundering illegal party donations to Helmut Kohl and his party, the CDU. Yet, this instance of political corruption is more a reflection of the power struggle within the institutional association of rule than an argument over how to finance the state. Offshore money laundering allowed conservative circles, especially industrialists from the Rhineland, to retain a stronghold within the institutional association of rule as the *Funktionselite* broadened with post-war democracy and a growing influence of social democratic politics. However, in the late 1990s, offshore tax evasion became so pervasive that it threatened the notion of Germany as a tax state. Successive governments at both state and federal level set out to curb it—successfully. Almost all interviewees pointed to a significant decrease in private offshore evasion between 2007 and 2015.

Corporate tax planning, on the other hand, has been restricted in its aggressiveness and scope. Although corporate financing has diversified in the past decades, corporate financing through own (family) capital and bank borrowing is still dominant compared to market financing. Consequently, it is rare for German corporations to access credit directly in the Euromarkets. Additionally, as an intrinsic and stable part of the association of rule, the money elite has, since the late 1990s, successfully aligned tax reforms with their interests. No other group of taxpayers has seen such a radical reduction of their tax burden since the beginning of the Berlin Republic. Moreover, true to the 'principle of performance', paying (relatively) high tax rates comes with returns in form of economic subsidies and other government support. In contrast, lower contributions to the state's tax revenue since the late 1990s has meant that the state became less lenient with regards to offshore tax planning. Throughout the 1990s and 2000s the German government passed unilateral defensive laws against aggressive tax planning and signed up to such laws at the European and international level. However, in the context of the OECD BEPS process, the strong link between the money elite and the *Funktionselite* was visible again. Defensive of their own multinational corporations, the German government practised the old strategy of committing to strong rules, whilst neglecting their enforcement and emphasizing the privacy of the individual corporate taxpayer. Germany is, for instance, the only European state that will not pub-licize the results of the now legally required country-by-country reporting of corporate annual results.[107] The institutional association of rule keeps a backdoor open.

The uses and abuses of offshore finance in Germany are marked by a com-bination of four elements. First, there is wide scope for individual tax evasion, and this has been implicitly accepted by the conservative elements of the *Funk-tionselite*. Second, there is relative restraint on corporate tax planning. The incentive structures are set against the unrestrained corporate offshoring as is practised in Britain. Third, a considerable amount of domestic political cor-ruption occurs, especially but not exclusively within the conservative elements of the *Funktionselite* and corporate corruption abroad. Here the politics of the invisible serves as means to cover up political crime. Fourth, there is con-siderable exposure to offshore money creation, something which has been especially embraced by social democrat governments. In summary, offshore money creation, money laundering, and tax planning became established practices in the Bonn and Berlin republics.

Yet, German state power has been resilient against the volatilities inherent in offshoring. Individual offshore tax planning aligned with the state's inter-ests. In addition, income from social security and therefore funding for welfare state policies was largely safeguarded from the effects of offshore finance. Once individual tax planning became fiscally and politically expensive, it was successfully reined in by the state. Corporate tax planning is compara-tively restrained, for corporate offshore debt issuance was limited and onshore taxation was favourable.

The important exception to this overall picture was the Euromarket expo-sure of the *Landesbanken* and Deutsche Bank pre-2007. The crisis response was politically and economically expensive. It strained the hitherto close relationship between the money and the *Funktionselite*. Post-2009, the *Landes-banken* retreated from the Euromarkets. The export-orientation of Germany's economy does not allow for a full retreat from the Euromarkets. Eurodol-lar exposure is now concentrated almost exclusively in Deutsche Bank. The German state's crisis response reigned in offshore money creation. In some instances, especially regarding the mitigation of the distributional conflict over the costs and benefits of money creation and taxation, it has even strengthened state power.

---

[107] Author's interview with employee of OECD, Paris, July 2017; with civil society organization, Berlin, January 2017.

The German case allows for four interesting observations about the relationship between offshore finance and state power.

First, as in Britain, in Germany the relationship between offshore finance and state power is not straightforward. There are instances when offshoring undermines state power, although they have mostly limited or indirect effects. In line with the theoretical considerations in Chapter 2, during the global financial crisis 2007–09, Germany's Eurodollar banks transmitted the volatility of the unregulated offshore markets into the domestic economy. However, there are also instances when offshoring strengthens state power. For it eases the distributional conflict over the costs and benefits of money creation and taxation and allows the state to pursue contradictory policies—open markets abroad in combination with a more regulated economy at home—without being questioned about them. In addtion, the state has profited from preferential liquidity to finance the costs of reunification.

Second, the nature of the effects varies between countries, but also within them. As the historical analysis suggests, the German state has not always been resilient to the effects of offshore finance. During the Weimar Republic, when the institutional association of rule struggled to keep up the cycle of money, tax, and debt, offshore finance did undermine the power of the state to finance its political goals.

Third, the German case suggests that there may not be a direct link between the scope of exposure to offshore finance and its effects on state power. Despite its considerable demand for offshore financial services, German state power, in the contemporary period, remains resilient. It found a successful way to mitigate offshore finance's effects by reaping the benefits domestically and externalizing the costs. Finally, again as in the British case, it is the democratic state that embraces the politics of the invisible most strongly.

# 5

# Brazil

## Inflation and Eurodollar dependency

With this chapter, I leave Europe, the cradle and catalyst of offshore finance, and turn to Latin American, one of the regions supposedly most badly affected by its existence.[1]

Brazil is the region's largest economy. Despite phases of profound growth, it is still a developing economy and faces important governance problems, including pervasive corruption. At the same time, compared to the other case study countries, Brazil's economy is not as fully open. Capital controls, for instance, remain a regular policy tool. It is also the only case study country that is geographically removed from major offshore financial centres.

Analysing the relationship between offshore finance and state power in Brazil from the money view, I find that offshore financial services have a deep impact on state power. As in Britain and Germany, that relationship is not straightforward. Likewise, although offshore finance affects Brazilian state power through both sides of the balance sheet—taxation and money creation—it is offshore banking that is more consequential.

In Brazil, offshore finance has become an integral part of the domestic cycle of money, tax, and debt. In this regard it is similar to Britain and different from Germany. Starting in the 1960s, offshore banking replaced, to a significant extent, onshore money creation. Offshore banking enhanced state power by providing access to preferential liquidity. It helped finance the institutional association of rule's political goals, including its economic miracle in the late 1960s to early 1970s. It also boosted Brazil's economy in the late 1990s to early 2000s.

At the same time, as in the British and German cases, offshore banking undermined state power in times of financial crisis, especially in 1982. However, similar to Germany and unlike Britain, the Brazilian state has built a set of defensive measures against offshore finance. It protected its tax base through a mix of domestic and international measures. More importantly, it effectively mitigated the risks of offshore banking through regulation and

[1] Zucman 2015.

*Offshore Finance and State Power.* Andrea Binder, Oxford University Press. © Andrea Binder (2023).
DOI: 10.1093/oso/9780192870124.003.0005

central bank interventions. Over time, Brazilian state power proved resilient towards offshore finance. Nevertheless, given the structural dependence on offshore banking, and the level of corruption it enables, offshore finance remains a double-edged sword for Brazilian state power.

This chapter analyses the relationship between offshore finance and state power in the long run and from the money view. Brazil, like Germany, is shaped by frequently changing regimes: monarchy (1822–89), oligarchic rule (1889–1930), autocracy (1930–45), military dictatorship (1964–85), and democracy (1946–64 and 1985 to today). However, from the money view, two critical junctures in Brazil's history are more relevant for the offshore finance–state power relationship than the different regimes. These junctures are (1) independence from Portugal in 1822, starting the long struggle to establish a functional sovereign money and (2) the 1994 monetary reform, which finally did so.

## 1  Brazilian state power from the money view

The genealogy of Brazil's institutional association of rule and the strategies to finance its politics differs from both the British and the German experience (Chapters 3 and 4). Brazil is the only colony in history whose independence had been declared by a family member of the colonizing power's royal court.[2] From independence in 1821 to the 1994 monetary reform, the Brazilian state has been characterized by short-lived cycles of money, tax, and debt. The fragile nature of money creation in Brazil has its roots in the long-standing tensions between an urban political elite and an oligarchic rural economic elite in a continental country. It is this uncomfortable relationship between the political and economic elites which has shaped the distributional conflict over the costs and benefits of money creation and taxation. It began with Brazilian independence.

In 1821, Dom Pedro, residing as prince regent in Rio de Janeiro, received an order from the Portuguese crown to return to Lisbon. The order was against his will and when a petition from local elites reached him with a request to stay, Dom Pedro seized the opportunity. He declared Brazil an independent monarchy and himself emperor. Yet, the relationship between the urban monarch and the rural planter-merchant elite was not as cosy as this episode of independence suggests. The provincial oligarchs, spread out across Brazil's vast coastline, sought independence from Portugal but had no inclination to

---

[2] Skidmore 2010.

upset the prevailing social order. They did not intend to share their power and wealth with the new emperor, nor to mobilize the masses to overthrow him. Dom Pedro, for his part, aimed to build a central state with the planter-merchant class contributing to its revenue. Neither side could win this power struggle.

The constitution of 1824 finally presented a compromise between the urban monarch and the rural oligarchs. The merchant-planter oligarchy was represented, nearly exclusively, in parliament. Parliament had the right to tax, spend, go into debt, and regulate how the national debt would be financed. The monarch, in turn, had the right to dismiss parliament, should he disagree with its fiscal policies. Dissolving parliament entailed, of course, the risk of creating even more opposition to the emperor's fiscal plans as the new parliament would be, by default, populated by members of the same economic elites.[3]

In Imperial Brazil, the bargain over how to finance the state was structured around the demands of the oligarchs' parliament for state spending in support of their sugar, coffee, and mining businesses, and their unwillingness to contribute to state finances via taxation or lending. Consequently, spending was financed through international borrowing and inflation. The emperor borrowed, especially from the British, in return for the country's mineral wealth.[4]

Domestically, Dom Pedro relied on the *Banco do Brasil*. Comparable to the early incarnation of the Bank of England, the *Banco do Brasil* was a government bank without being a central bank in the contemporary sense. It had the right to issue legal-tender paper money. It helped to finance the government by buying government debt with money that it created in the first place. However, with no tax revenue to speak of, the cycle of money, tax, and debt could not begin. Instead, government debt and inflation quickly spiralled out of control. It sealed Dom Pedro's political fate. Seven years after independence, the parliament revoked *Banco do Brasil*'s licence to print money and removed Dom Pedro from power.[5]

The conflict between Brazil's small rural economic elite and the urban political elite over the mobilization and centralization of state revenue remained a common theme of Brazilian politics well into the twentieth century. Then as now, the economic elite did not intend to share power with the political leaders. It aimed to rule through them.[6]

---

[3] Calomiris and Haber 2014, chs 12–13.
[4] Skidmore 2010.
[5] Calomiris and Haber 2014, ch. 12; Skidmore 2010.
[6] Author's interview with defence lawyer, São Paulo, April 2017, author's telephone interview with tax lawyer, Rio de Janeiro, April 2017, see also: Calomiris and Haber 2014.

This conflict shapes the nature of Brazil's institutional association of rule. Irrespective of regime type, the political elite always faced the same trilemma: do not tax and remain a weak central power in a continental country; or strengthen the state by taxing the wealthy elite and lose their political support; or finance the inevitable deficits via inflation and risk popular discontent.[7]

Most Brazilian governments have opted for the last option. As a result, in the past 200 years, Brazil developed average inflation rates that were among the world's highest.[8] Respective governments have dealt with the ensuing popular discontent via a combination of measures: highly exclusive decision-making processes, focusing economic policies on keeping unemployment low, and outright repression. As tax revenues remained low, the governments coaxed the wealthy elite and foreigners into providing credit by keeping interest rates high. Consequently, interest rates, just like inflation rates, were among the highest in the world. Brazil's problems with (hyper)inflation can be interpreted as an expression of the longstanding conflict between the urban rulers and the rural oligarchy over how to finance the state. The bank and tax bargain are a reflection of that conflict as the subsequent two sections detail.

## Bank bargain

The fate of the *Banco do Brazil*, one of the country's most important banks, mirrors the continuity and change of the relationship between the state and its financiers. Essentially, the *Banco do Brasil* has had, throughout Brazilian modern history, three incarnations.

In its first incarnation, the father of Dom Pedro II founded the bank in 1808 to help finance the build-up of the Brazilian kingdom's military and administrative infrastructure. Its post-independence existence was short-lived as the costs of money creation for the financiers were not matched by any benefits. After *Banco do Brasil*'s conclusion in 1829, Brazil's banking system remained miniscule for the coming two decades and did not allow for a broad access to credit. The lack of liquidity was more of a problem for the state than for the economic elite. Living off the land and natural resources and exploiting the largest slave community in the Americas, there was no high demand for credit among the rural economic elite. Money creation was not a power they aspired to. With expenditure running at twice the tax revenue, the state had to find international financiers to finance its political goals.[9]

---

[7] Calomiris and Haber 2014, chs 12–13.
[8] Ibid., 390.
[9] Ibid., ch. 12; Skidmore 2010.

The political elite resurrected the *Banco do Brasil* in 1850, when it gained the upper hand in the struggle over funding the state through money creation. The state merged two privately owned banks into the new *Banco do Brasil*, now majoritarian state-owned. To soothe the remaining minority shareholders, the state endowed the *Banco do Brasil* with far reaching privileges: a monopoly to issue notes and favourable reserve requirements. These privileges earned the private shareholders attractive rents. The benefits of creating money became apparent—even though this power had to be shared with the state. The second incarnation of the *Banco do Brasil* thus became a unifying force in the otherwise chronically tense relationship between economic and political elites within the institutional association of rule.

Nevertheless, the banking system outside the *Banco do Brasil* remained small and the demand for capital low. This state of affairs fundamentally changed with the abolition of slavery in 1888. Now the oligarchy needed money. Through the *Banco do Brasil* Dom Pedro II provided it in the form of government-subsidized credit. This policy, as a side effect, expanded the Brazilian banking system. However, it did not save the ailing emperor from republican pressures. In 1889, the military forced Dom Pedro II into exile, ending the Brazilian empire.[10]

The military government maintained the emperor's strategy to buy political support from the economic elite through subsidized credit. Without the backing of meaningful tax revenue on the left-hand side of the government's balance sheet, this credit boom soon gave rise to a bank run. The collapse of the banking system in 1900 took with it the *Banco do Brasil* and many of the other newly established banks.[11]

In 1906 the now republican government nationalized a large private bank and turned it into the third incarnation of the *Banco do Brasil*. Again, the state acted as a majority shareholder. Likewise, the state again aligned the use of the *Banco do Brasil* closely with the interests of the economic elites; this time especially of the coffee growers, Brazil's largest economic sector at the time. The *Banco do Brasil* helped to prop up the coffee sector when it came under pressure because of falling international coffee prices. The benefits of the shared power of money creation were now such that the rural-planter oligarchy started to favour a larger state.[12]

This third incarnation of the *Banco do Brasil* survived the 1930 military coup which brought Getúlio Vargas to power. Vargas, first as an authoritarian ruler from 1930 to 1945 and then as the democratically elected president

---

[10] Calomiris and Haber 2014, chs 12–13.
[11] Ibid.
[12] Ibid.; Maxfield 2001; Skidmore 2010.

from 1950 to 1954, left important imprints on Brazil's modern bank system. As his predecessors, he used the *Banco do Brasil* to unify the political and economic elites within the institutional association of rule. As the coffee business declined and the industrial sector rose in Brazil's economy, the beneficiaries of the *Banco do Brasil* changed. Vargas used the bank to appeal to industrialists by financing their enterprises. He also used it to keep class warfare at bay by financing welfare state policies for urban industrial workers. In addition, Vargas turned the *Caixa Econômica Federal* into a government-backed system of saving banks. Now the growing Brazilian working class contributed to financing the state via debt. Vargas also laid the foundations for the *Banco Nacional de Desenvolvimento Econômico e Social* (BNDES), the government-owned development bank. The BNDES provided cheap credit to selected, large companies that provided employment. The BNDES was used, both during Vargas' reign and under military rule, to keep popular discontent in check by funding employment-supporting policies that went along with repression. Vargas also attempted to create a central bank. However, the rural-planter oligarchy and later the São Paulo industrialist elite, who were among *Banco do Brasil*'s shareholders, successfully resisted that move. They feared a loss of the power to create money with the establishment of a central bank.[13]

Brazil's banking system now produced credit for the economic elite. All other economic actors and the government were, however, still short of it. From 1964 onwards, the Brazilian military government thus began to engage with the nascent offshore money markets. It developed an explicit approach to link domestic banks with the Eurodollar system—codified in Resolution 63 and subsequent laws. This approach is still the foundation of the country's offshore dollar transactions today.[14] It is built around four central elements.

First, the government limited engagement in the Eurodollar markets to a handful of banks, including *Banco do Brasil* and commercial banks such as *Banco Real* and *Banespa*.

Second, Resolution 63 allowed Brazilian banks to borrow US dollars internationally and then pass on the corresponding amount in local currency to industrial and commercial firms.[15] Offshore money creation complemented the onshore cycle of money, tax, and debt.

Third, Resolution 63 regulated the Eurodollar activities of participating banks to minimize the risks of overleverage and of maturity mismatches. The remaining risks could be transferred from leveraged corporations and

---

[13] Calomiris and Haber 2014; Maxfield 2001, ch. 8.
[14] Author's interview with BNDES banker, Rio de Janeiro, April 2017. See also Alvarez (2020) and Frieden (1987).
[15] Alvarez 2020.

banks onto the central bank's balance sheet. This transfer of risk was done through various mechanisms, including currency swaps and the possibility to deposit US dollars with the central bank. The central bank covered the related exchange risks and the charges of foreign lenders.

Finally, the government incentivized banks and large corporations to participate in these markets. For instance, it offered through BNDES subsidized credits to large corporations to give them the leverage needed to engage in offshore borrowing.[16] The government also abandoned reserve requirements for all transactions conducted under Resolution 63.[17]

In the 1970s, investors seeking to recycle their petrodollars considered Brazil, due to its rapid growth, increasing levels of industrialization, and political stability under the military dictatorship to be a creditworthy country.[18] The Brazilian state could borrow in London at negative real rates of interest.[19] And so it did, in the words of Rocha,[20] 'embark on a gigantic borrowing spree on world-capital markets ... to drive development'.

However, it was not only the Brazilian government that went offshore. Well-off Brazilian individuals and corporations routinely used offshore accounts to hedge against inflation and other risks, to circumvent capital controls and other regulations. At that time capital controls included a prohibition on holding capital abroad or exchanging it into foreign currency.[21] The offshore transactions were often facilitated by *doleiros*, money traders who would illegally exchange domestic currency into US dollars.[22]

Brazil's dream of cheap international debt ended in 1982. Yet, for Brazil, unlike for Mexico, 1982 was not a sovereign solvency crisis. It was a Eurodollar liquidity crisis.[23]

In the months before the 1982 crisis, Brazilian banks' aggregated offshore assets in London alone amounted to US$1.3 billion. These numbers exclude the offshore dollar business in Cayman Islands and the Bahamas. Despite this considerable exposure, Brazilian banks were largely resilient to the Eurodollar liquidity squeeze resulting from the Mexican declaration that it could no longer service its international debt. The reason for the resilience was Brazil's regulation of Eurodollar business. It emphasized cross-border over interbank financing. According to Alvarez,[24] the ratio was roughly 3:1. Consequently,

---

[16] Author's interview with tax lawyer, Rio de Janeiro, April 2017.
[17] Frieden 1987; Alvarez 2020.
[18] Altamura 2017.
[19] Cardoso and Fishlow 1989; Skidmore 2010.
[20] Rocha 2002, 6.
[21] Goldfajn and Minella 2005.
[22] Author's interview with defence lawyer, São Paulo, April 2017.
[23] Alvarez 2020.
[24] Ibid.

Brazil, unlike Mexico, did not suffer a systemic meltdown of its banking system.[25]

Nevertheless, the losses in the interbank markets were tangible and accumulated in just two banks: *Banco do Brasil* and *Banespa*.[26] These banks' foreign offices had no access to emergency funding either through the Federal Reserve in New York or through the Bank of England in London (see Chapter 2). As their liabilities were in a foreign currency there was also little the Brazilian central bank could do for them. Instead, the government decided to default on its foreign liabilities, including those it had towards its own banks operating in the offshore money markets. In response, the Brazilian government was excluded from international financial markets.

The pressure on the government to finance itself domestically grew. However, this did not mean that the Brazilian government severed the link between the domestic economy and the Eurodollar system so carefully crafted by the military regime in the 1960s and 1970s. Instead, that link was improved in two ways.

First, the government devised a division of labour between the domestic and the offshore banking system. The domestic banking system provided long-term credit nearly exclusively to the government. The offshore markets provided long-term credit to Brazil's corporate sector.[27] That is, the Brazilian government—again consciously—facilitated a link between the domestic economy and the Eurodollar system.[28]

This time, however, it focused on providing direct access for Brazilian corporations to the Eurodollar system. The transition was made possible because of the transformation of Brazil's state capitalism in the late 1980s and early 1990s. Through these reforms the state no longer acted as the owner, but as a shareholder of companies.[29] These reforms increased the trust of international investors. Furthermore, building on an approach pioneered in the 1960s—increased in scale and scope—the government subsidized domestic credit to a selected number of large Brazilian multinational corporations. It supported the so-called national champions, via the BNDES.[30] Thanks to these policies, the private sector was back in the Euromarkets from the early 1990s

---

[25] Alvarez 2015.
[26] Alvarez 2020.
[27] Author's interview with banker, Rio de Janeiro, April 2017.
[28] Author's interview with banker, Rio de Janeiro, April 2017. Author's interview with financial market expert, Rio de Janeiro, April 2017.
[29] Musacchio Farias and Lazzarini 2014.
[30] Author's interview with financial expert, Rio de Janeiro, April 2017; author's interview with financial journalist, São Paulo, April 2017. See also McCauley (2005).

onwards. The Eurodollar system now provided large Brazilian corporations directly with access to funding at lower interest rates than at home.[31]

The second improvement was that the central bank built a system back-stopping corporate Eurodollar borrowing by building up US dollar reserves[32] and setting up central bank swap lines. Complementing the onshore cycle of money, tax, and debt with offshore money creation became permanent.

## Tax bargain

The Brazilian tax state was a long time in the making. Yet, from the money view, its history is quickly told. The high concentration of wealth and power in the hands of Brazil's rural oligarchy made taxation a difficult affair. Between independence and 1994 only two regimes managed to gain the upper hand in the struggle between the rural economic elites and the urban rulers over how to finance the state: the autocratic *Estado Novo* under Getúlio Vargas (1937–45) and the military regime (1964–85).

Vargas's main goal was to strengthen the central government by central-izing taxation. The federal states had successfully increased their share of government revenue between the end of Imperial Brazil and during the First Republic.[33] Now Vargas was adamant to regain fiscal power from the federal states. The financial crash of 1929 and the Great Depression provided him with a window of opportunity for tax reform. The rural coffee growers and early industrialists needed financial support from the government. In return, they could finally be won over to support a larger central state. Additionally, building-up an administration run by technocrats, and relying on the military to maintain stability, Vargas succeeded in the fifteen years of his autocratic reign to centralize taxation.[34]

About three decades later, the military regime (1964–85) attempted the next tax reform, betting on Vargas's strategy: centralizing tax collection, profession-alizing tax administration and insulating the tax authority from the political struggles between the urban rulers and the rural wealthy elite. As a result, the *Secretaria da Receita Federal* (RFB) became one of the most well organized parts of the Brazilian administration.[35]

---

[31] Author's interview with BNDES employee, Rio de Janeiro, April 2017. Author's interview with financial market expert, Rio de Janeiro, April 2017.
[32] Alami 2018.
[33] Goldsmith 1986.
[34] Skidmore 2010.
[35] Weyland 1998.

Another important result of the 1965 tax reform was the introduction of VAT, split between the state and the federal levels.[36] Brazil was one of the first countries in the world to introduce a dual VAT. It was an efficient way to appease the states while broadening the central government's tax base. Introducing a general consumption tax finally included the large poor population into the rank of taxpayers. Even before offshore financial services entered the scene, in Brazil the lower classes had to pick up the tax bill the wealthy were unwilling to foot.

The military government was also clever in other ways. As corporations became ever better at avoiding taxation under conditions of inflation by pushing their payments into the future, the RFB indexed tax payments to inflation and introduced a pay-as-you-go tax structure. Helped by Brazil's 'economic miracle' between 1968 and 1973, with average annual growth rates around 10 per cent, these measures finally flushed some money into the state's coffers.[37]

During the period covering the autocratic regime of Getúlio Vargas to the time of the military regime, Brazil's economy transformed from agrarian to industrialized. Consequently, the institutional association of rule between the government and the rural oligarchy extended to include industrialists, mostly based in São Paulo. In addition, Vargas and his administration created a government-directed, corporatist social organization. The aim was to address questions of social welfare for the growing number of urban workers and to avoid class warfare.[38]

As a result, the tax system of the *Estato Novo* and the military regime was determined by the special interests of different social groups. The question of how to finance the state's political goals through taxation became one that was less about who must pay how much. Instead, it was about who could negotiate exceptions or tax breaks for its own social group. By the mid-1970s, tax breaks for different business sectors amounted to 65 per cent of corporate income tax revenue or to about 13 per cent of the federal government's revenue. This number excludes the loss of corporate income tax through tax evasion, which was also widespread.[39]

By the mid-1970s, the private sector had, essentially, stopped paying tax. After half a century, the tax state that Vargas and the military had built reached its limits. However, access to the Eurodollar could gloss over the fiscal problems and spared the military regime paying the political price for properly taxing the wealthy or cutting spending on urban workers. A decade later, by the

[36] Longo 1994; Melo, Barrientos, and Canuto Coelho 2014.
[37] Weyland 1998.
[38] Skidmore 2010.
[39] Weyland 1998.

mid-1980s, high inflation, low growth, and the fiscal and debt crises reflected that the institutional association of rule had not reached a sustainable agreement on how to finance the state. The wealthy were unwilling to pay through either tax or debt. As the state disintegrated, it took with it the military regime.

## 2  Contemporary exposure to offshore finance

Offshore finance has historical roots in Brazil, as the previous analysis has demonstrated. I now turn to the country's contemporary exposure to offshore finance which coincides with the country's process of democratization.

For a short time between 2007 and 2016, financial transparency around offshore finance was high in Brazil compared to Britain or Germany. By law every Brazilian corporation and individual with external assets worth US$100,000 or more is required to report these assets. Between 2007 and 2016, the *Banco Central do Brasil* has made that data publicly available as part of the annual Brazilian capital abroad (CBE) survey.[40] However, for reasons of comparability, I analyse Brazil's exposure to the offshore world as I did in the previous cases. Based on the BIS locational banking statistics, interview results, and the above historical analysis, this section provides a rough estimate of overall offshore exposure.

The analysis covers the time from 1994, the second critical juncture in the development of Brazil's institutional association of rule, until 2020. Quantitative data are available only from 2002 onwards, when Brazil started to report to the BIS. Again, the quantitative data must be treated with caution. It cannot portray a full picture of the offshore world. Additionally, I share the core assumptions of estimating the tax loss with the larger literature on finance—all offshore assets are untaxed and would be taxed if they were onshore—knowing that they simplify a complex world. Appendix 1 describes the methodological details of the rough estimate, including its limitations. In addition, the CBE data allow us to take a more nuanced look at Brazilian offshore assets and their implications for tax revenue.

### The uses and abuses of offshore finance

What is relevant from the money view, are all financial flows between Brazil and offshore financial centres. These flows reflect the scale and pattern of

---

[40] See Appendix 1 for details.

Brazil's exposure to offshore finance. As in the previous cases, claims represent money held in offshore financial centres, as well as liabilities for debt issued there.

Figure 5.1 depicts Brazil's overall exposure to offshore finance. As established earlier, offshore claims (assets) and liabilities (debt) affect the ability of the state to finance its politics differently, but collectively. The graph therefore depicts both sides of the balance sheet separately and in total. It is the sum of claims and liabilities that represents overall offshore exposure.

According to the BIS data, Brazilian offshore exposure developed from 4 per cent of GDP (or US$18.6 billion) in 2002 to 6 per cent of GDP (or US$116 billion) in 2019. Between 2002 and 2009, offshore liabilities outweighed offshore claims. Brazil is a net borrower in the offshore markets—as it has been historically.

After 2009 offshore claims grew strongly. In the decade between 2009 and 2019 the growth rate, in absolute terms, was about 20 per cent annually. By 2014 claims exceeded liabilities and Brazil became a net lender in the offshore markets. In the context of the interview results, this pattern of offshoring suggests that up until the global financial crisis, Brazilian economic actors used offshore financial services more to access credit than to invest or protect their money. The relationship reversed during the financial crisis and especially so since the economic contraction Brazil has experienced since 2010. Now Brazilians, while still borrowing more than at any time before the financial crisis, go offshore more to invest and to protect their money.

Disaggregating Brazil's offshore exposure by currency denomination, Figure 5.2 shows that between 2002 and 2019 the Eurodollar has been dominant in Brazil's offshore exposure. Except for the years 2005–09, the Eurodollar's share has always been above 80 per cent.

This pattern of offshoring is in line with the historical analysis, however the scale—4 to 6 per cent of GDP—appears small given the historical importance of the Eurodollar markets.

As indicated above, between 2007 and 2016, the *Banco Central do Brasil* published the results of the CBE survey online.[41] These historical data were disaggregated by counterparty country, allowing onshore and offshore transactions to be distinguished. The CBE survey data provide a unique opportunity, for the case of Brazil, to come to a more realistic quantitative estimate of offshore exposure. Nevertheless, the CBE data has its own limitations, most obviously that it is no longer publicly available and that it covers only assets, not liabilities. Figure 5.3 presents the difference between offshore assets reported through the BIS and offshore assets reported through the CBE.

---

[41] With a reform of national accounts reporting in 2017, the CBE data are no longer available online.

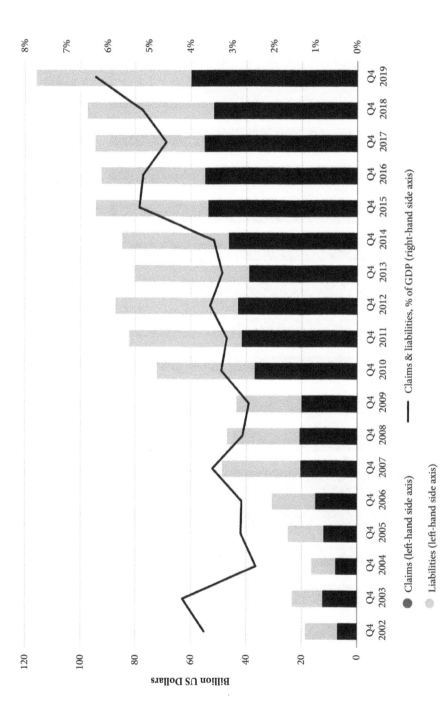

**Figure 5.1** Brazil's exposure to offshore finance

*Source:* BIS locational banking statistics, World Bank, own calculations.

**Figure 5.2** Currency breakdown of Brazil's exposure to offshore finance
*Source:* BIS locational banking statistics, own calculations.

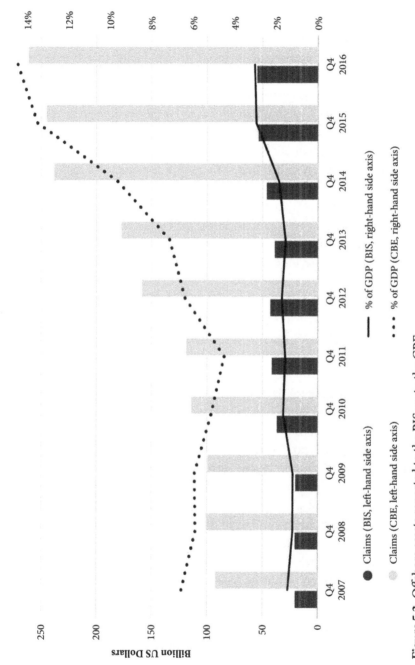

**Figure 5.3** Offshore assets reported to the BIS vs. to the CBE

*Source:* BIS locational banking statistic, Banco Central do Brasil, World Bank, own calculations.

According to CBE data, offshore assets developed from 7 per cent of GDP (or US$92 billion) in 2007 to 15 per cent of GDP (or US$261 billion) in 2016. The increase in offshore claims visible in the BIS data is also present in CBE data. However, CBE data reflect a much larger scale. As a share of GDP, the assets held offshore are three to five times higher than is reflected by the BIS data. Partially, the difference is related to reporting. In January 2016, the Brazilian Congress passed an amnesty law allowing Brazilian individuals to regularize their legally obtained, but non-reported foreign assets. These assets were in breach of Brazilian currency exchange and tax regulations. In response, Brazilian households reported an additional US$54 billion to the central bank. Once integrated into the survey, this amount led to the marked growth of external assets between 2013 and 2014.[42] The amnesty coincided with Brazil's decision to join the OECD's automatic exchange of information regime. Lawyers advised individuals with undeclared external assets to come clean before the new regulation would take effect in October 2016. It is hence highly likely that the CBE survey now covers close to all legally obtained offshore assets.[43]

Unfortunately, the CBE data do not cover offshore liabilities. However, interviewees working in foreign exchange markets suggested that the Eurodollar market is the largest international funding market for Brazilian firms.[44] Given the importance of offshore money creation before the 1982 debt crisis, it likely still plays an important role today. Next to offshore assets, the BIS offshore liabilities may also underestimate offshore money creation.

By the early 1990s, Brazil's longstanding cycle of low tax, high inflation, high debt, and even higher interest rates had gotten out of control. Inflation peaked at 1430 per cent per year.[45] Three years later, a team of economists around the newly appointed finance minister Fernando Henrique Cardoso understood the problem underlying Brazil's past predicament: Brazil had no trusted means of accounting for and settling debt, including tax debt, domestically. Between 1942 and 1994, the country had eight different currencies, most of which did not even last for a decade.

Cardoso's aides devised a currency reform. They split, for a time of transition, the two functions of money: means of payment and unit of account. The then official currency, the *cruzeiro real*, remained the means of payment, while

[42] Banco Central do Brasil 2017.
[43] Author's interview with defence lawyer, São Paulo, April 2017.
[44] Author's telephone interview with financial analyst, May 2017; author's interview with banker, Rio de Janeiro, April 2017.
[45] Averbug 2002.

a newly introduced virtual currency, the *unidade real de valor* (URV), became the new unit of account. Brazil's central bank, the *Banco Central do Brasil*, determined the exchange rate between the two daily. After prices expressed in URV had nominally stabilized, making Brazilians trust the currency reform, the two functions were merged again and the new currency, the Brazilian real (R$), was floated in the summer of 1994.[46] Twenty-seven years later, the Brazilian Real is the longest serving currency in modern Brazil.

As is to be expected from Ingham's theory of money (see Chapter 2), the debt-to-GDP ratio increased significantly after the currency reform, particularly from 1995 onwards. Importantly, this growth was driven by domestic debt issuance. External public debt, on the contrary, fell from 18 per cent of GDP in 1994 to 1 per cent in 2005. Domestic public debt, on the other hand, rose from 18 per cent in 1994 to 49 per cent of GDP in 2005.[47] Before the introduction of the Brazilian real, external debt usually outpaced domestic debt. With the currency reform and the steady growth of tax income, domestic financiers were finally willing to lend to the government.[48] Brazil's circle of money, tax, and debt was finally running.

As a result, there were two fundamental changes in Brazil's engagement with the Eurodollar system compared to the pre-1982 period. First, the government withdrew significantly from those markets. Indstead of issuing debt in the Eurodollar markets, it now issued it domestically. It also started building up US dollar reserves. This change in approach meant the government backed the Eurodollar engagement of banks and large corporations, while staying out of these markets itself. The move was made possible by the successful introduction of the Brazilian real and the resulting willingness of domestic financiers to lend to the government. It was also made possible by an export-oriented development and increasing oil revenues leading to an increase in US dollar reserves.

Second, unlike the government, corporations now moved forcefully into the Euromarkets. Private sector borrowing gained momentum in the early 2000s and after the global financial crisis as was demonstrated in the previous section (see Figure 5.1).

What has developed since the 1990s, against the backdrop of a proper sovereign money, is an institutionalized division of labour between the domestic and the offshore banking system with regards to long-term credit. The domestic banking system provided long-term credit almost exclusively to

---

[46] Ibid.
[47] Ferreira and Bonomo 2006.
[48] Ibid.

the government. The offshore markets provided long-term credit to Brazil's corporate sector.[49]

In addition to these domestic reasons, the banking regulation and litigation laws in the United States are an important set of motivations for why Brazilian corporates issue dollar-denominated debt in Europe. US American banking regulation is so demanding that it excludes most Brazilian firms from issuing in the US markets. According to the interviewees, even more of a deterrent than the banking regulations is US litigation law.[50] In the words of one interviewee:

> [T]o comply with all the rules when dealing with the American authorities, it really is a nightmare for the lawyers. And when talking with the management of the companies ... they know that if anything goes wrong, we will be prosecuted in the US and next time we visit Disneyland or New York, we cannot.[51]

However, the Eurodollar system has even more perquisites for creditors. It provides them with access to exactly those US investors, to which they have no access in the US market. Particularly since the global financial crisis, institutional investors from the United States were under pressure to find viable investments abroad as their own financial environment was marked by low interest rates and high liquidity. Searching beyond the US market, they invest in emerging economies, prime among them China and Brazil.[52] Moreover, issuing bonds offshore is an effective and widely used tool among Brazilian corporations for tax planning via intracompany loans.[53] In-line with these findings, the BIS reports that Brazilian intracompany loans co-move with offshore dollar debt issuance.[54]

Based on the explicit policy choice of the Brazilian government and central bank to continue to engage in the Eurodollar markets and to develop a backstop for potential crises, the country's access to Eurodollar liquidity in absolute terms was growing in the early 2000s (see Figure 5.1 above). During that time, Brazil's industrial production and domestic income grew at unprecedented levels. Other than subsidizing offshore credit, there was little need for the

---

[49] Author's interview with banker, Rio de Janeiro, April 2017.

[50] Author's telephone interview with investment banker, May 2017; with tax lawyer, London, June 2017; with tax lawyer, Mexico City, November 2015.

[51] Author's interview with banker, Rio de Janeiro, April 2017.

[52] Author's interview with banker, Rio de Janeiro, April 2017; author's telephone interview with investment banker, May 2017.

[53] Author's telephone interview with corporate tax lawyer, April 2017.

[54] McCauley, McGuire, and Sushko 2015.

government to intervene. This absence changed fundamentally with the global financial crisis in 2007. Brazil's banks and corporations were confronted with a considerable US dollar gap. This time, the Brazilian central bank was ready to respond. A combination of capital controls and swap lines with the Federal Reserve helped to effectively cover Brazilian banks' US dollar gap during the crisis.[55] Consequentially, the global financial crisis had comparatively limited negative effects on Brazil's banking sector.[56] Backstopping the Eurodollar exposure turned out to be an effective policy choice.

In 2009, dollar credit was still short in the United States, but Eurodollar credit was again flowing freely to Brazil. These flows were mainly driven by investors in search for yields in a low-interest environment.[57] The Brazilian private sector happily borrowed. Petrobras, the partially state-owned oil company, is a case in point. In 2009, Petrobras became the largest net issuer of Eurobonds in the world. With two issuances of US$8 billion and US$6 billion between 2009 and 2014, the oil company became one of the most indebted corporations globally.[58] Yet, the expansion of offshore credit no longer correlates with economic growth as it did before the financial crisis. Quite to the contrary, the Brazilian economy experienced its worst recession in decades. The *Banco Central do Brasil* considered the economic crisis a result of monetary tightening in the United States in 2011 and more strongly in 2013. Consequently, the central bank set out to defend the private sector's access to US dollars. Between 2013 and 2014, the central bank provided US dollar swaps to its own banking system from its reserves. The programme amounted to more than US$90 billion or about a quarter of Brazil's total foreign reserves.[59] Once again, the Brazilian authorities made a conscious policy decision to stabilize offshore money creation.[60] These efforts maintained access to US dollar liquidity. Yet, for almost a decade since, they have not been sufficient to meaningfully increase productivity.

Next to offshore money creation, offshore exposure is a precondition for economic actors to plan taxes. Again, to keep it comparable with the other cases, Figure 5.4 depicts the estimated tax loss based on BIS and CBE data.

Under the assumption that all offshore assets go untaxed and would be taxed at the full nominal rates if moved onshore, the tax loss for the Brazilian

[55] Allen 2013; Chamon and Garcia 2016.
[56] Author's interview with financial sector expert, Rio de Janeiro, April 2017.
[57] Author's interview with financial market expert, Mexico City, November 2015. Author's telephone interview with investment banker, May 2017. See also McCauley, McGuire, and Sushko 2015.
[58] McCauley, McGuire, and Sushko 2015.
[59] Chamon, Garcia, and Souza 2015.
[60] Alami 2019.

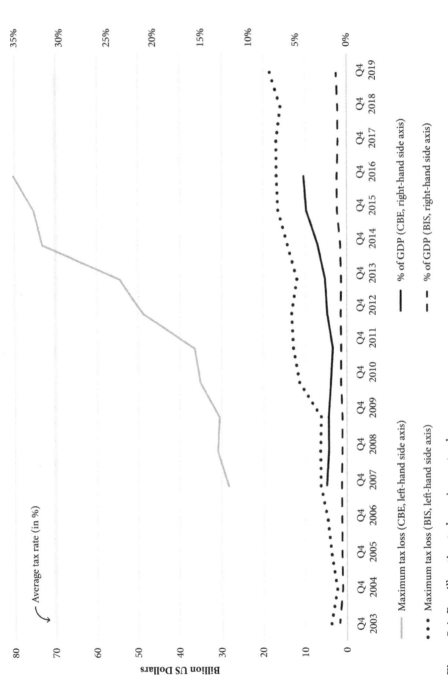

**Figure 5.4** Brazil's estimated maximum tax loss

*Source:* BIS locational banking statistics, CBE, World Bank, own calculations.

government ranges between 0.4 per cent of GDP (or US$2 billion) in 2002 and 1 per cent of GDP (or US$17 billion) in 2019, if we base the estimate on the BIS data. The tax loss estimate based on the CBE data amounts to 2 per cent of GDP in 2007 (or US$30 billion) to 5 per cent of GDP (or US$63 billion) in 2019. However, given that all assets reported to the CBE survey are declared, it is unlikely that they have all been untaxed and would be taxed at the full rate if moved onshore. The discrepancy between the BIS and the CBE data suggests that we underestimate the volume of offshore assets and overestimate the related tax loss by assuming that everything that is offshore goes untaxed and would be taxed at the full rate if repatriated.

Yet, the estimate of the potential tax loss covers only tax planning through offshoring assets. Interviewees reported, however, that Brazilian corporations also use offshore debt to plan their taxes. Here, it is even harder to come to conclusive estimates, not least because offshore credit is particularly strongly concentrated in Brazil's oil, gas, and mining sectors. The extractive industries need considerable pre-financing. It is thus impossible to distinguish between 'proper debt', issued to finance operations and 'artificial debt' issued to avoid taxation in Brazil. Nevertheless, it is clear that the extractive sector structures its debt in a tax efficient manner via offshore issuance. The following quote from a Brazilian corporate tax lawyer describes a classic scheme:

[W]e get pre-export finance from the group so instead of going to the bank market, we get credit from our group, which is based in Luxembourg.... Luxembourg is, since 2011, no longer considered a tax haven in Brazil anymore, so ... our withholding tax rate for any sort of business we have with Luxembourg is 15 per cent. If Luxembourg were considered a tax haven, we should pay withholding taxes of 25 per cent. The group has money to finance itself— that is why we get money from our [group]. So, it is easier for us to make the export processes. The money that we get, we consider as a debt, so these are expenses to the company. So, from the tax perspective, those expenses are deductible.... The money that we pay as an interest for the group it should be taxed in Luxembourg, but as we have a very huge income tax loss there it doesn't have any sort of impact...[61]

As established in Chapter 2, the tax system reflects the institutionalized relationship between the state and its taxpayers. In Brazil, this relationship is today less contentious than in the past. Brazil is now Latin America's most successful

---

[61] Author's telephone interview with corporate tax lawyer, Rio de Janeiro, April 2017.

tax state. As for the bank bargain, for taxation too, the introduction of the Brazilian real in 1994 was a turning point. With the establishment of sovereign money, the government's tax receipts increased remarkably. Between 1993 and 1994 it rose from R$3.6 million to R$102 million—nearly thirtyfold.[62] The tax-to-GDP rate also grew steadily from 21 per cent in 1992 to 32 per cent in 2015, peaking at about 35 per cent in 2007. Since then, it has oscillated around the OECD average of about 32 per cent.[63] In the 1990s, Brazil became a tax state comparable to that of OECD countries.

Nevertheless, there are five ways in which the contemporary Brazilian tax system is a continuation of the past. First, all democratically elected governments have effectively extracted money from taxpayers. However, as in the past, the economic elites have contributed little towards the Brazilian tax state. Democratic governments have found a way to tax the growing middle classes and the country's poor instead. In 2014, they collectively contributed about three-quarters of the tax revenue. Taxes on corporate income, profits, and property roughly contributed the remaining quarter.[64] In contrast to Britain and more like Germany, the Brazilian Workers Party's rise to power did not transform the nature of the tax bargain.[65] Improvements for the poor and the middle classes were paid for by these classes themselves.

Second, onshore tax avoidance and evasion illustrates that the economic elite remains unwilling to subordinate itself to the state's fiscal power. A common way for corporations to avoid the taxman is to use the intricacies of Brazilian tax law. Corporations often appeal to the Supreme Court to clarify a specific clause. Such an appeal can take between ten and twenty years before being addressed by the Court. In this way, a corporation can legally postpone paying taxes. By the time the case is addressed the tax debt might have expired by limitation, the law might have changed in the corporations' favour, or inflation—still comparably high in Brazil—may have devalued the tax debt.[66] The poor, the majority of Brazil's population, also tried to get away from the taxman. The easiest way to do so is informality. However, unlike curbing corporate tax avoidance, the government succeeded in reducing informality—and with it tax avoidance—from about 46 per cent of the labour force in 1999 to 37 per cent in 2013.[67]

Third, although social spending towards the poor, for instance with the social cash programme *Bolsa Família*, has grown to unprecedented levels,

---

[62] Ferreira and Bonomo 2006.
[63] OECD 2016.
[64] OECD 2015.
[65] Bianchi and Braga 2005; Baer and Love 2009.
[66] Author's interview with defence lawyer, São Paulo, April 2017.
[67] Cardoso 2016.

the old practice of government support for corporations through subsidized credit continues too.[68] Brazilians' have come to call these subsidies *Bolsa Empresario*.[69]

The fourth reminder of the past in contemporary taxation is the sheer amount of tax privileges and taxes that are earmarked for specific sectors.[70] In the words of Mello and Spektor:

> Legislators and the president alike regularly raise taxes not so they can invest in better public services but so they can replenish the war chests they use to please the special interest groups that help them stay in power. With government spending benefiting thin slices of the electorate rather than the majority of Brazilians, the discrepancy between revenue and the quality and extent of public services is enormous.[71]

The fifth and final legacy of the past relationship between the government and its taxpayers is Brazil's strong tax administration. Brazilians call the RFB *o leão*, the lion, and it is considered an attractive place to work for tax lawyers and accountants. The RFB is one of the technically most modern tax administrations in the world. Moreover, strong institutional insulation from other government agencies protects the RFB's work from the politics of patronage that marks other political institutions.[72]

Brazil's fight against harmful tax competition started in 1994. The government introduced defensive measures. These measures include withholding taxes on source-based income in Brazil. The withholding tax rate is at 15 per cent,[73] unless the income is passive, and its beneficiary is resident in a tax haven (according to the tax authority's blacklist). In this case, the withholding tax rate increases to 25 per cent. The withholding tax increases the transaction costs of cross-border flows such that it makes shifting money solely for tax purposes less attractive.

Furthermore, Brazil introduced CFC rules, which are among the most stringent in the world. The purpose of the CFC rules was to increase tax income, regardless of the reason for why corporations may be offshore.

The Brazilian government also added rules with regards to transfer pricing. Brazil is famous for deviating both from the OECD and the US approach to

---

[68] Melo, Barrientos, and Canuto Coelho 2014.
[69] Leahy 2015.
[70] Author's interview with banker, Rio de Janeiro, April 2017.
[71] Mello and Spektor 2014.
[72] Author's telephone interview with corporate lawyer, Rio de Janeiro, April 2017; author's telephone interview with tax lawyer, São Paulo, April 2017, author's telephone interview with public investigator in the Lava Jato scandal, Rio de Janeiro, April 2017. Author's interview with former banker, Rio de Janeiro, April 2017.
[73] Services are subject to 25 per cent.

transfer pricing. Rather than working with the arm's length principle, requiring comparable prices which are often difficult to come by, the RFB works with maximum values for import prices and minimum values for export prices. This system is easier to navigate for the Brazilian tax administration. In addition, because it is so different from what the rest of the world does, it increases the transaction costs for shifting profits through transfer pricing.

Finally, in 2010, the RFB added thin capitalization rules.[74] Their purpose is to limit the amount of debt that is deductible from a corporation's tax debt— one of the commonly used routes for offshore tax planning. A legacy of Brazil's extensive capital controls is the extensive reporting requirement for international capital flows. These data, in combination with the advanced tax and banking technology, help to enforce laws and regulations.[75] That is, the Brazilian tax administration has come up with effective domestic measures to curb base erosion and profit shifting.[76]

Nevertheless, there remain ways for corporate tax advisers to circumvent the rules and regulations legally. The best way to do so is through the network of Brazil's double tax agreements, commonly called 'treaty shopping'. To counter this practice, Brazil was, as a non-member, actively involved in the OECD BEPS process. Despite not being a member, Brazil started implementing a considerable part of the agreement. Most importantly, Brazil created a register of beneficial ownership. The information is not publicly available though.[77]

As is the case for tax planning, the financial flows between Brazil and offshore financial centres as shown in Figure 5.1 are also a precondition for offshore money laundering. As in the other cases it is, however, impossible to determine which share of the flows are related to illicit sources. Offshore money laundering is therefore analysed based on interview data and information that emerged from the official investigation into the *Lava Jato* corruption scandal. These qualitative data provide comprehensive insights into the abuses of offshore financial services.

Ownership of offshore companies, bank accounts, and assets are legal in Brazil if they are reported to the relevant authorities. Hence, ownership in itself does not indicate any wrongdoing. Since the liberalization of capital controls in the 1990s, many offshore accounts have been regularized. Nevertheless, for those who seek to hide ill-gotten gains or evade taxes, collaboration with

---

[74] Falcao 2012; Rigoni 2014; Estellita and Silva Bastos 2015; Valerdi 2017.
[75] Author's interview with defence lawyer, São Paulo, April 2017.
[76] Rigoni 2014; Estellita and Silva Bastos 2015.
[77] See: https://star.worldbank.org/sites/star/files/bo_country_guide_brazil_final_0.pdf, last accessed 10 May 2021.

*doleiros* and the use of offshore accounts is still the bread and butter of their illicit financial transactions. Investigations into the *Operação Lava Jato* (Operation Car Wash) started off with a *doleiro* and soon moved on to the offshore world.

*Operação Lava Jato* started in March 2014 with an investigation into a corruption scheme involving a cartel of big Brazilian construction companies, the majority state-owned oil company Petrobras, and an illegal party financing system. By April 2017, the *Lava Jato* investigation had, in one interviewee's words, gone 'through 35 stages, each with a different corruption scheme, some extremely complex, some extremely simple; but in nearly every stage, offshore played an essential role'.[78] The investigations show that offshore banks and offshore shell companies in particular were an essential part of the corruption scheme.[79]

Offshore banks were necessary to process the large financial flows. The case of the construction corporation Odebrecht, one member of the cartel, reflects the actual volumes involved. Between 2001 and 2016, the construction firm dispersed US$788 million in bribes, out of which US$348 million went to politicians and political parties in Brazil and across eleven countries in Latin America and Lusophone Africa.[80] Given the large amounts and globally dispersed beneficiaries involved, Odebrecht needed a trusted bank. The company's 'Structured Operations Department', exclusively responsible for handling bribes, chose an Austrian bank in Antigua. When this bank faced liquidity troubles, the head of Structured Operations simply bought the bank to ensure that Odebrecht's payments remained hidden.[81] Next to Antigua, Odebrecht worked with banks in New York, Belize, Panama, and the British Virgin Islands. Odebrecht's offshore network included thirty-three different banks and more than seventy bank accounts in Antigua alone.[82] Also, the middlemen's bank account and even that of the final beneficiary of the bribe were often held offshore: 'Just today', one interviewee told me, 'there was a plea bargain of the marketing director of the last presidential campaign of the PT (*Partido dos Trabalhadores*), the Workers' Party. He testified that Odebrecht paid his salary offshore for ten years.'[83] Offshore shell companies, on the other hand, were used to get the money undetected into and out of Brazil. The shell companies were used to forge documentation of fictitious imports of fictitious

---

[78] Author's telephone interview with a senior investigator, April 2017.
[79] Author's telephone interview with civil society organization, April 2017.
[80] Capers and Weissmann 2016.
[81] Smith, Valle, and Schmidt 2017.
[82] Capers and Weissmann 2016.
[83] Author's interview with anti-money laundering expert, São Paulo, April 2017.

products to justify money flows between the bribing corporation and the bank account of middlemen, who would then pass on the money (after deducting their own share) to the final beneficiary of the bribe. Often, the money would pass through three or four layers of offshore structures.[84] To get the money back into Brazil, according to a defence lawyer, the final beneficiary

> would have a company in Brazil which has a partner that is not really a partner, usually the maid, who holds 1 per cent of the company and the other partner, an offshore company, holds 99 per cent. And this offshore company would make an investment in Brazil, which is not taxable and then you have the money here. For instance, in one of my cases in Rio [de Janeiro], this company bought famous paintings and art objects.[85]

'But' the lawyer pointed out, 'these days in Brazil we only talk about *Lava Jato* and Odebrecht, but in almost all my cases on big tax fraud, about 90 per cent of the time there was an offshore structure involved.'[86] Abusing offshore financial services is part and parcel of corruption, tax evasion, and other financial crimes committed by Brazilian corporations and individuals. The quantitative volume of the money involved remains invisible. But the extent to which offshore finance facilitates political and economic crime in Brazil has been dragged into the light of day and into the public debate through the *Lava Jato* investigations.

In sum, the contemporary exposure to offshore finance reveals that in the case of Brazil access to credit via the Eurodollar system, distancing corporate and individual wealth in times of crises, and abuses of offshore secrecy are the most important uses of offshore financial services. Offshore tax planning is also relevant but less significant than offshore banking in its legal and illegal incarnations. After having established the scale and pattern of the uses and abuses of offshore financial services by Brazilian corporations and wealthy individuals, the next section turns to an analysis of how it affects state power in Brazil.

## 3  The encounter

The Brazilian state, the institutional association of rule, is marked by a fundamental tension between the rural economic and the urban political elites. Throughout Brazil's history, the economic elites were never quite willing to

---

[84] Author's telephone interview with senior investigator, April 2017. See also: Capers and Weiss-mann, 2016; Pacheco 2017.

[85] Author's interview with defence lawyer, São Paulo, April 2017.

[86] Author's interview with defence lawyer, São Paulo, April 2017.

contribute to the central state either through debt or taxation. The Brazilian state is contested from within in ways in which the British and German states are not.

It was government-subsidized credit via the *Banco do Brasil* and later the BNDES that provided the essential glue for the post-slavery institutional association of rule. To this day, the three government-backed or government-owned banks *Banco do Brasil*, *Caixa Econômica Federal*, and the BNDES are the bedrock of Brazil's banking system. They are the state's central tool to implement monetary, industrial, and redistributive policies.[87] The Brazilian state was a debt state before it became a tax state.

Consequently, it took a long time to get a smooth cycle of money, tax, and debt going. The state struggled to mobilize and centralize the resources to finance its political goals domestically. Tapping into money created off-shore, partially by domestic banks' offshore offices, complemented—at times even substituted—money created onshore. Meaningful taxation became possible only as industrialization had produced a middle-class, and dual VAT had brought the lower classes into the tax net. The Brasilian tax bargain is thus largely one between the state and the middle and lower classes. These classes pay taxes and social security contributions with which the state—to a certain extent—finances the welfare state. While the Brazilian middle and lower classes are also prone to tax evasion and avoidance, their channel of choice is not offshore finance, but informality.[88]

Again, as in the previous two cases, offshore finance can affect state power through both sides of the balance sheet: taxation and banking. As in Britain and Germany, the key mechanism through which offshore finance affects state power in Brazil is, however, banking—in its legal and illegal forms. In terms of potential tax losses relative to GDP, taxation plays an even more subordinate role than in Britain and Germany.

As in the previous two cases, having determined the mechanism through which offshore finance affects state power, the next section turns to the question of the nature of these effects.

## Strengthening state power

Historically, the Brazilian central state faced a trilemma when aiming to mobilize and centralize resources to finance its political goals. It could choose not

---

[87] Author's interview with former banker, São Paulo, April 2017; author's interview with BNDES staff, Rio de Janeiro, April 2017.

[88] Author's interview with tax expert, Rio de Janeiro, April 2017.

to tax the wealthy and therefore stay a weak central power in a continental country. It could tax the wealthy elites to strengthen its central power but lose their political support. Or it could finance the inevitable deficits of the state via inflation and risk popular discontent.[89] The availability of offshore credit helped the state to overcome this trilemma.

Access to Eurodollar could gloss over the state's fiscal problems. It spared successive governments paying the political price for properly taxing the wealthy, or for cutting expenses for urban workers. For about two decades, offshore money creation by Eurobanks appeared to be a good replacement for onshore money creation. The offshore money fulfilled its purpose: it financed the state and it financed production. And it did so at better terms than those available in the onshore economy at home or abroad. As was the case for Britain and Germany, offshore banking strengthened state power in the good times.

In contrast to Britain and Germany, however, offshore banking became a fundamental element of the onshore economy. During the military regime (1964–85) especially, issuing debt offshore was a politically convenient and economically successful way to finance the Brazilian state's developmental ambitions. Eurodollars financed the Brazilian 'economic miracle'. And, once Brazil had overcome the consequences of the 1982 crisis, in the late 1990s, during the early 2000s offshore dollar liquidity again became the grease of Brazil's economy. The power-enhancing effects of offshore finance were profound.

In is unsurprising then, that the Brazilian state developed a policy-framework to engage with the Eurodollar markets. During the military regime and post-1982, the government's support for Eurodollar borrowing was an explicit policy choice. Post-1982, the government considered it an effective way for Brazilian corporations to access funding. And to do so at lower interest rates than at home or in the United States.[90] As a result, in contrast to Britain and Germany, the politics of the invisible had no place in Brazil's approach to offshore banking. The Brazilian state overtly supported large corporations to issue debt offshore.

However, compared to the times of the military regime, the state's ability to influence its relationship with offshore finance was one level removed in the post-1982 world. It was now corporations, not the government directly, which borrowed offshore. Corporations' debt strategies were largely outside the state's immediate influence. Nevertheless, from the mid-1990s to 2007,

---

[89] Calomiris and Haber 2014, chs 12–13.
[90] Author's interview with BNDES employee, Rio de Janeiro, April 2017. Author's interview with financial market expert, Rio de Janeiro, April 2017.

the production of offshore credit money replaced onshore credit money quite adequately. Brazil's industrial production and domestic income grew at unprecedented levels. The power-enhancing effects of offshore finance were felt once more.

The state's abstinence changed fundamentally with the global financial crisis. Building on the lessons from 1982, however, this time the Brazilian state was prepared. The central bank combined capital controls with swap lines—a central bank currency swap line with the Federal Reserve and one between the *Banco Central do Brasil* and domestic banks with US dollar shortages. The measures helped to mitigate the effects of the global financial crisis on the Brazilian banking sector and economy.[91] Unlike in Britain and Germany, the global financial crisis did not affect the Brazilian state financing its political goals at scale.[92]

In 2009, dollar credit was still short in the United States, but Eurodollar credit was again flowing freely to Brazil. These flows were mainly driven by investors in search for yields in a low-interest environment.[93] The Brazilian private sector happily borrowed as the example of Petrobras, the partially state-owned oil company, exemplifies. With two issues of US$8 billion and US$6 billion between 2009 and 2014, Petrobras became the largest net issuer of Eurobonds in the world.[94]

## Undermining state power

In Chapter 2, I argue that offshore finance has the potential to undermine state power by inflicting revenue losses on its budget, and by imposing the burdens of unregulated offshore banking. The empirical analysis revealed, however, that in Brazil, comparable to contemporary Germany, offshore finance unfolds its destructive powers for the state when the inherent volatility of these markets flips into outright financial crises. It is during the bad times that the woes of the drain of preferential liquidity appear with full force. Unlike Britain and Germany, Brazil—and Mexico—experienced the power-undermining effects of offshore finance already with the 1982 crisis.

When the Eurodollar markets froze in late 1982, Brazil's access to preferential liquidity was revoked. The Latin American crisis of 1982 pushed the

---

[91] Allen 2013; Chamon and Garcia 2016.

[92] Author's interview with financial sector expert, Rio de Janeiro, April 2017.

[93] Author's interview with financial market expert, Mexico City, November 2015. Author's telephone interview with investment banker, May 2017. See also McCauley, McGuire, and Sushko 2015.

[94] McCauley, McGuire, and Sushko 2015.

Brazilian state to default on its international debt and experience a 'lost decade' in terms of growth and development. However, during Brazil's recovery, the global role of the US dollar only increased. If Brazil wanted to participate in the global economy, it needed access to US dollars. The easiest way was still to tap into the preferential liquidity in the offshore markets, especially because domestic private sector credit was still scarce and expensive. The domestic banking system could not provide sufficient and affordable domestic or US-dollar-denominated credit to allow for capitalist expansion.[95]

Instead of withdrawing from the Eurodollar markets entirely, the Brazilian government developed policy tools aimed at better managing the risks related to the domestic banking system and the economy. With the financial support of the BNDES and hence ultimately the Brazilian taxpayer, large Brazilian corporations thus turned again to the Eurodollar system for credit.[96]

## A mixed blessing

Brazil has financed its economic development in the Eurodollar markets. These markets provided liquidity when the domestic financiers were unwilling to do so. The availability of offshore money bridged the chronically tense relationship between the rural economic and the urban political elites. From the beginning, the Brazilian state therefore carefully crafted a strategy to reap the benefits of offshore money creation while guarding against its potential risks. Nevertheless, the 1982 debt crisis demonstrated the destructive forces of freezing Eurodollar markets. During Brazil's recovery the *Banco Central do Brasil* developed a set of policy tools that successfully defended the domestic banking system as the Eurodollar markets froze again in 2007. This time, the defence worked. Offshore money creation has become a permanent complement to the onshore cycle of money tax and debt, actively managed by the central bank. The Brazilian state has learned how to manage the volatilities of the Eurodollar markets.

What it could not anticipate, however, was that the global financial crisis would structurally alter offshore money creation for good. Post 2007–08, European banks retreated from offshore money creation. Non-bank financial institutions, such as institutional funds and asset managers, took up some of the slack by providing offshore credit to emerging market economies.[97]

---

[95] Calomiris and Haber 2014, chs 12–13.
[96] Musacchio Farias and Lazzarini 2014.
[97] Kreicher and McCauley 2016.

Nonetheless, overall Eurodollar liquidity has stagnated since the global finan-cial crisis.[98]

Brazil remains still stuck with a shallow and expensive domestic banking system. Yet, unlike in the past, offshore money creation post-financial crisis no longer led to enhanced production and growth. Indeed on the contrary, in 2013–15, the Brazilian economy experienced its worst recession in decades.

The reason why Brazil's access to credit did not translate into capitalist expansion is a contested topic. The *Banco Central do Brasil* interpreted the events as a result of the announcement of monetary tightening by the Federal Reserve in 2013. Consequently, the central bank set out to defend its currency and the private sector's access to Eurodollar. Between 2013 and 2014, the cen-tral bank drew again, as during the global financial crisis, on its reserves and started providing US dollar swaps that were settled in Brazilian real. The pro-gramme amounted to more than US$90 billion or about a quarter of Brazil's total foreign reserves. Despite these efforts, the Brazilian economy did not recover. According to a financial analyst, it could not, because the *Banco Cen-tral do Brasil*'s measures to bring down the price for offshore credit cannot make up for the shortage of offshore money creation since European banks retreated from the Euromarkets in 2009.[99] In the case of Brazil, offshore money creation has lost its potency.

The government's support for the private sector's offshore borrowing exposes Brazilian economic actors further to a Eurodollar system that does not deliver liquidity the way it did in the past. The institutionalized division of labour between domestic banks lending short-term to small economic actors and international banks lending long-term to large corporations has become problematic. Brazil's money creation has become too dependent on offshore money creation and US American willingness to support it in times of crisis.

The stagnation of offshore money creation and the resulting suppression of economic growth in Brazil revived the conflict over how to finance the state's political programme. It may no longer be enough to gloss over the tense relationship between rural economic and urban political elites. Unlike in the nineteenth century, however, Brazil's lower and middle classes now contribute towards financing the state, via both debt and taxation.

After the 1982 crisis, the Brazilian state has put sustained effort into estab-lishing the Brazilian real as a trusted sovereign money. The success of this cur-rency reform allowed the government to shift its debt from the Euromarkets

---

[98] Binder forthcoming.
[99] Snider 2017.

to domestic creditors. The 1994 monetary reform also stabilized the state's tax revenue, which it has safeguarded against offshore tax planning through domestic defensive laws. When it comes to offshore tax planning, *o leão* bares its teeth. However, part of the reason why the Brazilian state is resilient against offshore tax planning is also that the domestic tax system provides the economic elites with ample exemptions and advantages, making offshore structures less attractive. Moreover, even before offshore financial services were available, taxation in Brazil was strongly based on consumption taxes and government-organized social security contributions. Both types of taxes are evaded through informality, rather than offshoring. Finally, in some instances, the Brazilian state even supports offshore tax planning. For example, removing Luxembourg from the list of tax havens was an explicit policy choice that allows for tax planning via offshore debt issuance. Likewise, the state-owned development bank BNDES holds minority shares in several Brazilian multinational corporations that have extensive offshore structures. According to one interviewee, the central bank even encouraged BNDES itself to open a branch in the Cayman Islands, for reasons of efficiency. The BNDES decided to go to London instead.[100] In stark difference to Britain and Germany, the Brazilian institutional association of rule does not resort to the politics of the invisible when it comes to the legal uses of offshore financial services. It engages in and manages offshore banking and tax planning openly.

That does not mean, however, that the politics of the invisible has no place in Brazil. The currently running circle of money, tax, and debt testifies to a less contentious relationship within the institutional association of rule since the mid-1990s. Yet, Brazil's contemporary relationship between the executive and the legislative still echoes the old conflict between the urban political elites and the rural oligarchy.

The 1988 constitution grants the President far reaching powers, but every law must eventually pass Congress. The Brazilian Congress is made up of more than twenty parties, which are more loosely knit groupings than ideologically coherent platforms. As a result, the loyalty of members of parliament rests rather with their constituencies than with their party.[101] The ordinary Brazilian is mostly not part of these constituencies. They are dominated by the successors of the rural planter oligarchy: agribusiness and powerful corporate interests from other sectors. The political decision-making process in contemporary Brazil is still marked by the economic elite's desire to rule

---

[100] Author's interview with banker, Rio de Janeiro, April 2017.
[101] Mello and Spektor 2014.

through the state rather than be ruled by it.[102] Consequently, presidents must negotiate legislative proposals with individual lawmakers rather than having a stable majority or coalition that votes along with their suggested initiatives. Tax incentives or attractive contracts for large corporations in the parliamentarians' constituencies are bargaining chips in the negotiation.[103] And so are, as the *Lava Jato* corruption scandal exemplified, illegal kickbacks. It is here, in the abuses of offshore financial services, that the politics of the invisible is key.

Nevertheless, it does not undermine the state's power to finance its political goals. The politics of the invisible is, instead, a means of the economic elite to influence the shape of that political programme. As the court proceedings demonstrate, almost half of the money Odebrecht spent in the context of *Lava Jato* was dedicated to party financing—at home and abroad.[104]

On 9 April 2015, Márcio Martins de Oliveira entered the Brazilian Congress with a box full of rats.[105] He made his way to the Parliamentary Committee of Inquiry (CPI) which was investigating the *Lava Jato* scandal. The day Martins de Oliveira headed towards the CPI, it was to hear the testimony of João Vaccari Neto, the treasurer of the PT. Neto was accused of money laundering and bribery. At that point in time, he was one of 110 people the judicial investigation had accused of corruption, money laundering, and other financial crimes. Over fifty of the accused were members or former members of Congress. When the treasurer entered the room of the CPI, Martins de Oliveira released the rats, wreaking chaos among the deputies. After long minutes of disorder, armed security forces finally arrested Martins de Oliveira and seized the animals.[106] One deputy later lamented: '[This was an] action that testifies against the parliament, the armed circus shows the level we are at. Those who complain about the low acceptance of the government, should look at the acceptance of the parliament; it is even worse.'[107]

Despite over two decades of democratization, most Brazilians remain excluded from the institutional association of rule. Unlike in Britain and Germany, mass democracy has not substantially opened up the institutional association of rule. Offshore finance does not serve as an exit from a democratizing, widening institutional association of rule as in the case of Britain. It

---

[102] Author's interviews with former banker, São Paulo, April 2017, anti-money laundering expert, São Paulo, April 2017, defence lawyer, São Paulo, April 2017.
[103] Mello and Spektor 2014.
[104] Capers and Weissmann 2016.
[105] It later turned out that the rodents were hamsters and mice, not rats. But the news first reported them as rats see: Passarinho, Calgaro, and Salomão (2015).
[106] Passarinho, Calgaro, and Salomão 2015; Pacheco 2017; Sotero 2018.
[107] Cited in Passarinho, Calgaro, and Salomão 2015.

is also not a mechanism to sweeten the deal over the distribution of the costs and benefits of money creation and taxation for the money classes as in the case of Germany.

Offshore finance, in Brazil, is a means to complement a historically weak bargain over how to finance the state. As such, it is the mirror image of the German case: despite a comparatively small exposure to offshore financial services in absolute terms, and relative to its GDP, offshore money creation is highly consequential for state power in Brazil. Again, we cannot observe a direct link between the scope of the exposure and its effects on state power.

Likewise, as in Britain and Germany, we can observe that the nature of the effects of offshore finance on Brazilian state power varies between cases and within Brazil itself. Given Brazil's fundamental dependence on Eurodollar financing, the Brazilian state has found ways to mitigate the resulting risks for its domestic banking system and economy. In doing so, however, Brazil has also made itself ever more dependent on offshore money creation.

# 6

# Mexico

## Power without plenty

Mexico is the last of the four case studies considered in this book. It is a large country, geographically and economically. Mexico is Latin America's second largest economy and one of its most open. In 2015, for instance, Mexico's gross domestic product (GDP) was US$1.14 trillion and its currency, the Mexican peso, was the most traded emerging market currency in the world. It was over-taken by the Chinese renminbi only in 2016.[1] Despite its economic weight, though, Mexico is also a developing country and one with endemic problems of crime and corruption. Finally, Mexico is located close to the Caribbean, one of the world's largest offshore hubs. We would expect Mexico to have rampant exposure to offshore finance and offshore finance to affect state power in a significant way.

Analysing the relationship between offshore finance and state power in Mexico, I find for the contemporary period that, puzzlingly, Mexican eco-nomic actors rarely make use of offshore financial services. As with the previ-ous cases, however, the relationship between offshore finance and state power is not static across time. Mexico, like Brazil, financed its development in the Euromarkets in the 1960s and 1970s. At that time, it strengthened state power.

However, the 1982 Latin American debt crisis brought Mexico's access to the offshore dollar to a grinding halt. The costs of unregulated offshore banking hit Mexico with full force. Like Britain, Mexico's bank bargain had not given rise to institutions that could withstand offshore finance's power-undermining effects. As a result, Mexico's exposure to offshore finance has been short, intense, and politically extremely costly. The social, political, and economic fallout from the 1982 crisis was such that Mexico, unlike Brazil, withdrew from these markets for good. Of the four cases studied here, Mexico is the only one to have found an alternative to offshore money creation. It embedded its banking system with that of the United States. It now gets direct access to onshore US dollars.

---

[1] Cota 2015.

*Offshore Finance and State Power.* Andrea Binder, Oxford University Press. © Andrea Binder (2023).
DOI: 10.1093/oso/9780192870124.003.0006

It is thus, as in the other three cases, through banking rather than taxation that offshore finance's effects are transmitted. The reasons why that is, differ though. In Britain the effects of offshore tax planning did affect state power negatively. Only the effects of offshore banking, power enhancing and limiting, were much greater. Germany and Brazil, on the other hand, had built domestic institutions that would mitigate the effects of offshore tax planning. Money laundering is significant in both these countries, but they do not affect the state's ability to unite and centralize resources. In Mexico, offshore tax planning and money laundering do not affect state power as much as offshore banking because the informal sector provides ample opportunities to dodge taxes and launder money. With so many rents to be had domestically, there is little need to use sophisticated offshore structures.[2]

This chapter analyses the intense, short, and disastrous relationship between offshore finance and state power in Mexico. It also assesses how that relationship has been largely cut. Starting in the late nineteenth century, the chapter takes, as the previous chapters have done, a long view. Mexico's political order has undergone dramatic changes during that time span: from the autocratic reign of José Porfirio Díaz (1877 to 1911), known in Mexico as the *Porfiriato*; through a revolution (1910–20); to the dictatorship of the *Partido Revolucionario Institucional* (PRI)[3] (1928–97); and most recently a subsequent process of democratization. Despite these fundamental regime changes, the institutional association of rule remains impressively stable over time.

## 1 Mexican state power from the money view

From the money view, Mexico's modern statehood developed around the same time as that of Germany and Brazil. Mexico became independent from Spain in 1821, but it took another 50 years for the federal republic to stabilize, centralize, and exert territorial control in a manner that justifies speaking of Mexico as a modern state. In the first half of the nineteenth century, Mexico saw seventy-five presidents come and go. The governments had no tax revenue to speak of. They repeatedly defaulted on their debt and were thus excluded from international capital markets.[4]

It was President José Porfirio Díaz who, in the late nineteenth century, finally sustained Mexico's accumulated debt—and by extension his grip on power. He

---

[2] Binder 2019.
[3] The party was first named Partido Nacional Revolucionario, then Partido de la Revolución Mexicana and since 1946 trades under the current name of Partido Revolucionario Institucional.
[4] Centeno 2002; Flores Zendejas 2020; Maurer and Gomberg 2004.

was able to create a small cycle of money, tax, and debt thanks to Mexico's silver resources. In the absence of sovereign money, the precious metal helped to create a trusted means to account for and to settle debt.

From the money view, President José Porfirio Díaz's major achievement, one that would shape the Mexican state for more than a century, was his partnership of interest with Mexico's financiers.[5] Díaz convinced the wealthy Mexican elite to lend to his government in return for rents that arose from direct involvement in policymaking, deliberate restrictions on competition, and selective enforcement of property rights.[6] The rents could offset tax revenue as a means of coaxing the financiers into extending credit to the government. And so Díaz's tax revenues remained marginal. The bankers lent to the government despite its limited resources for repayment because of the sheer volume of the rent. According to Maurer and Gomberg, the financiers broke even if the government did not expropriate them via bank nationalization and reneging on debt payments more than twice in a decade.[7] With this arrangement, Díaz had found a formula to finance the state without taxing the wealthy.

His arrangement would not have been sustainable were it not for Mexico's natural wealth. Fortunately for Díaz and his government, Mexico's resources of precious metals meant that the country has had, for 400 years, a trusted currency—silver. Silver coins were used as tax payments and as a means to account for and settle debt long before the *Porfirato*.

However, by the early twentieth century this precious metal reached its limits as a currency. A drop in the price of silver brought Mexico's international creditors and investors to the scene. They feared for the repayment of their loans, and the devaluation of their investment. In 1905, under pressure from the US government, Porfirio Díaz implemented a far-reaching and domestically contested currency reform. He limited the coin production, introduced paper money, and put the country on the gold standard. With these measures, Díaz successfully stabilized the value of the (silver) peso.[8] But he still lacked the revenue to create a smooth cycle of money, tax, and debt.

So Díaz reached for the country's oil resources. Earlier in his presidency, he had already sought to develop the oil industry to generate government income and address the country's rising energy costs. In 1884, to promote investment into the development of the industry, his government granted the

---

[5] Calomiris and Haber 2014, chs 10–11.
[6] Maurer and Gomberg 2004.
[7] Ibid.
[8] Pessananti 2008; Sotelo 2008; Banco de México 2018.

owner of surface land the rights to subsurface petroleum resources. Unfortunately for Díaz, it took the US American and British investors a decade of exploration before they could profitably drill oil. By 1911, the time when Mexico emerged as one of the world's largest oil producers, Díaz's reign had already ended.[9]

During the *Porfiriato*, the Mexican institutional association of rule was very small. It essentially consisted of the president, his closest allies, and a handful of bankers and big businesses.[10] The rural poor and the urban middle classes, the overwhelming majority of Mexicans, were excluded from that association. The bargain over how to distribute the costs and benefits of money creation and taxation was skewed. The rents fully accumulated with the financiers. The rural poor and urban middle classes had to pay, directly or indirectly, for the rents that allowed Díaz to finance the state via debt.[11] The resulting problem of the state's legitimacy was solved—or rather postponed—through coercion and violence.[12] In November 1910, the educated middle classes joined forces with the rural poor in protest over Díaz's reign and took to the streets. Their protests ignited the Mexican Revolution, a 10-year armed struggle over political participation.[13]

Through that struggle, members of Mexico's old elite seized power. Unlike Díaz and his allies, they acknowledged, however, that the new regime needed a popular base. They created a one-party system and co-opted popular movements—small farmers, organized workers, and unionized public employees—into the emerging PRI. The country's economic elites, in contrast, were not included in the PRI. Rather, the PRI corrupted big businesses individually and resurrected Díaz's partnership of interest with the bankers. As a result, the spheres of political and economic elites developed as separate but interrelated.[14] The institutional association of rule now consisted of the PRI, its co-opted popular movements and—at arm's length—the economic elites. The glue that held the political and economic elites within the institutional association together was the same that connected the PRI with its popular base: a system of selective privilege and patronage.

The government provided the economic elites with decision-making power, monopoly rents, and tax exemptions in return for investment and access to credit. In the same vein, the party offered its popular base political influence,

---

[9] Haber, Maurer, and Razo 2003.
[10] Carmagnani 1994; Aboites 2003; Knight 2013; Calomiris and Haber 2014, chs 10–11.
[11] Calomiris and Haber 2014.
[12] Centeno 2002; Smith 2014.
[13] Hamilton 1982.
[14] Author's interview with economist, Mexico City, November 2015.

welfare programmes, tax exemptions, social mobility, and opportunities for personal enrichment in return for political loyalty.[15] Privilege and patronage ensured the PRI's quasi-total power from 1928 to 1997.

However, after more than fifty years of successfully mitigating the conflicts between the interests of the financiers and the co-opted social movements, the PRI model of organizing the state's finances through rents and debt met its limits in the 1982 crisis.

In 1982, most Mexicans, excluded from the system of privilege and patronage, paid for the debt crisis with sharply rising inflation and unemployment. The crisis rang in Mexico's *Década Perdida*. It was the end of the PRI's uncontested power.

The austerity measures that the government introduced undermined the system of privilege and patronage. They severed the party's link with its popular base. Moreover, the PRI's response to the crisis laid the foundation for the currency crisis of the mid-1990s, sealing the party's fate. After seventy-six years of uninterrupted reign, the PRI had to concede defeat in the presidential elections of July 2000. The winner was the opposition candidate for the presidency, Vincente Fox.

With Mexico's transition from a one- to a multi-party system, formal power in Mexico changed fundamentally.[16] Yet, the informal power networks between the government, the wealthy, and the co-opted social movements, built through the system of privilege and patronage, persisted. Despite political competition, the relationship between the government and the citizens continued to be mediated by 'political brokers' as Selee puts it.[17] Political opinion- and decision-making remained a process of intermediation through private networks, rather than parties and parliament. Mexico's democracy is more clientelist than representative. In other words, despite democratization the nature of the Mexican institutional association of rule changed little.[18] In the words of one interviewee:

> Most Mexicans consider the state as something that is external to them. The state is a set of institutions which are controlled by a small group of people. That is, you have two options. Either you become part of the state controlling group, which is difficult, or you stay away from the state as far as possible.[19]

[15] Knight 1990; Maurer and Gomberg 2004; Haber et al. 2008.
[16] Camp 2015.
[17] Selee 2011, 170.
[18] Selee 2011.
[19] Author's interview with civil society organization, Mexico City, November 2015.

## Bank bargain

Díaz's partnership with Mexican financiers did not only shape the institutional association of rule. It obviously also left its deep imprints on banking in Mexico. Díaz's 'crony banking system', as Calomiris and Haber term it, proved successful.[20] Although small, it was stable and provided the resources to finance Mexico's industrialization. It also created significant revenue, both in the form of rents and cash, for Mexico's moneyed classes. The wealthy and the government shared the power to create money—and the benefits that come with it.

By the 1890s, Mexico, hitherto the chronic defaulter, had the best credit rating in Latin America.[21] An important step on the way from chronic defaulter to creditor darling was the foundation of the *Banco Nacional de México* (Banamex) in 1884. Comparable to the early incarnation of the Bank of England and the *Banco do Brasil*, Banamex was the first national bank with the right to issue paper money, to act as the finance ministry's fiscal agent, and to run the mint. The underlying bank law was co-written between the government and Mexican financiers. They ensured it granted Banamex a monopoly of lending to the government by revoking the right of the states to issue bank charters. Through the foundation of Banamex, a semi-official bank, Díaz managed to successfully establish paper money as the main means of payment, including tax payments which were also collected through Banamex. The successful establishment of paper money allowed for capitalist expansion.[22]

Yet, the Mexican Revolution thoroughly disrupted Díaz's cycle of money, rent, and debt. Every party to the conflict printed its own bills with their validity limited to the territory they controlled at any given point in time. With the military ups and downs of these groups, the validity of the paper money changed constantly, undermining the credibility of paper money among the population. In response, Mexicans resorted to what they trusted: silver—and the US dollar. By 1916, even the government had given up on paper money. It now accepted only silver coins as tax payment. By law, workers had to be paid in precious metal too.[23] By the end of the revolution, the Mexican banking institutions and money creation were in shatters.

As noted above, after the revolution, the emerging PRI resurrected the partnership of interest in a move similar to Díaz's. It founded a bank that would

[20] Calomiris and Haber 2014, 337.
[21] Knight 1990.
[22] Calomiris and Haber 2014, chs 10–11; Banco de México 2018.
[23] Cardenas and Manns 1987; Banco de México 2018.

bring together the government and Mexican financiers. In 1925, they founded *Banco de Mexico*.[24] Initially, the *Banco de Mexico* was the same mix between a commercial and a central bank as Banamex. However, with this setup, the re-introduction of paper money proved difficult. To address this problem, the PRI removed, in 1931, the *Banco de Mexico*'s commercial powers and demon-etized precious metal. Silver coins were no longer accepted as tax payment. With these measures, the PRI established a central bank and re-established the cycle of money, rent, and debt. As under Díaz, the resulting banking system was small, but functional in terms of financing the institutional association of rule's political programme.[25] However, the system's smallness became a prob-lem when, in 1938, the government decided to make good on one of the most radical promises of the 1917 constitution: to privatize the oil industry.

Now the question of how to finance the state's political goals was a dif-ferent ball game. The government expropriated all foreign petroleum firms and merged them into one large state-owned company, *Petróleos Mexicanos* or PEMEX for short. Next to PEMEX, other central industries were also nationalized—although in a less dramatic fashion. Through the continuous acquisition of stocks, the government became either a minority or a major-ity shareholder of firms in the railway, tourism, telecommunication, and other sectors.[26]

Initially, the nationalization drew money into the state's coffers. Over time, however, inefficiencies in the state-owned companies became a strain on the budget.[27] Simultaneously, the costs for the system of patronage and privilege continued to rise. By the 1970s, debt began to outpace revenues. The govern-ment urgently needed more and cheaper money than the domestic financiers were willing to provide.[28]

The PRI was lucky. Thanks to rising petroleum prices and new discover-ies in the Mexican Gulf, government revenues were high enough to allow for borrowing in the international financial markets.[29] Even more importantly, a banking reform in 1974 allowed Mexican banks to internationalize. The banks, first among them Banamex and Bancomer, used the deregulations to get involved in the Euromarkets.

Participating in Eurodollar banking appeared to be a win–win situation between the banks and the government. It resembled an internationalized

---

[24] Banco de México 2018.
[25] Ibid.; Calomiris and Haber 2014, chs 10–11.
[26] MacLeod 2005.
[27] Ibid.
[28] Calomiris and Haber 2014, chs 10–11.
[29] Haber and Musacchio 2013.

version of Díaz's partnership of interest. On the one hand, the state profited from Mexican banks' Euromarket activities. Having access to international interbank loans, the Mexican banks expanded their domestic lending activities; between 1977 and 1982 domestic credit increased at an average rate of 38 per cent annually.[30] The credit was used, largely, to finance the state's political goals.

For instance, in September 1976 the Mexican government issued an US$800 million Eurodollar loan. This was Mexico's largest loan in the Euromarkets thus far; and it was one of the largest loans issued by any market participant that year. According to the government, the intent of the loan was to invest in infrastructure development, including in the oil sector.[31] Only one year later, Mexico topped this record with a new largest-ever Eurodollar loan. This time it was valued at US$1.2 billion. This loan came in addition to a separate Eurodollar loan issued by PEMEX the same year, seeking US$300 million, but ending up oversubscribed with US$350 million.[32] Again, the loans were sought to invest into infrastructure development.

All in all, in the decade between 1970 and 1979, Mexican economic actors issued 322 Eurodollar loans valued collectively at US$16 billion. Of the US$16 billion roughly one-third included Mexican banks as intermediaries.[33] These banks also profited from the new arrangement by increasing their business. Best of all, however, interest rates in the Euromarkets were about 40 to 60 per cent lower than domestically. With a *de facto* fixed exchange rate (under a managed floating exchange rate regime), Mexican banks could borrow cheaply internationally and lend on at higher prices domestically. In addition, in the Euromarkets the international branches of Mexican banks were not subject to reserve requirements. The rents through arbitrage were steep.

However, when oil prices collapsed in 1982, the Eurodollar bonanza came to sudden end. The Mexican government had to sign a moratorium and to negotiate a restructuring of its debt. The bargain over how to distribute the costs and benefits of money creation turned out to be lopsided. The state and the financiers could enjoy its benefits in good times. In bad times, the costs fell on everyone but the PRI. The state implemented a fierce domestic structural adjustment programme and—to avoid a collapse of the Mexican banking system—nationalized the banks. At the stroke of a pen, Mexico's long-lasting partnership of interest between the state and its financiers was finished.[34]

---

[30] Alvarez 2015.
[31] New York Times 1976.
[32] Riding 1977.
[33] Alvarez 2015.
[34] Calomiris and Haber 2014, chs 10–11.

Yet, negotiation between the Mexican state and its international creditors in 1982 entailed some small print that turned out to be important for the distribution of costs and benefits of money creation in the post-crisis years.

Interbank credit lines were kept frozen at the pre-moratorium level. After several prolongations of this agreement, in 1991, a newly created financial instrument was introduced: the so-called Floating Rate Privatization Note, a direct obligation of the Mexican government.[35] When President Carlos Salinas (1988–94), intending to stem the withdrawal of the propertied classes from domestic credit markets, re-privatized the banks the same year, the holders of the Floating Rate Privatization Note could use it to purchase shares in Mexican banks. In addition, Salinas tried to revive the partnership of interest and offered the financiers unlimited insurance against any loss the banks may incur in the future. This offer proved so attractive that the financiers were willing to pay US$12.4 billion, three times the book value of the banks, for the eighteen banks on offer.[36]

Facing little risk thanks to the government-bailout guarantee and the remaining access to the interbank market through the owners of the Floating Rate Privatization Note, Mexico's banks, in particular Banamex and Bancomer, were back in the Euromarkets in the early 1990s. During that time, economic actors were starved of credit to finance the lucrative acquisition of the public companies that were privatized as part of the structural adjustment programme. With the banks back in Eurodollar intermediation, Mexico's private sector moved from being a net creditor in 1990 to being a net borrower only one year later. The lending of Mexican banks in the Eurodeposit market alone increased from US$321 million in the third quarter of 1994 to US$2.7 billion in the last quarter of 1994.[37]

Unlike in the 1970s, this time the intermediation was mainly between Mexican banks and the Mexican private sector. The banks channelled US dollar liquidity into Mexican corporations, even if they had mainly peso denominated assets. When the peso collapsed in December 1994, nearly halving in value against the US dollar, Mexican firms' US-dollar-denominated loans doubled in value in the space of a few days. The firms could not serve their debt. The banks failed.

Only three years after the banks' re-privatization, the government of Ernesto Zedillo (1994–2000) nationalized the banks again, costing the country about 15 per cent of GDP. Via the Floating Rate Privatization Note and the bailout

---

[35] Alvarez 2015.
[36] Calomiris and Haber 2014, chs 10–11.
[37] Antzoulatos 2002.

guarantee, the financiers had won back a significant proportion of the price they paid for the shared power of money creation up until 1982. Now, the Mexican taxpayers were solely responsible for footing the bill for offshore money creation. The bailout—which transferred money from Mexican taxpayers to bank stockholders, some of Mexico's wealthiest individuals—killed the relationship between the PRI and its popular base. The PRI lost power first at the local level in 1997 and then at the federal level in 2000.

## Tax bargain

Due to Mexico's natural resources, the tax bargain is fundamentally different than in Britain, Germany, or Brazil. The possibility to create rents allowed the government to go into debt and create sovereign money, backed for centuries by silver. Porfirio Díaz's (1877–1911) partnership of interest with the financiers thus set in motion a circle of money, rent, and debt. Taxation remained marginal. However, that cycle would not have been sustainable if it were not for Mexico's natural resources.

Profitable oil drilling started a couple of years into the revolution. From then onwards it grew significantly—and with it tax revenue. In 1912, receipts from the oil sector accounted for less than 1 per cent of the government's total income. In 1917, the year of the new constitution, it made up 5 per cent. Five years later, in 1922, the government's income depended to more than 30 per cent on oil.[38]

Since then, the Mexican oil industry has experienced important changes. For instance, in the late 1920s, with the technology of the day, drilling companies could not maintain its previous levels of oil extraction. Mexico lost an important share of the international oil market. Once these problems were overcome, the PRI nationalized the oil industry in 1938. The 1970s, in turn, were a golden age for Mexico's petroleum industry with new discoveries in the Gulf of Mexico and roaring international oil prices. Despite these changes, what stayed the same in the long run was the contribution of the oil sector to the state's ability to mobilize and centralize revenue.[39] Since the early 1920s, the petroleum industry has contributed about one-third of state income.[40] Although not enough to finance the state, taxes from oil created the basis for a tax bargain marked by a low tax burden.[41]

---

[38] Haber, Maurer, and Razo 2003.
[39] Author's interview with economist, Mexico City, November 2015.
[40] Hall 1995; Aboites 2003.
[41] Haber et al. 2008.

In the words of Smith, 'the elites considered taxation as brazenness and peasants as another feudal load'.[42] Oil revenue allowed the PRI to avoid political conflict with its two power bases. Instead of taxing them, the state could finance its political goals through debt.[43]

Nevertheless, by the end of the 1940s, in order to be able to tax the oil sector, the PRI had developed a small, but modern tax system. Between the 1950s and the early 1980s, this system generated, on average, about two-thirds of the typical tax revenues in the rest of Latin America at that time. Before the mid-1970s the state's revenue was constantly less than 10 per cent of GDP. With Mexico's increasing income from oil revenues throughout the late 1970s and early 1980s, the ratio increased to about 15 per cent of GDP. By the early 1970s, government expenses finally started to outpace revenues, and the government urgently needed to mobilize resources to sustain its debt.[44] But in the system of patronage and privilege, taxing the wealthy or cutting expenditures for the popular base was politically unfeasible. The government decided to borrow on the Euromarkets, that is, to tap into money created offshore.

Despite the fundamental political and economic rupture of the 1982 and 1994 financial crises, Mexico's tax bargain is still shaped as it was in the old days. The wealthy elite is willing to lend to the government against rents. But they demand to be spared by the taxman.

## 2   Contemporary exposure to offshore finance

As in Britain, Germany, and Brazil, making use of offshore financial services dates back to the mid twentieth century. The reasons why economic actors do so have even longer historical roots. It is no different in Mexico. What sets the country apart from all other cases, as we shall see, is that its contemporary exposure to offshore finance is marginal. This section traces the contemporary uses and abuses of offshore financial services in Mexico and the reasons that explain their scope and pattern.

As in Britain and Germany, the Mexican government does not collect any statistical data on the uses of offshore financial services. The quantitative analysis of Mexican economic actors' exposure to offshore financial services is again based exclusively on BIS locational banking statistics. These quantitative data are complemented with data from qualitative expert interviews and contextualized in a historical perspective. Once more, it is important to

---

[42] Smith 2014, 261.
[43] Aboites 2003; Calomiris and Haber 2014, chs 10–11.
[44] Calomiris and Haber 2014, ch. 11; Smith 2014.

emphasize that all quantitative estimates are of a rough nature and cannot capture the full picture. Besides limitations in the available data, the underlying core assumptions—all assets offshore are untaxed and would be taxed if onshore—simplify a complex world. The methodological approach, including its limitations, is detailed in Appendix 1.

## The uses and abuses of offshore finance

As in the previous cases, what counts as relevant from the money view, are financial flows between Mexico and offshore financial centres. Again, claims represent money held offshore; liabilities debt issued there.

Figure 6.1 depicts the overall scale of offshoring in Mexico between 2003, the earliest year of reporting to the BIS, and 2019—in absolute US dollar and as a percentage of GDP. The figure shows the claims and liabilities between Mexico and the aggregate of all offshore financial centres. These are the uses of offshore financial services by all sectors of the Mexican economy: central government, financial, corporate, and households. As discussed before, offshore assets and debt affect state power differently, but jointly. For instance, offshore assets, if untaxed, lead to revenue loss. Offshore debt in turn transmits volatilities of the Eurodollar system into the domestic economy. The graph therefore depicts offshore claims and liabilities separately and as a sum. It is the sum that represents Mexico's overall exposure to offshore finance.

Mexico's exposure to offshore financial services developed from 0.04 per cent of GDP (or US$272 million) in 2003 to 0.1 per cent (or US$1.3 billion) in 2019. It peaked at 0.2 per cent of GDP (or US$2.6 billion) in 2010. Mexican exposure to offshore finance was by magnitudes lower than in any of the other case study countries. Britain's exposure peaked at 158 per cent, Germany's at 40 per cent, and Brazil's at 6 per cent.[45]

Between 2003 and 2011 offshore assets outweighed offshore debt (except for 2010). Then the trend reversed, and liabilities exceeded claims. Interviewees generally maintained that if Mexican economic actors did go offshore, it was to hedge against risks rather than to seek financing. They argue that the increase in offshore debt issuance between 2007 and 2010 was driven by supply. International investors were in search of investment opportunities and, given the state of the US and European economies, emerging market investments appeared attractive. However, the government and economic experts

---

[45] Brazil's value is based on BIS, not CBE data.

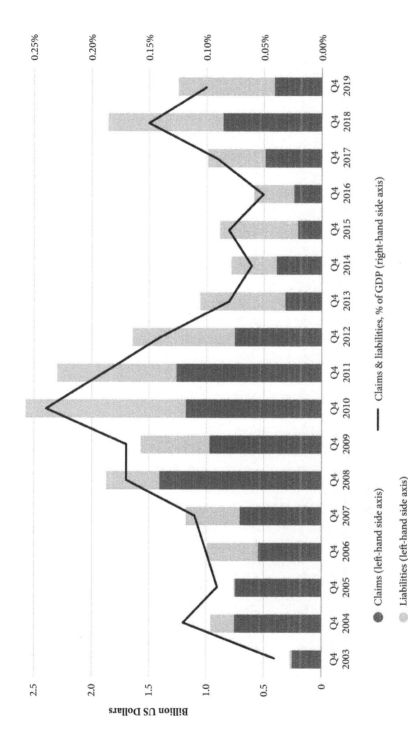

**Figure 6.1** Mexico's exposure to offshore finance

*Source:* BIS locational banking statistics, World Bank, own calculations.

remained wary of increased corporate sector leverage, denominated in US dollars.[46] Indeed, from 2010 to 2016, offshore debt issuance declined again. It is important to note, however, that what we can see in Figure 6.1 are mostly individual transactions. An interviewee from the central bank could even recall the banks responsible for each of the larger transactions and why they had a specific funding need.[47] It is difficult to infer trends from this data.

Disaggregating the data on offshore exposure by currency denomination, we see in Figure 6.2 that in Mexico—more than in the other three countries—the Eurodollar is fully dominant in the country's offshore exposure. Its share oscillates between 84 or 99 per cent. The low overall exposure of Mexico and the dominance of the Eurodollar within it, are a result of Mexico's past engagement with the Eurodollar markets and its destructive effects on Mexican politics.

The 1982 and 1994 financial crises put the PRI under existential pressure. Bracing for the PRI's demise, then-president Zedillo attempted to spur economic growth, for which he needed a new partnership with the bankers. As the relationship with the domestic financiers was ruined, Zedillo turned to foreigners. In 1996, for the first time since the *Porfiriato*, Zedillo allowed unrestricted foreign bank ownership. It took only a few years for the largest Mexican banks to be owned by foreign investors, particularly from the United States and Spain.[48]

The end of the partnership of interest between the Mexican government and its domestic financiers in the 1990s and the subsequent liberalization of the financial sector, disrupted banking in Mexico more substantially than the revolution did. In 1991, foreign banks owned 1 per cent of assets; by 2013, that number had grown to 74 per cent. Mexico became the country with the most rapid and far-reaching penetration of foreign banks in the world.[49]

According to Haber and Musacchio, the entry of foreign banks made Mexico's banking system more stable.[50] Access to credit for corporations and households became more easily accessible and cheaper. Still, financial inclusion remains small in Mexico; only 39 per cent of adults have a bank account.[51] The system also remains highly concentrated with seven banks, five of which are foreign owned, accumulating 73 per cent of market share.[52]

[46] Author's interviews with central bank staff, with economists, with a financial sector expert, Mexico City, November 2015.
[47] Author's interview with an employee of the central bank, Mexico City, November 2015.
[48] Haber et al. 2008; Calomiris and Haber 2014, chs 10–11.
[49] Haber and Musacchio 2013.
[50] Ibid.
[51] CONAIF 2016.
[52] Díaz-Infante 2013.

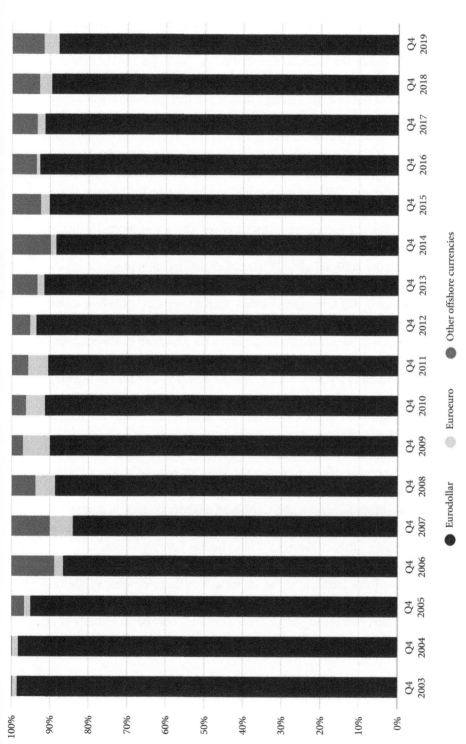

**Figure 6.2** Currency breakdown of Mexico's exposure to offshore finance

*Source:* BIS, own calculations.

● Eurodollar ● Euroeuro ● Other offshore currencies

As the ownership of the banking system developed from domestic-owned to foreign-owned, the issuance of Mexican sovereign debt developed in the opposite direction. Before the Mexican financial crises, 70–80 per cent of debt was issued abroad. Today that amount is issued domestically. The ownership structure, though, did not change. Mexico's debt is still foreign owned, since most of it is held by the foreign-owned banks and their pension funds.[53] The big change is that the debt is now denominated in Mexican pesos.[54] In other words, after three decades of offshoring debt with terrible consequences for Mexico's ordinary citizens, the government finally moved to create money onshore.

Likewise, after the 1994–95 peso crisis, the private sector became much more restrained in its borrowing in US dollars. Hence, for a considerable period after Mexico's successive financial crises, there was limited demand for US dollar-denominated debt and thus no reason to search for investors offshore. After the 2007–09 global financial crisis—which had severe effects on Mexico's economy but barely affected the banking system—the dynamic changed. Driven by US American investors' search for yields in the post-crisis, low interest-rate environment, Mexican private corporations found it easy to issue debt in international credit markets as the US American banks operating in Mexico could provide them with direct access to these markets.[55] Hence, an important contemporary reason for economic actors to go offshore—getting access to credit denominated in US dollars—is no longer present in Mexico in the way it had been in the past. The limited exposure to offshore money creation is a recent phenomenon.

Disaggregating data from Figure 6.2 by counterparty country, we find that the two most popular offshore centres for Mexican economic actors are the Cayman Islands and the Netherlands. They are followed at a distance by Guernsey and other European and Caribbean offshore centres. In contrast to what the literature suggests, Mexican economic actors do not necessarily prefer nearby Caribbean offshore centres.[56] They also use European ones.

Another notable observation is that interviewees usually mentioned Switzerland and the Netherlands as important offshore centres. While the Netherlands are indeed a popular offshore centre, Switzerland is used much less than the interviewees suggested. This difference may be an indication of illegal uses of Swiss offshore financial services. This is analysed further below

[53] Author's interview with central bank staff, Mexico City, November 2015; author's interview with economist, Mexico City, November 2015.
[54] Banco de México 2014.
[55] Author's interview with financial sector expert, Mexico City, November 2015.
[56] Blanco and Rogers 2014; Haberly and Wójcik 2015a.

in the context of money laundering. The Netherlands is, on the other hand, Mexico's second biggest investment partner, 'both, in substance and in form' as a corporate lawyer put it.[57] In substance, the Dutch are among Mexico's ten largest trading partners and with the trading real investment flows in the same direction. In form, the Netherlands is also one of the most prominent off-shore financial centres used to structure investment from and into Europe in a tax efficient manner.[58] And indeed, the Netherlands account for 25 per cent of Mexican outward investment. A number that appears disproportionately high in comparison to the real economic relations between the two countries. Mexican investors channel their equity investments into Europe, mostly to Germany and Spain, through holdings in the Netherlands. These holdings give them, as one tax lawyer put it, an 'excellent exit strategy' to sell shares without paying tax for the proceeds in either Mexico or the final destination country of the investment.[59]

Yet, unfortunately, the FDI data cannot tell us how much of the pie is real investment into the Netherlands and how much of it is virtual investment that ends up in Germany or Spain. Summing up the uses of offshore finance by Mexican economic actors one interviewee said:

> You know, a lot more money is probably parked in apartments in Miami than it is in Jersey or Bahamas. The destination is the United States, or Spain ... if I were to look at where the money is, it is there.[60]

This insight brings us to a question that is particularly relevant for the Mexican case study: the role of United States' sub-national offshore financial centres. With no income tax on individuals and trusts, a very low state estate tax, no inheritance and no gift taxes, Florida is certainly a low-tax jurisdiction. However, it is not an offshore financial centre according to the concept discussed in Chapter 2. The favourable tax laws are not exclusively provided to non-residents, but also to United States citizens (no ring-fencing). Furthermore, Florida is not among the country's secrecy jurisdictions. According to the financial secrecy index these are Delaware, Nevada, and Wyoming.[61] These US offshore financial centres have not been mentioned in the interviews at all and hence there is neither quantitative nor qualitative data on their importance for Mexican firms and individuals. Finally, with a good three-hour flight from

[57] IMF n.d.
[58] Garcia-Bernardo et al. 2017.
[59] Author's interview with tax lawyer, Mexico City, November 2015.
[60] Author's interview with economist, Mexico City, November 2015.
[61] Tax Justice Network 2018c.

Mexico City, the wealthy indeed spend time in their Miami apartments.[62] The Miami holiday home for rich Mexicans is the equivalent to the Swiss Chalet for rich Germans. The line between capital flight and offshoring can be a fine one. Importantly, however, all of the Mexican money in the United States is under the jurisdiction of the Federal Reserve and the US Treasury. The US dollars in the Bahamas and Cayman Islands are not.

Mexico's withdrawal from the offshore markets post-1994 had consequences for offshore tax planning too. As argued in Chapter 2, offshore financial flows are a precondition for offshore tax planning to happen. With the limited flows to offshore financial centres come limited opportunities for Mexican firms and individuals to plan taxes there.

Assuming, as in the previous cases, that all offshore money is undeclared, but would be taxed at the full average tax rate if onshore, the potential maximum loss for Mexican tax revenue ranges, as Figure 6.3 shows, between an annual minimum of US$67 million (or 0.01 per cent of GDP) in 2015 and a maximum of US$394 million (or 0.04 per cent of GDP) in 2008. In a country with a large proportion of the population living in poverty and lacking basic services, this is no trivial amount. Yet, it is hardly a fatal blow to the Mexican tax state.

According to the OECD, in Mexico taxes on personal income make up a smaller proportion of tax revenue than in any other member state. As in previous times, the wealthy are spared from contributing more significantly to the state's treasury. Likewise, social security contributions account for a much smaller share in the tax mix, expressing the association of rule's limited willingness to contribute to the welfare of the larger population.[63] Mexico's nearly entirely privatized health, pension, and social security systems create much lower spending needs than in either the OECD or other Latin American countries.[64] Next, consumption taxes make up about 39 per cent of tax revenue. This share is lower than the Latin American average of more than 50 per cent,[65] but is an explicit attempt by the government to increase its revenue by taxing poor people in Mexico's informal economy.[66]

Finally, the share of corporate income taxes is considerably higher than in the OECD world. Corporations contribute 20 per cent to the tax revenue, much more than their OECD peers. A high tax burden for corporations is common in developing countries, as these taxes are easier to collect than

[62] Author's interview with economist, Mexico City, November 2015.
[63] Author's interview with tax expert at a civil society organization, Mexico City, November 2015.
[64] OECD 2015.
[65] Ibid.
[66] Author's interview with tax expert at a civil society organization, Mexico City, November 2015.

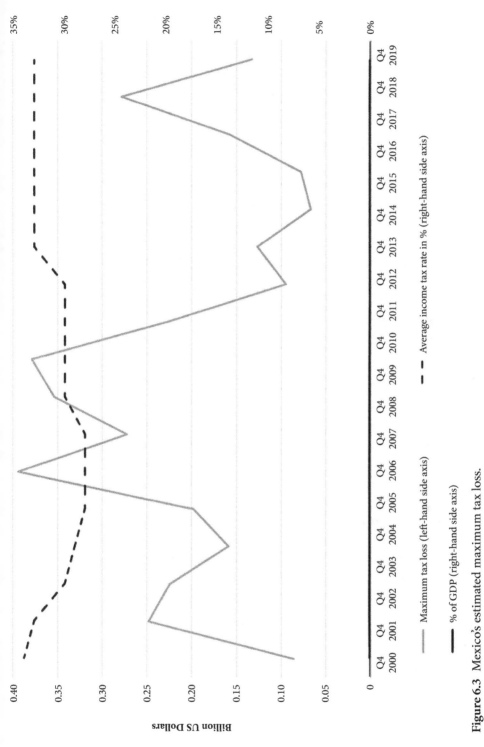

**Figure 6.3** Mexico's estimated maximum tax loss.

*Source:* BIS locational banking statistics, World Bank, own calculations.

— Maximum tax loss (left-hand side axis)

- - - Average income tax rate in % (right-hand side axis)

— % of GDP (right-hand side axis)

others.[67] Yet, in Mexico it must be seen against the background of an overall significantly lower tax burden than in any other OECD country. Mexico still has the OECD's lowest tax-to-GDP ratio. In 2016, its tax revenue amounted to 17 per cent of GDP compared to the OECD's average of 34 per cent and the Latin American average of 22 per cent.[68] That is, Mexican corporations contribute a larger share to a much smaller pie than corporations in other OECD countries.

This setup reflects the above-described fact that businesses were not part of the PRI's system of privilege and patronage but were corrupted individually. In contemporary Mexico, the high corporate tax rates are matched by equally high rates of corporate onshore tax avoidance. Businesses negotiate individual tax exemptions at the municipal and state levels[69] adding up to a considerable tax loss at the federal level.[70] That is, Mexico's contemporary tax institutions reflect the preference of the institutional association of rule: limited spending on the poor and ensuring a low tax burden for the wealthy. Within that agreement, however, the government has the capacity to enforce the rules.[71] For instance between 2004 and 2015, evasion of VAT came down from 35 to 19 per cent of the possible tax revenue and evasion of income tax dropped even more from 49 to 26 per cent.[72]

The contemporary shape of Mexico's tax institutions has two implications for the use of offshore financial services. First, Mexico's exceptionally low tax burden limits corporations and wealthy individuals' demand to go offshore. Second, almost 40 per cent of tax revenue comes from consumption taxes. These taxes do not lend themselves to being evaded offshore. Mexicans dodge them through the country's large informal economy instead.[73]

In Mexico, it is the informal sector, not offshore financial centres, that help the criminal and the wealthy to engage in the politics of the invisible. The informal economy provides similar opportunities as offshore financial services; except that it avoids the cost and effort of hiring the lawyers and accountants needed to go offshore. As in the past, Mexico's tax state is weak by design. The ensuing shortage of tax revenue is offset, again as in previous times, by revenues from petroleum[74] and debt.[75] This approach to financing the Mexican

---

[67] Genschel and Seelkopf 2016.
[68] Numbers for Latin America are from 2014.
[69] Author's interview with tax lawyer, Mexico City, November 2015.
[70] San Martín Reyna et al. 2016.
[71] Author's interview with tax auditor, Mexico City, November 2015.
[72] San Martín Reyna et al. 2016.
[73] ILO 2014; Buehn and Schneider 2016.
[74] Aboites 2003; Sobarzo 2011.
[75] Calomiris and Haber 2014, chs 10–11.

state exposes public finances to the volatility of international debt and oil markets. Yet, it reflects the preferences of the still exclusive Mexican state.

Next to tax planning, financial flows between Mexico and offshore financial centres are a precondition for offshore money laundering. Limited offshore exposure implies limited offshore money laundering. Indeed, the interviewees maintained their general claim about the limited uses of offshore finance in Mexico even with regards to money laundering. They argue that Mexican criminals use the onshore informal economy rather than offshore financial services for money laundering purposes. Informality coupled with the low inclusion of Mexican households into the financial sector, creates a largely cash-based economy.[76] The use of cash, going down internationally, is on the rise in Mexico.[77]

A cash economy creates formidable spaces for onshore money laundering. For instance, paying workers without a bank account in cash is a cheap and efficient way for firms to keep financial flows below the state's radar. Although the Mexican authorities are well aware of these money laundering schemes and have highly developed systems to detect them, law enforcement is wanting.[78] That is, Mexican criminals employ classic onshore money laundering schemes such as 'cuckoo smurfing', succinctly described by a former employee of HSBC Bank:

> My experience was ... that all these criminal networks ... have singular persons involved in these money laundering systems. They pay, for example, a cleaning lady ... and her only job is to go daily to a different branch of HSBC to make a deposit of 500 pesos.... They collect 1,000 cleaning ladies doing that daily to different accounts. The owners of the accounts are ... the sons or nephews of the main capos and outside of Mexico. Maybe he is in England, studying in Oxford, or in Harvard and they ... make the shift of transactions of thousands, of millions of dollars to other branches of HSBC.[79]

Although there is no publicly available data to quantify illegal offshore uses, the data of the Swiss National Bank on fiduciary funds can help to test the plausibility of the interview results.

As noted above, there is a notable difference between what the interviewees said and what the data showed regarding the importance of Switzerland as

---

[76] Del Angel 2016.
[77] FATF and GAFILAT 2018.
[78] Ibid.
[79] Author's interview with financial sector expert, Mexico City, November 2017.

a popular offshore financial centre. Interviewees usually mentioned Switzerland as one of the most important offshore financial centres, while the data demonstrate that other centres are far more important. One reason for the discrepancy of these numbers with the interviewees' impression could be that transactions are off-balance sheet, not showing up in the BIS statistics. For instance, fiduciary funds and trusts can make offshore money statistically invisible (see Appendix 1).

Unlike fiduciary deposits, trusts are not allowed under Mexican law. Famously, Switzerland is the prime location globally for fiduciary funds.[80] For a criminal who wants to hide her money while still being able to invest it, a Swiss fiduciary deposit account is a good option. The Swiss National Bank publishes an annual breakdown of the country of origin of the fiduciary funds.[81] If criminal Mexicans were hiding their money in Switzerland, it is likely it would show in this data set.

According to the Swiss National Bank, Mexican fiduciary deposits amounted to CHF1.2 billion in 1987 and more than halved to CHF476 million in 2016.[82] The data on fiduciary deposits, in combination with Swiss efforts to reduce dirty money flowing into its banking system suggest that it is unlikely that Mexican economic actors hide large amounts of money in Switzerland.[83] The discrepancy of the interviewees' perception of the role of Switzerland and its contemporary importance may, however, reflect past scandals.

For instance, in the early 1990s, Raúl Salinas, the brother of former President Carlos Salinas (1988–94), transferred around US$100 million to Switzerland and the UK. After the Mexican government was able to show that a large amount of this money was actually public funds, the Swiss government froze Raúl Salinas's accounts and handed back US$74 million to the Mexican government.[84] In sum, all available data—quantitative and qualitative—point to limited use and abuse of offshore finance in Mexico in the contemporary phase.

### 3  The encounter

Mexico's institutional association of rule, the state, is marked by the legacy of the partnership of interest between the government and its financiers. It is also

---

[80] Zucman 2015.
[81] Swiss National Bank 2017.
[82] Ibid.
[83] Sharman 2017.
[84] GAO 1998; Swissinfo 2008.

marked by creating legitimacy through a system of patronage and privilege that favours the few above the many. No other state analysed in this book has resisted the expansion of the institutional association of rule as much as the Mexican. Throughout history, Mexico's economic elites were willing to lend to the central state against rents from natural resources and monopoly power. Mexican modern statehood thus emerged out of debt and political violence.[85] It did not emerge, as usually attributed with reference to the European experience, from external warfare and the mobilization and centralization of taxes.[86] It established a cycle of money, tax, and debt backed by the revenue from its natural resources, above all silver and oil. That cycle is functional but small. Historically, the Mexican state has been weak by design, not because of a lack of capacity.

The availability of rents from monopoly power and natural resources influences how offshore finance affects state power. In Britain, Germany, and Brazil we have seen that, in line with the arguments made in Chapter 2, offshore finance can affect state power through both sides of the balance sheet: taxation and banking. In all three cases, however, offshore banking was more consequential for state power than offshore tax planning. In Mexico, due to the low tax burden on the wealthy and high informality among the poor, offshore tax planning plays a negligible role. Offshore banking is the exclusive mechanism through which offshore finance affects Mexican state power.

As in the previous case studies, after having established the mechanism through which offshore finance affects state power, this last section turns to the quality—enhancing or limiting state power—of that effect.

## Strengthening state power, then destroying it

When in the 1960s offshore credit first became an option for Mexico, it presented, as in the case of Brazil, an opportunity for the Mexican state to finance its political goals. Better still, it could do so at preferential conditions compared to domestic or regular foreign debt.

In the 1970s especially, the Mexican government and state-owned corporations borrowed extensively in the Eurodollar markets. Profiting from high oil prices, offshore borrowing was made possible by the Mexican central bank, which allowed domestic banks to establish affiliates abroad.[87] As in the other

---

[85] Centeno 2002.
[86] Tilly 1990; Schumpeter 1991.
[87] Alvarez 2015.

cases, banks' offshore business was not done against, but with support of the state.

Just as was the case in Brazil, access to Eurodollars allowed Mexico to finance its economic development. Moreover, it helped the PRI to sustain the system of privilege and patronage beyond its means. The Eurodollar markets provided more credit at better conditions than domestic or US American investors were willing to advance. The Mexican state went in enthusiastically. As in Brazil, the early days of offshore finance strengthened state power by directly providing money to the state and large corporations (often at least partially state-owned). Again, as in Brazil and in contrast to Britain and Germany, the politics of the invisible had no role in strengthening state power via offshore finance. It was all about preferential liquidity. Mexico, when it participated in offshore finance, did so openly.

Unlike Brazil, however, it engaged without any meaningful defensive measures.[88] So when the 1982 financial crisis hit, the encounter between offshore finance and Mexican state power turned destructive. The effects of offshore finance on state power were once more subject to an alteration of good and bad times. In good times, offshore finance enhanced state power. As in Brazil, it financed Mexican economic development. When the inevitable bad times arrived in 1982, in the absence of defensive measures and insufficient alternative income to Eurodollar debt, offshore finance destroyed Mexican state power.

The century-old partnership of interest between the Mexican state and its domestic financiers broke down. The Mexican state retreated from borrowing in the Eurodollar markets and nationalized the banks. Yet, Mexico's small banking system still did not create enough money to allow the private sector to take part in a globalized trading system ever more dominated by the US dollar. Thus, large Mexican banks were back in the Eurodollar markets by the early 1990s. The banks passed on the US-dollar denominated offshore credit to the Mexican private sector. This second round of Mexico's exposure to offshore banking ended with the 1994 peso crisis. The price Mexico paid for offshore money creation was two severe financial crises in the span of a decade. Politically, the 1982 crisis cost the state its relationship with the financiers and that of 1994 the backing of its popular base. As a result, the PRI's power, uncontested for seventy-six years, vanished.

What makes Mexico stand out, compared to Britain, Germany, and Brazil, is the centrality of offshore banking as the key mechanism in combination with

---

[88] Alvarez 2020.

an absence of defensive measures and an unsustainable tax bargain. As a result, the destructive forces of offshore finance on state power were so strong and persistent that it turned contemporary Mexico into a counterintuitive case.

Today, the country exhibits all the factors that are commonly associated with an important demand for offshore financial services. Mexico is large, has an open economy, is located closely to important offshore financial centres and wrestles with problems of crime and corruption. And yet, as the empirical data discussed above demonstrate, contemporary Mexico has little exposure to the Eurodollar market. Tax avoidance and money laundering are done through the country's large informal economy. Mexican economic actors make little use of offshore financial services. Considering offshore finance as a purely contemporary phenomenon, as most studies do, would leave us puzzled why Mexican economic actors do not go offshore.

It is the historical perspective that reveals that Mexico's offshore restraint is a contemporary phenomenon. In the 1970s and late 1980s/early 1990s the Mexican state and Mexican corporations issued debt in the Eurodollar markets like no other country. Today's constraint is a lesson learned from offshore finance's distructive effects in the past.

## A lesson learned

After the 1982 and 1994 financial crises, the Mexican state onshored money creation. Opening the Mexican banking sector to foreign banks increased the possibility for domestic debt issuance for both, the state and the private sector. All newly issued debt, sovereign and corporate, was now denominated in the Mexican peso.[89]

Abstaining from offshore money creation remains an explicit policy of the Mexican government.[90] Next to political will, this move was possible for two reasons. First, though small, Mexico's cycle of money, debt, and rent backed by silver and oil has been comparatively stable since the nineteenth century. It made the peso an accepted sovereign currency. Second, the integration of Mexico into the North American Free Trade Agreement (NAFTA), its shared border with the United States, and the opening of the banking system towards US American banks created onshore access to the US dollar as

[89] Author's interviews with central bank staff; with financial sector expert, Mexico City, November 2015.
[90] Webber 2019.

and when needed.[91] Leaving the Eurodollar markets behind increased the Mexican state's ability to conduct a monetary policy that was supportive of its politics. Mexico's response to the financial crises was to withdraw from offshore banking. No other country studied in this book did this.

The limited flows to and from offshore financial centres naturally limits the use of offshore tax planning and money laundering. Offshore tax planning is also limited by Mexico's comparatively low tax burden on income and wealth. Instead of building legally complicated offshore structures, tax planning and money laundering are done at home.

The low overall tax burden in Mexico—it is still only at about 17 per cent of GDP[92]—reflects a tax bargain that aims to avoid pushing the cost of financing the state's political goals onto either the wealthy classes or the state's popular power bases. Nevertheless, the Mexican state demonstrated that—if need be—it can fight onshore and offshore tax avoidance and evasion. The significant drop in VAT and personal income tax fraud as well as Mexico's early implementation of the OECD BEPS standards testify to the tax state's potential strength. Nevertheless, large corporations use the opportunities that arise from in- and outflows of offshore FDI to plan taxes. It does not threaten the Mexican state's ability to finance its political goals, though.

Next to the nature of Mexico's tax system, the informal economy is an important factor in explaining the limited demand for offshore services—in the past as today. It allows criminals to launder their ill-gotten gains from tax evasion, corruption, or drug trafficking without too much risk of being detected. For the wealthy, the informal economy provides similar rents as offshore finance, but without having to spend money on accountants and lawyers to set up sophisticated offshore structures. At the same time, the informal economy provides a hideout for the poor who feel—not unjustifiably—that Mexico's tax system is skewed too much against them.[93]

Even today, it matters for the relationship between offshore finance and the state, that Porfirio Díaz forged a partnership with the bankers *before* establishing a modern tax system. This chronology laid the foundations for an institutional association of rule shaped by debt rather than tax. The state, in Mexico, unites resources by going into debt against expected revenue from natural and mineral resources rather than by taxing its wealthy elite. Consequently, but counterintuitively, the nature of money creation has been more consequential for the level of using offshore financial services than formal

---

[91] Author's telephone interview with banker, May 2015.
[92] OECD 2017b.
[93] Author's interview with tax expert in civil society organization, Mexico City, November 2015.

democratization. In sum, banking and taxation institutions in Mexico are shaped such that in the contemporary period, there is limited demand for off-shore financial services. In the absence of significant uses of offshore finance, their effect on state power is, naturally, limited too.

Once more, Mexico's experience supports the theoretical argument (Chapter 2) that there is no straightforward effect of offshore financial ser-vices on the state's ability to mobilize and centralize resources to finance its political goals. It can enhance state power in good times and undermine it in bad times. Which of these it does depends on domestic institutions that help to weather the storm. Banking regulation as in Brazil, or a ring-fencing of tax and bank bargains from the effects of offshore finance as in Germany, can insulate a country from the excesses of offshore finance. Consequently, how strongly offshore finance affects state power varies within countries and between them.

Mexico exhibits both these variations. Comparing Mexico with Britain, Germany and Brazil, highlights that it is not exclusively the financial crises emanating from the volatility of offshore money markets that undermine state power. It is also the specific crisis response, conditioned by the nature of the institutional association's strategy to distribute the costs and benefits of money creation across different groups of society. In Mexico, the short-term response to the costs of offshore money creation was politically, socially, and economi-cally destructive. The long-term effect was a unique decoupling of the Mexican state from offshore finance.

# 7

# Conclusion

The encounter between offshore finance and state power is, indeed, like a house of mirrors. Mexico's contemporary uses of offshore financial services are considerably smaller than the literature would suggest. In Brazil, both its economic development and large-scale corruption would have been impossible without offshore finance. Germany's substantial role in the Eurodollar markets often goes unnoticed. The size of Britain's use and provision of offshore financial services may not surprise comparatively, but the absolute numbers are nonetheless dizzying. Coming at the offshore phenomenon from the money view proved a useful guide through that house of mirrors.

The money view emphasizes the shared power of money creation between the state and banks as one crucial feature of modern statehood.[1] Money creation is the result of a set of creditor–debtor relationships between the state, its financiers, and taxpayers.[2] From this analytical vantage point, state power is the ability of the institutional association of rule (*Herrschaftsverband*) to mobilize and centralize resources to finance its political goals. These resources can be in the form of tax, debt, rents, loot, or a combination thereof, as we have seen across the case studies. The resources securitize the state's credit-money creation. State power depends on the ability of the state to mediate successfully the distributional conflict over the costs and benefits of taxation and money creation across different groups of society.[3] This notion of state power underlines the relational nature of power, while being agnostic towards its purpose. It highlights state autonomy over state influence[4] and material over ideational perspectives.

The purpose of the money view in this book has been to balance the necessity to account for the historical and geographical contingencies of different states[5] with the possibility of identifying larger patterns through comparison. This balance is especially important when analysing the impact of global

---

[1] Vogl 2015.
[2] Ingham 2004.
[3] Levi 1989; Calomiris and Haber 2014.
[4] Cohen 2013.
[5] Skinner 2009.

*Offshore Finance and State Power*. Andrea Binder, Oxford University Press. © Andrea Binder (2023).
DOI: 10.1093/oso/9780192870124.003.0007

phenomena—such as offshore finance—on individual states with significantly different paths to modern statehood—as is the case for Britain, Germany, Brazil, and Mexico. Offshore finance is a clearly circumscribed instance of financial globalization. It is a set of cross-border financial services marked by the non-resident principle, low or no taxation and regulation, and invisibility. Offshore finance is not any financial flow outside a specific jurisdiction, and it is hence also not simply capital flight. It is a set of financial services deliberately codified in law such as to circumvent national regulation in a mostly invisible way.[6] In asking how offshore finance affects state power, the book considered the mechanics—how does it work?—and the outcome of this effect—is it enhancing or limiting state power?

This concluding chapter walks the tightrope between taking seriously historical and geographical contingencies and identifying larger patterns about state power in the age of offshore finance through comparison. Contrasting the experiences of Britain, Germany, Brazil, and Mexico, it refines the arguments made in Chapter 2 about how offshore finance affects state power. It then moves on to explain under which conditions offshore finance either undermines or strengthens state power. It spells out what the theoretical and empirical findings mean for our understanding of state power in the age of offshore finance. The book ends by lifting our gaze beyond the money view, deliberating on the effect of offshore finance on the legitimacy of the democratic state.

## 1   How offshore finance affects state power

In Chapter 2, I argued that there is no straightforward relationship between offshore finance and state power. Theoretically, offshore finance can enhance state power through preferential liquidity—credit at better conditions than at home or in regular foreign markets—and by providing the possibility for a politics of the invisible—a means for the state to obscure the true nature of the bank and tax bargains. On the flip side, offshore finance can limit state power by depriving the state of tax revenue and by transmitting the volatility of unregulated offshore banking into the domestic political economy.

Empirically, we saw that, indeed, offshore finance affects state power through both sides of the balance sheet—claims (tax) and liabilities (debt). Unexpectedly, however, the tax loss related to offshore tax planning did not

---

[6] Pistor 2020.

deprive the state of power in any of the four cases. Instead, the case studies confirmed Genschel's[7] argument that international tax competition does not fatally harm the tax state but leads to a redistribution of the tax burden. In all four cases offshore banking was more consequential for state power. Despite the distinct histories of offshore tax planning and offshore banking, the latter has become the enabler of the former. Today, the main purpose of offshore finance is to create money, not simply to hide it. Offshore finance's potency in affecting state power lies in its ability to create and access global credit-money.

Next to the mechanism, how offshore finance affects state power, the case studies also provided insights into the quality of the effect. They confirmed that offshore finance can strengthen or undermine state power. Empirically, we could also see, however, that offshore finance does not enhance or limit all states' power in equal measures. The effect was also not constant over time. It varied across space and time. Weimar Germany was differently affected by offshore finance than the contemporary Berlin Republic. The same is true for Brazil and Mexico before and after the Latin American financial crises of the 1980s and 1990s. Britain, too experienced different effects of offshore finance on state power between its onset in the 1950s and today.

However, the empirical results of the comparison of offshore finance's effect on state power across cases also help to refine the theoretical arguments in two respects.

First, the comparison highlighted that the benefits of offshore finance are not equally important in all cases. In the Latin American cases, the question of liquidity provision was more important than the politics of the invisible. In the European cases it was the reverse.

In Brazil and Mexico, the central benefits of offshore money creation included direct state financing and corporate access to US dollars, vital to participate in international trade. Compared to general foreign debt, offshore debt comes with better conditions: although denominated in US dollar, offshore debt is settled under British commercial law. British commercial law is more lenient towards debtors than US American litigation law.[8] With this setup, offshore finance increases access to US dollars, while decreasing the political and economic costs in case of default. While pronounced in the Latin American cases, Britain and Germany also made use of the preferential liquidity available offshore. In Germany it contributed towards the costs incurred by reunification. First and foremost, however, Germany and Britain were suppliers of

---

[7] Genschel 2005.
[8] Author's interview with tax lawyer, London, September 2017.

preferential liquidity in the offshore world: Britain as the premier offshore banking hub in the world; Germany furnishing one of the largest offshore banks. As the offshore banker to the world, the British state can exert international influence beyond its actual political and economic weight.[9] Better still, it can do so without having to conduct a monetary policy that must balance domestic with international considerations.

In the European cases, the politics of the invisible—the strategy of the state to use offshore finance to cover up the actual distribution of the costs and benefits of money creation and taxation between different groups of society—has been central to state power. For instance, the politics of the invisible afforded the German state the possibility to constrain its large banks in the domestic economy, while providing them with the opportunity to engage in profit-creating business offshore. Offshore finance does not do away with the inescapability of prioritizing one set of interests over another. Yet it spares the government political conflict over the chosen prioritization. The politics of the invisible played a smaller role in Brazil and Mexico. Their large informal sectors provide space for a domestic politics of the invisible.

Second, the comparison made clear that offshore banking transmitted, as suggested in Chapter 2, the volatility of unregulated offshore markets into the domestic political economy. It also revealed, however, why the volatilities of offshore money creation undermine state power.

Preferential liquidity dried up for those actors using it and created trouble for the balance sheets of those actors providing it. In both scenarios, the costs of offshore money creation outpaced its benefits. The ability of the state to finance its political goals took a severe hit in Britain, Germany, Brazil, and Mexico during financial crises. The Latin American and global financial crises, in particular, were not external shocks, but were deeply rooted in the Eurodollar system.[10] Financial crises are indeed endogenous to the offshore system. The intensity and longevity of the hit and its political consequences varied strongly between the four cases.

Pre-2007 and pre-1982, Britain and Mexico engaged in the Eurodollar system unhedged. In both cases the economic and political fallout was severe. The crisis response limited the ability of the British and the Mexican states to finance their respective political programmes. Moreover, the bailout of the banks revealed the actual nature of the bank bargain: the banks (and in extension the state) had reaped the benefits of money creation in good times. In

---

[9] Green 2020.
[10] Alvarez 2015; Altamura 2017; Tooze 2018; Hardie and Thompson 2020.

bad times, the costs were distributed widely across society. The experience of Brazil in 1982 was similar to the British and Mexican ones, but the defensive measures the Brazilian state had set up from the beginning of its engagement in the Eurodollar markets did soften the effects compared to Mexico.[11]

Financial crises related to offshore money creation undermine state power in two ways. For one, it revokes the preferential liquidity or creates trouble for the banks providing it. Solving these issues produces enormous economic costs. Additionally, the response to the crisis reveals what has been hidden by the politics of the invisible—the true nature of the bank and tax bargains. Financial crises nullify the politics of the invisible. Consequently, the power of the state to finance itself becomes contested economically and politically. That is, the same reasons that strengthen state power in good times—preferential liquidity and invisibility—undermine state power in financial crises and their aftermath.

In short, the empirical analysis reveals that offshore finance provides the state with an extraterritorial vehicle that enables a cover up of the deep political conflicts over how to finance the state or to what extent the revenue is used to mitigate class conflict. Brazil and Mexico's benefits from offshore finance manifested in overcoming the economic elite's resistance to finance the state via taxation. Britain's and Germany's benefits from offshore finance took the form of overcoming conflicts over redistributional policies. That is, in the age of offshore finance, the constitution of state power is not relegated exclusively to the domestic realm. Instead, states use the offshore world with its low-regulatory, low-tax regimes that make financial flows invisible, to advance their own political goals. Offshore finance transforms the constitution of state power.

At the same time, in all cases, capitalist expansion through offshore money creation increased the risks of broken promises. For offshore money entails the promise to pay back *and* the promise to get access to US dollars if need be. Once that double-promise is questioned and banks with an exposure to offshore money can no longer refinance themselves in the interbank offshore markets, crisis erupts. This happened in Latin America first; Europe followed about two decades later. Besides different chronologies, the empirical analysis also demonstrated that the severity of the effect depends on the crisis response. Underexplored in the offshore literature, the historical-institutionalist analysis revealed the agency that states have in their relationship with offshore finance. The next section therefore interrogates this observation in more detail by contrasting, once more, the experiences of Britain, Germany, Brazil, and Mexico.

---

[11] Alvarez 2020.

## 2  Making offshore finance work for the state

Offshore finance can strengthen state power in good times. It comes at the price of combined economic and political crises when preferential liquidity recedes, and the politics of the invisible becomes transparent. The state has, therefore, an incentive to make offshore finance work in its favour. Any strategy to do so faces a trade-off between maximizing the benefits of offshore finance and limiting its risks. Depending on which balance a state strikes, offshore finance does not enhance or limit all states' power in equal measures.

This finding explains why, at first sight counterintuitively, the quantitative analysis revealed that more offshoring does not necessarily mean stronger effects. British exposure to offshore financial services equals the size of the country's economy. Before the 2007–09 global financial crisis, it even stood at 1.5 times the economy's size. Given the pre-eminence of the City of London in global finance, it hardly comes as a surprise that exposure to offshore financial services in the other countries is a different ball game. In Germany, the largest of the four economies, the overall exposure to offshore finance peaked in 2008 at 40 per cent of GDP and then fell after the global financial crisis to 24 per cent in 2019. Brazil's exposure to offshore financial services ranges between 4 per cent in 2002 and 6 per cent in 2019. In Mexico offshore exposure between 2003 and 2019 is negligible. In case of a direct link between scale and outcome, we would expect Britain's state power to be more strongly strengthened and more strongly undermined by offshore finance. Followed by Germany, Brazil, and then Mexico.

We cannot observe a proportional impact of scale on the effect. There is no ground on which to argue, for instance, that Britain was affected by the financial crisis four times more than Germany. Or on the contrary, that before the crisis its power was strengthened four times more than Germany's. In addition, Brazil's scale of offshoring is smaller compared to the size of its economy than Germany's. Nevertheless, both enhancing and limiting effects are more pronounced in Brazil than in Germany. In the contemporary period, the German state simply was more effective in making offshore finance work in its favour. It could, as Palan[12] argues, indeed 'have [its] cake and eat it'. Size does not matter. Institutions do.

In Germany from the mid-nineteenth century onwards, the development of modern banking merged industrial and financial capital into a money elite which was separate from but close to the country's *Funktionselite*, an elite of

---

[12] Palan 1998, 625.

public functionaries. The money elite has been remarkably stable ever since. The *Funktionselite* has been replaced with each regime change in Germany. It is the elite of functionaries that broadened with the arrival of a post-war democracy, while the money elite remains exclusive. This elite constellation influenced Germany's tax and bank bargain.

At its outset, imperial Germany had very little in the way of public finances. It started free of debt and almost free of any spending needs. Military expenditure was supposed to be met with the gold seized from France.[13] In the first decades of its existence, the strategy to finance the federal German state was built around loot. Only during the Weimar Republic (1918–33) did federal tax and—more hesitantly—debt make a serious entry onto the central stage of German politics. Once established, however, the German tax state became an ideal-type, while sovereign debt remained contested. The 'principle of performance'—the idea that the economic elites who contribute to financing the state should have, in return, a high degree of influence over what the tax was spent on—shaped the tax bargain. To this day, the interests of the money elite is that the state spends its revenue on supporting industry and the welfare of labour. Importantly, the German welfare system is mainly based on co-financed insurance schemes. It is not overly redistributive. A substantial share of the welfare system's costs is borne by the working classes themselves. The employers' share constitutes a corporate cost that does not directly reduce the capital owner's private wealth. Moreover, compared to tax-financed welfare measures, insurance schemes limit the state's discretion over how to spend that money. Even with the rise of mass democracy and the welfare state in post-war Germany, the money elite had been influential enough to mitigate onshore the class conflict such that its own interests were still dominant. At the same time, unlike taxes, social security contributions are difficult to avoid via offshoring. The insurance companies are publicly owned, and the contributions are directly deducted at source. Law enforcement is strict. If German economic actors dodge social security contributions, they do it through informality, not offshoring. With this setup, offshore tax planning by the money class, though considerable at the individual level, remained non-threatening for German state power.

The bank bargain, in turn, was historically a relatively balanced distribution of costs and benefits of money creation. It led to the sufficient creation of liquidity but limited the banks' ability to make a profit from it. In the 1950s and 1960s offshore banking, then, allowed large German banks to make

---

[13] Macdonald 2003.

a profit, while the domestic banking system could remain insulated from international markets. Throughout its engagement with offshore banking, Germany's exposure to the Eurodollar markets took place outside the country, mostly in London and Luxembourg. This distance to the Eurodollar markets is as much the result of design as of chronology. Germany was, compared to Britain anyway, a latecomer to large-scale offshore money creation. Although German banks had provided liquidity to the developing offshore markets in the 1960s, the *Bundesbank*'s conservative outlook on financial innovation tempered Germany's engagement in the growing Eurodollar markets.

This situation changed substantial only in the late 1990s when the introduction of the euro allowed *Deutsche Bank* to develop a global quasi-monopoly for foreign exchange business between the euro and the US dollar.[14] It was then also *Deutsche Bank* (and to a certain degree the *Landesbanken*) which made German state power vulnerable to the global financial crisis. However, despite its sizeable engagement in the Eurodollar markets, Germany had successfully ring-fenced its domestic banking system from the potentially destructive forces of offshore banking.

Offshore money creation happened outside the state. As a result, the political and economic consequences of the crisis were limited compared to Britain. *Deutsche Bank*, the only remaining Eurodollar bank in Germany, came out of the crisis economically weakened, but politically unscathed.

In short, in Germany offshore finance plays a secondary role in the tax and bank bargains. It simply sweetens the deal for the money elite. Offshore tax planning allows them to reduce their tax burden and offshore money creation opened-up profits for the country's big banks. The state moulded the engagement with offshore finance such that it leveraged some of its benefits, while shielding state power. This stands in contrast to the time of the Weimar Republic when offshore finance was a means for the money elite to distance their wealth from the *Funktionselite*. The ability of the state to mitigate the effects of offshore finance may change over time.

Britain's approach to balancing the benefits of offshore finance against its risks was fundamentally different. Here we can observe historically a near-identity between the economic and political elites that make up the state. A state shaped by the identity between political and economic elites meant that borrower and lender, taxman and taxpayer were identical too.[15] This very close relationship between the state, its financiers, and taxpayers established in

---

[14] Author's interview with banker, Munich, November 2018.
[15] Macdonald 2003.

Britain a smooth and stable cycle of money, tax, and debt that should last from the late seventeenth century to today. Careful elite reproduction preserved a high degree of homogeneity within Britain's institutional association of rule. The homogeneity thus remains present even as the state becomes more inclusive towards members of the lower classes with the arrival of mass democracy and the first Labour government after the end of World War II.

Nevertheless, tensions between the broadening political elite and the old economic elites arose. Compared to Germany, the post-war tax and bank bargains were less aligned with the interests of an economic elite rooted in finance. The more strongly tax-based financing of the welfare state and tax policies in general were firmly redistributive. Moreover, bank regulations and the growing importance of US American finance undermined the financial elites' traditional way of making money. In this context, offshore finance became a common project of the political and economic elites. For the political elite, it was a means of keeping capital engaged in financing the welfare state. For the economic elites it was a means of recreating the dominance over money creation and taxation they had lost with the advent of mass democracy. Together, the political and economic elites enjoyed the fact that offshore money creation maintained the state's international ambitions beyond its currency's diminished power. They hence worked together to make Britain the heartland of offshore finance.

From the British perspective, the offshore credit markets worked smoothly. Running the offshore system from the City of London worked in the state's favour. It therefore took limited measures to mitigate the effects of offshore finance on state power. The Bank of England, when first allowing offshore banking in the City of London, made it clear that, should the business go wrong, the banks would not be bailed out. To make its point, the Bank of England did not impose reserve requirements on Eurodollar transactions. Reserve requirements, they argued, indicated the possibility for bailout in case the Eurodollar business caused problems—an impression that the Bank of England was adamant to avoid. When the offshore markets finally froze in 2007–09, London-based banks had become so exposed that the Bank of England could not stick to its word. The banks were bailed out. The fallout for the British state was enormous. Across time, offshore finance never left the power of the British state unaffected. Rather, Britain reaped the full benefits in good times and paid accordingly when the bad times finally hit.

Brazil's approach to mitigating the effects to offshore finance has more similarities with Germany's than with Britain's. Brazil's regulatory laws and social security systems intend to mitigate the most harmful effects of offshore finance on state power. However, what sets Brazil apart from all other cases is that the state is contested in ways the other three are not. The institutional association of rule has been marked since the country's independence in 1821 by a fundamental tension between the rural economic elites, spread out along the country's immense coastline, and the urban central political elites. The arrival of mass democracy did broaden the urban central political elites but did not change the tense relationship with the rural oligarchs. Historically, the economic elites were unwilling to contribute to the central state's finances through either tax or debt. Here it was the exploitation of land and slaves that kept the need for credit money limited and allowed a modern state to develop that was more of a predator state than a tax or debt state. The glue that held the political and economic elites together was, from the beginning of the twentieth century, government-subsidized credit. Without tax income on the other side of the balance sheet, high inflation became a constant in Brazilian politics. It took well into the middle of the twentieth century to establish a smooth and stable cycle of money, tax, and debt. However, banking remained suppressed. Foreign lenders filled the void. Foreign debt became a central element of the Brazilian state's strategy to finance itself. Brazil was a debt state before it became a tax state.

Then, in the 1960s and 1970s, offshore money creation came along. It was a game-changer. Brazil could borrow in London at negative real interest rates. The Brazilian state could finance its politics through credit from foreigners, but at better conditions than with regular foreign debt. The Eurodollar became a complement to the country's small cycle of money, tax, and debt. Therefore, the military government set out to make the Eurodollar system work for Brazil. It passed regulations that allowed Brazilian banks to engage in cross-border business, but not in interbank lending. These measures helped to soften the impact of the 1982 Latin American debt crisis relative to Mexico.[16] It did not, however, protect the power of the state. With the Eurodollar being an intrinsic part of the domestic cycle of money, tax, and debt, the Brazilian state reinforced its effort to make offshore finance work in its favour. A combination of foreign reserves, swap lines, and capital controls now mitigate the effects of Brazil's exposure to offshore finance. Compared to 1982, the economic fallout of the global financial crisis was indeed mitigated and did not have major political repercussions. Nonetheless, the financing of large, employment-generating corporations, both publicly

[16] Alvarez 2020.

and privately owned, remains dependent on preferential offshore liquidity. Therefore, despite Brazil's regulatory grip on offshore banking, offshore money creation still involves the risk of undermining Brazilian state power.

Mexico, like Britain, never seriously attempted to mitigate offshore finance. From the beginning, offshore money creation seemed to work in the interest of the Mexican state. It provided—at preferential conditions—liquidity not available at home. Backed by oil revenue, Mexico could lend in London, even at negative interest rates. The Eurodollar system provided the resources needed to rule through privilege and partnership even as that system had become economically unsustainable. In the 1960s and 1970s, Mexico went full in, reaping the benefits of offshore finance. Mexico's banks, state, and state-owned companies all became exposed to offshore finance. With no meaningful mitigation measures in place, the 1982 and 1994 financial crises effectively destroyed state power. Subsequently, Mexico established the most effective protection against the fallouts of offshore finance. It withdrew from the Eurodollar markets.

With defensive measures in place in Germany and Brazil and the withdrawal of Mexico from the Eurodollar markets, there are instances when offshore finance left the power of these states unaffected. In a more consequential way, mitigating the effects of offshore finance on state power is what made offshore tax planning less challenging to the state's ability to finance its politics than expected. All four countries effectively hedged against harmful effects through shifting from direct to indirect taxation and social security contributions, law enforcement, and multilateral initiatives. Britain and Germany were so effective in that strategy that, combined with the politics of the invisible, offshore tax planning even enhanced state power. It spares the state visibly taking sides in the conflict over how to distribute the tax burden across different groups of taxpayers, while systematically aligning with the interests of wealthy individuals and large firms.

Weighing the benefits against the potential costs of offshore finance, states may strive to make offshore finance work to their advantage. They mould the encounter with offshore finance such that it provides the wealthy classes and itself with the benefits of offshore while protecting state power. It is important, however, to emphasize that the elite constellation and the tax and bank bargains change within a country across time. Take Germany and Brazil as examples. The two countries are, in the contemporary phase, comparatively successful in making offshore finance work in the state's interest. However, both countries were less successful in the past. To determine the effect of offshore finance on state power, we must, as Skinner[17] suggests, consider the state's historical and geographical contingencies.

### 3  Institutions matter

In conjunction, the theoretical arguments and empirical analysis reveal that the relationship between offshore finance and state power is not straightforward. They also demonstrate that offshore banking is more consequential for state power than offshore tax planning.

Offshore finance provides preferential liquidity—access to money created not available at home, at cheaper prices, in combination with the opportunity to minimize taxes, and under a legal framework that is more lenient towards debtors—and the politics of the invisible—the opportunity to implement contradictory policies without being questioned about it. Outside of financial crises, preferential liquidity and the politics of the invisible can strengthen state power. During times of crises, and in their aftermath, severely reduced offshore liquidity and the exposure of the politics of the invisible can unfold destructive forces on state power.

At the same time, states can mitigate these effects. Any mitigation strategy involves a trade-off between reaping the full benefits of offshore finance and reducing the potential risks. Which balance a specific country strikes, and how successfully, depends on two elements. It depends on the position of the wealthy in the domestic bank and tax bargains today relative to the past. It also depends on the state's ability to ring-fence its tax and banking systems from the fallouts of offshore finance. These findings challenge the literature on offshore finance in three central aspects.

First, the empirical assessment of the relationship between offshore finance and state power questions the literature's strong focus on offshore tax planning to the detriment of offshore banking. Contrary to conventional wisdom, offshore banking is the core mechanism that links offshore finance and state power.

Second, the book's findings challenge accounts that maintain that offshore finance robs the state of power. Offshore finance can enhance and limit state power. Moreover, domestic institutions can mitigate the power-undermining effects of offshore finance. These findings help to develop a more nuanced understanding of the relationship between offshore finance and state power.

---

[17] Skinner 2009.

However, they are also relevant for an understanding of why states have been reluctant to effectively regulate offshore finance. It is not so much a matter of capacity, but one of political will. Money creation, onshore as well as offshore, is a shared power between the state and banks. The state therefore has its own vested interests in offshore finance.

Finally, the book supports the argument that offshore finance does not affect the power of all states' in equal measure. The historical analysis revealed how important the constellation of political and economic elites as well as the tax and bank bargains are in explaining a specific state's relationship with the off-shore world. These findings reinforce arguments that account for historically grown domestic institutions and politics when analysing the global economy.[18] At the same time, they challenge accounts that see variation in a country's structural characteristics—size, economic openness, proximity to offshore financial centres, and level of development. As the case studies demonstrated, these structural variables have difficulties explaining the varying outcomes of offshore finance on state power between countries and within them across time. Institutions and politics, however, can.

## 4  Beyond the money view

The book has explicitly taken a money view on the state. Money, I argued is the glue that holds state power and offshore finance together. Consequently, the effect of offshore finance on state power has been framed in terms of the institutional association of rule's ability to centralize and mobilize resources to finance its political goals. This notion of state power emphasizes the state's financial autonomy over its ability to make others do what it wants.[19] It reflects that the state's capacity to mobilize, centralize, and use resources in an autonomous way is a precondition for it to exert influence. Furthermore, the notion highlights the relational nature of power. It is grounded in the premise that politics is about the conflict over different groups' interests. These conflicts are reflected in and shaped by historically grown institutions which inescapably—but not unchangeably—privilege some interests over others. This notion of state power deliberately puts a spotlight on material dimensions. That focus is warranted, I argued, because the shared power of money creation and the role of taxation herein has received insufficient attention in the study of international political economy.

---

[18]  see Hall and Taylor 1996; Swank 2003; 2016.
[19]  Cohen 2013.

Naturally, such a focused perspective misses out on crucial aspects of reality. It disregards, for instance, how offshore finance affects people outside of the institutional association of rule. In this last section of the book, I therefore briefly lift the gaze beyond the money view and discuss the implications of offshore finance on democratic politics.

A notion of state power focused on the state's ability to finance its politics has its limits. These limits are most obvious regarding offshore money laundering. In Germany and Brazil economic and political actors systematically used off-shore financial services to cover up political and economic crimes. Of course, money laundering is a practice that is much older than the offshore world.[20] Yet, its offshore embodiment, obviously, depends on money flowing through offshore financial centres. With its propensity to differentiate between residents and non-residents, to have little regulation and taxation, and to provide statistically invisible services, offshore finance is attractive for those who made fortunes through drug trafficking, tax fraud, corruption, or plain robbery.

The re-introduction of illicit money into the licit economy is a precondition for the criminal to enjoy her wealth. She cannot pay with suspicious money for the world-class education of her children in Britain or for that nice beach-side apartment in Rio de Janeiro. Yet, using offshore financial services to launder money requires an important level of legal and accounting sophistication. The resulting higher transaction costs lead to a crowding out of small amounts of ill-gotten funds. Offshore services are particularly relevant for so-called 'high-end money laundering' involving large sums whitewashed through the professional and financial services sectors.[21] Therefore, offshore money laundering is often related to grand corruption and organized transnational crime.[22] These large amounts of ill-gotten funds accumulate on the asset side of banks' balance sheets and hence balance offshore banks' credit-money creation. They become an integral part of offshore banking. And yet, from the perspective of state power as advanced in this book, offshore money laundering simply does not affect the state's ability to finance its political goals.

In Germany, offshore money laundering allowed conservative circles, especially industrialists from the Rhineland, to retain a stronghold within the institutional association of rule as the *Funktionselite* broadened with the advent of post-war democracy. In Brazil, offshore money laundering is a means of the economic elite to influence the shape of that political programme beyond what

[20] Gelemerova 2009.
[21] NCA 2018, 39.
[22] Sharman 2011; 2017.

is constitutionally possible. In democracies this state of affairs cannot be the end of the story.

Weber's notion of the modern state as a *Herrschaftsverband* highlights that the ruling elite's power is not absolute. The ruler can only rule if considered legitimate by the ruled.[23] Yet, as Thompson[24] emphasizes the state cannot serve the interests of all groups of society at the same time. It has to side with some over others. The quest for legitimacy is therefore innate to democratic politics. Offshore money laundering does not undermine the power of the state, it bereaves the state of legitimacy. This effect, however, is not limited to the abuses of offshore financial services. Since their inception, offshore financial services promoted the free movement of money across borders.[25] The freely flowing money peaked with the offshore dollar markets integrating into one global market in the late 1980s and early1990s. Offshore money markets appear to be essentially capitalist. They efficiently create liquidity through competition, free of state intervention. Instead, the analysis demonstrated that offshore finance propels into the twenty-first century historically grown oligopolistic and oligarchic structures, which democracy and free market economics were supposed to upend. This process has been aided by the state.

In all cases the institutional associations of rule have supported the use of offshore financial services. At the very least, they have looked the other way. In consequence, the state systematically sided with one group—the wealthy and large corporations—over everyone else, including small and medium-sized companies. Counterintuitively, the politics of the invisible was less pronounced in Brazil and Mexico, the more exclusive democratic states. Germany and Britain are more inclusive towards the lower classes and are more deeply involved in the politics of the invisible. The inclusiveness of the institutional association of rule decreases the dominance of the economic elites within the state, heightening the conflict with capital. Offshore financial services help to lessen this conflict. The diversion via offshore financial centres is less necessary in more exclusive democratic countries such as Brazil and Mexico. Here, political institutions are formally democratic, but opinion- and decision-making are organized through private informal networks rather than parties and parliament.[26] Taxation of the wealthy and money creation remains off the political agenda. Economic elites can still more easily shape political

---

[23] Weber 1994.
[24] Thompson 2010.
[25] Palan, Murphy, and Chavagneux 2010.
[26] Selee 2011.

decisions over tax, debt, and spending in line with their interests. More inclusive democratic states do not put a limit on the politics of the invisible. They beget it.

The systematic privileging of the interests of one group in society over everyone else is a larger threat to the state's legitimacy in more inclusive democratic states. The governments of these states cannot be seen corrupting democratic politics and furthering inequality. Consequently, these governments reach for the politics of the invisible. It has its roots in British gentlemanly capitalism.[27] Building on the infrastructure of empire, the economic elites set out to preserve offshore the influence that they began to lose onshore. To protect the basis of their influence—property—the financiers resorted to a politics of the invisible. Except for land, most of their wealth and earnings were invisible by nature.[28] The trust then helped to obscure ownership even of land and industrial plants, usually visible from afar. The trust also helped to move wealth offshore without having to relocate the assets physically.[29] In Germany and Britain, the more inclusive democratic states, the politics of the invisible obscured the growing divergences between nominal and effective tax rates[30] and the real distribution of costs and benefits of money creation. Consequently, it undermines voters' ability to build preferences based on the actual situation.

Popular ways to capture the offshore world are a product of the politics of the invisible. The mainstream account of offshore finance alleges that there is something sinister about it. The commonly used language around offshore finance reflects that well. There is talk of 'dirty' or 'dark' money that accumulates in shadow banks. There is a system of tax havens which are, according to Zucman[31] a 'scourge' on the international economy. Thanks to the so created 'Moneyland', Bullough[32] informs us, the 'thieves and crooks now rule the world'. These accounts create dichotomies: the notion of 'dirty' or 'dark' money implies an existence of 'clean' or 'clear' money; the notion of shadow banks implies that somewhere at the other end of the spectrum are respectable banks that do not dread the daylight; the scourge of tax havens implies that if we only closed them down, the international economy would somehow be free of trouble; the notion that offshore finance has led to crooks and thieves *now* ruling the world, evokes a better past, when upright men (there are rarely any women populating this better past) took care of the state's affairs. As this book

[27] Cain and Hopkins 2015.
[28] Ibid.
[29] Harrington 2016b.
[30] Zucman 2014; Tørsløv, Wier, and Zucman 2018.
[31] Zucman 2015.
[32] Bullough 2018.

has shown, the dichotomy between an onshore world and an offshore world, if it ever existed, certainly ceased to exist when the volume of offshore created US dollars surpassed that of the onshore created US dollars in the late 1980s. False dichotomies are unhelpful in analytical and in political terms.

Take Brazil as an example. It is unlikely that, without offshore finance, Brazil's 'economic miracle' (1968–74) would have happened. Likewise, without offshore finance, the *Lava Jato* corruption scandal would not have developed its epic proportions. To govern offshore finance in the interest of the common good, those inherent tensions must be acknowledged. As the world economy outside the United States runs on the Eurodollar, and the Eurodollar is created offshore, we cannot 'simply' do away with it.

Moving forward, research on offshore finance must address the centrality of the Eurodollar markets. Loved by bankers and tolerated by governments, the Euromarkets grew until they were, possibly, probably, bigger than the onshore financial system. If offshore is the new normal, it raises the empirical question about the true size of the Eurodollar system. It may well be, as the interviewees claimed, that our current macroeconomic and banking statistics capture the smaller piece of the pie. If that is indeed the case, the current governance system—ranging from the OECD BEPS project to the BIS financial stability monitoring to national monetary policies—likewise focuses its attention on the smaller piece of the pie. Offshore tax planning practices have become more visible in recent decades. The Eurodollar markets, on the other hand, remain largely invisible. Here too it is time to meet the politics of the invisible with attempts to achieve transparency.

# A cautionary tale about quantitative data on offshore finance

The reason for offshore to exist is to make financial transactions invisible. Therefore, analysing offshore transactions means to reverse-document what has been made invisible—a daunting task. In essence, researchers choose one of three different approaches to deal with this challenge. One group of scholars works with formal models and applies those models to individual countries. The second group of scholars estimates the total global scope of offshore finance and then apportions parts of that global total to individual countries.[1] The third group of scholars works based on interviews, literature review, or archival work.[2] Each of these approaches has contributed to a better understanding of the offshore phenomenon. However, they also come with important limitations. First, the formal models only cover a single aspect of offshore finance, for instance corporate taxation or foreign investment, leaving out all other—equally vital—aspects of the phenomenon. To remedy that problem, the second approach combines different macroeconomic data sets ranging from national accounts data, over investment data, to tax and banking data. This approach provides a more sophisticated view of offshore finance in its entirety but creates a second problem. For each data set the authors use, the underlying concepts and their statistical expressions are contested. Moreover, the quality of the data is compromised precisely because of the offshore phenomenon.[3] The IMF, for instance, estimates that 30 to 40 per cent of global foreign direct investment is 'phantom investment' in offshore financial centres.[4] Combining different sources of quantitative data creates a comprehensive perspective on the offshore world, but it also leads to combining conceptual and statistical shortcomings. Qualitative approaches, on the other hand, come with their own problems. Most importantly in our context, they cannot tell us how big the phenomenon is. Yet, it is impossible to make a judgement about the impact of offshore finance on state power without knowing, at least roughly, how big the phenomenon is. The quantitative estimates presented in this book exclusively serve this purpose: to have a rough idea about the size of the phenomenon, in comparative perspective. The estimates do not and cannot contribute to the debate about how best to quantify the demand for offshore financial services.

The estimates are based on the BIS locational banking statistics. The advantage of bank data over other macroeconomic statistics is its balance sheet approach. Each economic interaction between economic actors in a specific state and an offshore financial centre, whether it is trade or investment, real or virtual, of legal or illegal origin, is recorded through the related financial transaction of the involved banks. That is, rather than dealing with contested concepts and their statistical expression, bank data record how money changes its location on banks' balance sheets as cross-border economic activity unfolds. Moreover,

---

[1] See e.g. Henry 2012; Alstadsæter, Johannesen, and Zucman 2018; Tørsløv, Wier, and Zucman 2018.
[2] See e.g. Palan 1998; Palan, Murphy, and Chavagneux 2010; Altamura 2017; Braun, Krampf, and Murau 2020.
[3] Linsi and Mügge 2019.
[4] Damgaard, Elkjaer, and Johannesen 2019.

building on central bank data, the BIS statistics are of equal quality for all four case studies. Finally, the BIS has a coherent definition of what offshore money is. It distinguishes two types of Euromarkets: pure offshore and round-tripping. In pure offshore transactions 'the residence of the placer of funds, the residence of the borrower of funds, the booking location of the deposit and the loan, and the jurisdiction governing the transaction are all outside the US' as He and McCauley[5] put it. However, the funds may still flow through the United States' banking system.[6] Round-tripping means that residents of the United States deposit US dollars with banks outside the country, who then lend the money back to residents in the United States. For the most part of the history of Euromarkets, pure offshore transactions were significantly more important than round-tripping.[7] This book focuses on pure offshore transactions.

Obviously, the BIS data come with limitations. To begin with, as with all data sets dealing with offshore finance, the question is which jurisdiction counts as an offshore centre and which does not. The BIS classifies a number of countries as offshore financial centres, but the list excludes important European offshore centres such as Switzerland, the Netherlands, or Luxembourg. The estimates provided in this book use the BIS list and adds to it the missing European jurisdictions identified as offshore financial centres in Garcia-Bernado et al. (see below).[8] Besides the question of who is and who is not an offshore financial centre, another shortcoming of the BIS data is that they miss out on off-balance sheet transactions. For instance, fiduciary funds and trusts are two asset-holding structures that are legally off a bank's balance sheet. However, both structures are valued vehicles for individual and corporate offshore investments.[9] Likewise, the locational banking statistics exclude the bond market, which is covered by the BIS international debt statistics (IDS). The BIS IDS do not allow, however, a distinction to be made between domestic and foreign bonds and therefore cannot help in quantifying offshore financial services. In addition to these statistical intricacies, it is important also to see the numbers for what they are in a historical context. The German, Brazilian, and Mexican cases demonstrate that the contemporary level of exposure to offshore finance is a snapshot, not a static, universal fact. The BIS data provide us with a coherent idea of the face of the offshore system while being oblivious to its underbelly. From the perspective of state power, these quantitative intricacies are of secondary importance only. Beyond a general sense of the scale of the uses and abuses of offshore financial services through quantitative data, it is first and foremost the interview results and historical analyses that help to determine the effect of offshore finance on state power in the case study countries.

I designed the interviews as open-ended expert interviews structured around two sets of questions. One set of questions was the same for all interviews, and the other set was specifically tailored to the expertise of the respective interviewee. This approach allowed identifying recurring patterns, while covering the different aspects of offshore finance. All interviewees had everyday experience with offshore finance, be it as lawyers, bankers, wealth mangers, policymakers, or civil society activists. I conducted the interviews between November 2015 and July 2019 in the four case study countries. To ensure that individual insights are visible as such, I attribute statements to individual interviewees in anonymized

---

[5] He and McCauley 2012, 36.
[6] The same logic applies to other offshore created currencies.
[7] He and McCauley 2010.
[8] Garcia-Bernardo et al. 2017.
[9] Zucman 2015; Harrington 2016a.

form. If certain themes or arguments came up in all or most interviews within a case study country, I report them in the text as 'interview results' or attribute them to 'the interviewees'.

## 1  List of offshore financial centres

Table A.1 lists offshore financial centres, in alphabetical order. The list is based on BIS locational banking statistics and completed by European offshore financial centres as identified by Garcia-Bernardo et al.[10]

**Table A.1**  List of offshore financial centres

| Caribbean offshore | Asian offshore | European offshore | Other offshore | Complemented European offshore[11] |
|---|---|---|---|---|
| Aruba | Hong Kong | Gibraltar | Bahrain | Cyprus |
| Bahamas | Macao | Guernsey | Lebanon | Ireland |
| Barbados | Singapore | Isle of Man | Samoa | Liechtenstein |
| Bermuda | | Jersey | Vanuatu | Luxembourg |
| Cayman Islands | | | | Malta |
| County of Curacao | | | | Switzerland |
| Netherlands Antilles | | | | |
| Panama | | | | |
| West Indies United Kingdom | | | | |

## 2  The special case of Britain

Unlike any other country, Britain is at the same time a large economy with domestic economic actors using offshore financial services elsewhere and one that offers offshore financial services to foreigners. This double identity as a user and provider of offshore financial services makes Britain a crucial case—and a tricky one. Some researchers argue that because Britain is a central node in the international web of offshore financial centres, it should be studied in the same vein as classical offshore financial centres such as Switzerland, Luxembourg, or Ireland.[12] Most others who go through the pain of determining which countries are offshore financial centres and which are not, do not include Britain in their lists.[13] Both approaches are reasonable but flawed in the context of this book, for they would create biases in the data. I therefore work with a middle ground. I consider Britain an offshore banking centre, but not a tax haven. Despite low corporate income tax rates, I do not consider Britain a tax haven, since its tax rules are not systematically different for residents and non-residents and—though large—the financial sector remains but one important sector in the British economy. Offshore tax services are not as crucial for the British economy as they are, for instance, for Ireland. This approach reflects Britain's important role in the

[10] Garcia-Bernardo et al. 2017.
[11] Garcia-Bernado et al (2017) also include Monaco, but Monaco does not report to the BIS and is hence not included in my estimates.
[12] Garcia-Bernardo et al. 2017.
[13] See Dharmapala and Hines 2009; Johannesen and Zucman 2014; Gravelle 2015.

Euromarkets, while keeping it apart from the classical tax havens. Although I consider Britain an offshore banking centre, I do not include it in the list of offshore counterparts for transactions by German, Mexican, and Brazilian economic actors for the BIS data cannot be disaggregated by sector. Therefore, treating Britain as an offshore counterpart for the other case study countries would mean labelling all economic interaction between them, including trade, as offshore transactions. However, Britain's financial sector is only one of several economic sectors and even within the financial sector not all transactions are off-shore services. Given the overall size of the British economy, this approach would create a considerable bias towards overestimating offshore services. Given that the City of London's status as an important offshore financial centre is uncontroversial in the literature, a rough and biased quantitative estimate would not add any value to the analysis.

## 3  Estimating overall exposure to offshore financial services

The BIS locational banking statistics allow us to determine the cross-border flow of money between reporting institutions in the reporting country (i.e. Britain, Germany, Mexico, and Brazil) and reporting institutions in counterparty countries (i.e. the countries listed in Table A.1). Reporting institutions include banks, non-bank financial institutions, non-financial corporations and the non-financial sectors (i.e. government and households). I refer to all bank and financial sector institutions as banks to facilitate the analysis. With these data, we can see the financial flows between, say, Germany and offshore banks. German claims towards offshore financial centres represent assets that German economic actors hold offshore. German liabilities towards offshore financial centres represent debt that German economic actors issued offshore. Offshore assets may be held offshore, for instance, to avoid taxation. Debt, on the other hand, may be issued offshore because in the country of residence, banks would or could not lend to the economic actor in need of money. However, offshore debt may also be used for intra-corporate financing and hence be used again to plan taxes. As a result, offshore claims and liabilities affect the power of the state differently, but collectively. A country's offshore exposure is thus the sum of its claims and liabilities towards offshore financial centres.

## 4  Currency denomination

To be considered a part of the Eurosystem, a transaction must fulfil two conditions: it must be denominated in a foreign currency, and it must happen between reporting institutions from the case study country and an offshore financial centre. However, the BIS locational statistics do not allow a breakdown of bilateral financial flows by currency. The estimate therefore needs to proceed in two steps. First, I use the BIS locational banking statistics data to determine the share of foreign-currency denominated cross-border transactions between the case study country and the rest of the world. Second, I apply this share to transactions between the case study country and offshore financial centres.

## 5  Estimating the potential tax loss

Income taxation in all case study countries is a complicated affair with different rates depending on the type and volume of income and a long list of exceptions to the rule. Given the above-described purpose of the estimate, I aim for a straightforward, transparent, and simple approach. This meant not building on existing more sophisticated approaches that also come with greater methodological challenges. This includes the insightful work of Alstadsæter et al.[14] which estimates the amount of money held offshore by individuals as a means to improve existing measurements of inequality; the study of Tørsløv et al.[15], which estimates the amount of profit-shifting based on macroeconomic data from tax haven countries; the work of Crivelli et al.[16] and of Cobham and Janský,[17] which estimate profit-shifting via tax differentials between tax havens and high tax countries based on International Monetary Fund (IMF) data. What I do have in common with those more sophisticated approaches is that my estimate applies an average tax rate between corporate and individual income tax rates to the assets held offshore as reported to the BIS. This approach is based on three assumptions. The first assumption is that all money that is offshore is not taxed at all. How well this assumption reflects reality differs from country to country. In all cases, tax lawyers maintained that it is more accurate for individual than for corporate tax planning. The second assumption is that all money that is offshore would be taxed at the full applicable rate if onshore. Again, it is unlikely that this is the case as there are plenty of onshore tax planning opportunities, including sub-national tax havens. The third assumption is about the applicable tax rate. Given that different taxpayers (individuals and corporations) hold different asset classes offshore, it is difficult to determine which tax rate would apply onshore. Therefore, most estimates, including mine, work with an average tax rate. Taken together, estimates of tax loss related to offshoring tend to be biased towards overestimating the loss.

## 6  Money laundering

It is impossible to tell, based on the BIS data, which of the reported transactions are of legal and which of illegal origin. One reason is that money laundering is a 'derivative crime'.[18] It depends on the laws that regulate the underlying activity. As the law changes regarding these activities, the nature of the money changes, too. For instance, paying bribes to foreign businesses was, until the late 1990s, considered a business expense in many OECD countries. It was thus not only legal, but also tax deductible.[19] Once the practice was outlawed, the funds became illicit and, if still paid, needed to be laundered. The combination of the obscure nature of offshore financial services and the illusiveness of money laundering makes the quality of quantitative data on the matter questionable. To build on it would mean furthering a 'politics of numbers', to quote Andreas,[20] rather than to further scientific enquiry. My assessment of offshore money laundering therefore exclusively builds on qualitative data and considers offshore money laundering a part of offshore banking.

[14] Alstadsæter, Johannesen, and Zucman 2018.
[15] Tørsløv, Wier, and Zucman 2018.
[16] Crivelli, De Mooij, and Keen 2015.
[17] Cobham and Janský 2017.
[18] Sharman 2011, 28.
[19] Sharman 2017, 1–21.
[20] Andreas 2008.

# Bibliography

Aboites, Luis. 2003. *Excepciones y privilegios: modernización tributaria y centralización en México, 1922–1972.* 1st ed. México: El Colegio de México, Centro de Estudios Históricos.

Alami, Ilias. 2018. Money Power of Capital and Production of 'New State Spaces': A View from the Global South. *New Political Economy* 23 (4): 512–529.

Alami, Ilias. 2019. Taming Foreign Exchange Derivatives Markets? Speculative Finance and Class Relations in Brazil. *Development and Change* 50 (5): 1310–1341.

Allen, Bill. 2013. *International Liquidity and the Financial Crisis.* Cambridge; New York: Cambridge University Press.

Alstadsæter, Annette, Niels Johannesen, and Gabriel Zucman. 2018. Who Owns the Wealth in Tax Havens? Macro Evidence and Implications for Global Inequality. *Journal of Public Economics* 162: 89–100.

Alstadsæter, Annette, Niels Johannesen, and Gabriel Zucman. 2019. Tax Evasion and Inequality. *American Economic Review* 109 (6): 2073–2103.

Alston, Philip. 2018. *Statement on Visit to the United Kingdom, by Professor Philip Alston, United Nations Special Rapporteur on extreme poverty and human rights.* Geneva: United Nations Office of the High Commissioner of Human Rights. Available at <https://www.ohchr.org/Documents/Issues/Poverty/EOM_GB_16Nov2018.pdf>. Accessed 19 October 2022.

Altamura, Carlo Edoardo. 2017. *European Banks and the Rise of International Finance: The Post-Bretton Woods Era.* 1st ed. Routledge explorations in economic history. London; New York: Routledge, Taylor & Francis Group.

Alvarez, Sebastian. 2015. The Mexican Debt Crisis Redux: International Interbank Markets and Financial Crisis, 1977–1982. *Financial History Review* 22 (1): 79–105.

Alvarez, Sebastian. 2020. *International Banking and Financial Fragility: The Contrasting Experience of Brazil and Mexico in the Lead-up to the 1982 Crisis.* Oxford Economic and Social History Working Papers. Oxford: Oxford University. Available at <https://www.economics.ox.ac.uk/materials/working_papers/5247/176januaryalvarez.pdf>. Accessed 31 March 2020.

Andreas, Peter. 2008. *Sex, Drugs, and Body Counts.* 1st ed. Cornell University Press. Available at <http://www.jstor.org/stable/10.7591/j.ctt7zg8b>.

Antzoulatos, Angelos A. 2002. Arbitrage Opportunities on the Road to Stabilization and Reform. *Journal of International Money and Finance* 21 (7): 1013–1034.

Aubry, Manon, and Thomas Dauphin. 2017. *Opening the Vaults: The Use of Tax Havens by Europe's Biggest Banks.* Oxfam International. Available at <https://www-cdn.oxfam.org/s3fs-public/bp-opening-vaults-banks-tax-havens-270317-en_0.pdf>. Accessed 8 June 2021.

Augar, Philip. 2008. *The Death of Gentlemanly Capitalism: The Rise and Fall of London's Investment Banks.* London: Penguin Books.

Avdjiev, Stefan, Michael Chui, and Huyon Song Shin. 2014. Non-financial Corporations from Emerging Market Economies and Capital Flows. *BIS Quarterly Review* 2014 (4): 67–77.

Averbug, Andre. 2002. The Brazilian Economy in 1994–1999: From the Real Plan to Inflation Targets. *The World Economy* 25 (7): 925–944.

Bach, Stefan. 2016. *Unsere Steuern: wer zahlt? Wie viel? Wofür?* Frankfurt/Main: Westend.

Bach, Stefan. 2019. *100 Years of the Modern German Tax System: Foundation, Reforms, and Challenges.* 46, 47, 48. DIW Weekly Report. Berlin: Deutsches Institut für Wirtschaftsforschung. Available at <https://www.diw.de/documents/publikationen/73/diw_01.c.698419.de/dwr-19-46-1.pdf>. Accessed 9 June 2021.

Baer, Werner, and Joseph L. Love. 2009. Introduction. In *Brazil under Lula*, edited by Joseph L. Love and Werner Baer, 1–5. New York: Palgrave Macmillan US. Available at <http://link.springer.com/10.1057/9780230618374_1>. Accessed 12 May 2021.

Banco Central do Brasil. 2017. *Brazilian Assets Abroad.* Brasilia: Banco Central do Brasil. Available at <http://www4.bcb.gov.br/rex/CBE/Ingl/CBE2013Results.asp>. Accessed 22 January 2018.

Banco de México. 2014. *Financial System Report.* Mexico City.

Banco de México. 2018. *The History of Coins and Banknotes in Mexico.* Mexico City, D.F.: Banco de México. Available at <http://www.banxico.org.mx/billetes-y-monedas/material-educativo/basico/%7B2FF1527B-0B07-AC7F-25B8-4950866E166A%7D.pdf>. Accessed 5 June 2018.

Bartels, Charlotte. 2017. Top Incomes in Germany, 1871–2013. WID world Working Paper Series. Berlin: Deutsches Institut für Wirtschaftsforschng.

Basinger, Scott J., and Mark Hallerberg. 2004. Remodelling the Competition for Capital: How Domestic Politics Erases the Race to the Bottom. *American Political Science Review* 98 (2): 261–276.

Berenskoetter, Felix. 2016. *Concepts in World Politics.* Thousand Oaks, CA: Sage Publishing.

Berghoff, Hartmut. 2018. 'Organised irresponsibility'? The Siemens Corruption Scandal of the 1990s and 2000s. *Business History* 60 (3): 423–445.

Berghoff, Hartmut, and Ingo Köhler. 2007. Redesigning a Class of its Own: Social and Human Capital Formation in the German Banking Elite, 1870–1990. *Financial History Review* 14 (1): 63.

Bianchi, A., and R. Braga. 2005. Brazil: The Lula Government and Financial Globalization. *Social Forces* 83 (4): 1745–1762.

Binder, Andrea. 2019. All Exclusive: The Politics of Offshore Finance in Mexico. *Review of International Political Economy* 26 (2): 313–336.

Binder, Andrea. 2022. Relational Claims: Offshore Dollar and Sovereign Debt. In *Capital Claims: Power and Global Finance*, edited by B. Braun and K. Koddenbrock. New York: Routledge.

Black, Susan, and Anella Munro. 2010. Why Issue Bonds Offshore? BIS Working Papers. Bern: Bank for International Settlements. Available at <https://www.bis.org/publ/work334.pdf>. Accessed 12 November 2014.

Blanco, Luisa R., and Cynthia L. Rogers. 2014. Are Tax Havens Good Neighbours? FDI Spillovers and Developing Countries. *The Journal of Development Studies* 50 (4): 530–540.

Blouin, Jennifer, and Leslie Robinson. 2019. Double Counting Accounting: How Much Profit of Multinational Enterprises Is Really in Tax Havens? SSRN Electronic Journal. Available at <https://www.ssrn.com/abstract=3491451>. Accessed 6 April 2021.

Bonney, Richard. 1999. Introduction. In *The Rise of the Fiscal State in Europe, c. 1200–1815*, edited by Richard Bonney, 1–17. Oxford: Oxford University Press.

Borio, Claudio, and Piti Disyatat. 2011. Global Imbalances and the Financial Crisis: Link or No Link? BIS Working Papers. Bern: Bank for International Settlements. Available at <https://www.bis.org/publ/work346.pdf>. Accessed 7 May 2020.

Braun, Benjamin, Arie Krampf, and Steffen Murau. 2020. Financial Globalization as Positive Integration: Monetary Technocrats and the Eurodollar Market in the 1970s. *Review of International Political Economy* special issue: 794–819.

Brooks, Richard. 2014. *The Great Tax Robbery. How Britain Became a Tax Haven for Fat Cats and Big Business.* London: Oneworld.

Browne, James, and David Phillips. 2010. Tax and Benefit Reforms Under Labour. 2010 Election Briefing Note No 1. Institute for Fiscal Studies. Available at <https://ifs.org.uk/bns/bn88.pdf>. Accessed 8 June 2021.

Buehn, Andreas, and Friedrich Schneider. 2016. Size and Development of Tax Evasion in 38 OECD Countries: What do we (not) know? *Journal of Economics and Political Economy* 3 (1): 1–11.

Bullough, Oliver. 2018. *Moneyland: Why Thieves & Crooks Now Rule the World & How to Take It Back.* London: Profile Books.

Bundesbank. 1997. The Role of the Deutsche Mark as an International Investment and Reserve Currency. Bundesbank Monthly Report. Frankfurt a.M.: Bundesbank. Available at <https://www.bundesbank.de/Redaktion/EN/Downloads/Publications/Monthly_Report_Articles/1997/1997_04_international_investment.pdf?__blob=publicationFile>. Accessed 26 July 2018.

Burn, Gary. 1999. The State, the City and the Euromarkets. *Review of International Political Economy* 6 (2): 225–261.

Burret, Heiko, Lars Feld, and Ekkehard Köhler. 2013. Sustainability of German Fiscal Policy and Public Debt: Historical and Time Series Evidence for the Period 1850–2010. In *Jahrbücher für Nationalökonomie und Statistik*, Vol. 3, 233. Stuttgart: Lucius and Lucius.

Büschgen, Hans E. 1995. Deutsche Bank from 1957 to the Present: The Emergence of an International Financial Conglomerate. In *The Deutsche Bank 1879–1995*, edited by Lothar Gall, Gerald D. Feldman, Harold James Carl-Ludwig Holfrerich, Hans E. Büschgen. London: Weidenfeld & Nicolson.

Cain, P. J., and A. G. Hopkins. 2015. *British Imperialism: 1688–2015.* 3rd ed. New York: Routledge.

Calomiris, Charles W., and Stephen H. Haber. 2014. *Fragile by Design: The Political Origins of Banking Crises and Scarce Credit.* The Princeton Economic History of the Western World. Princeton, NJ; Oxford: Princeton University Press.

Camp, Roderic Ai. 2015. Democratizing Mexican Politics, 1982–2012. In *Oxford Research Encyclopedia of Latin American History*, Vol. 1, edited by Stephen Webre. Oxford: Oxford University Press. Available at <http://oxfordre.com/latinamericanhistory/view/10.1093/acrefore/9780199366439.001.0001/acrefore-9780199366439-e-12>. Accessed 21 December 2018.

Capers, Robert L., and Andrew Weissmann. 2016. *United States of America vs Odebrecht S.A.* https://www.justice.gov/criminal-fraud/file/920096/download. Accessed 20 October 2022.

Cardenas, Enrique, and Carlos Manns. 1987. Inflation and Monetary Stabilization in Mexico during the Revolution. *Journal of Development Economics* 27: 375–394.

Cardoso, Adalberto. 2016. Informality and Public Policies to Overcome It. The Case of Brazil. *Sociologia & Antropologia* 6 (2): 321–349.

Cardoso, Eliana, and Albert Fishlow. 1989. The Macroeconomics of the Brazilian External Debt. In *Developing Country Debt and the World Economy*, edited by Jeffrey D. Sachs, 81–100. Chicago: Chicago University Press.

Carmagnani, Marcello. 1994. *Estado y mercado: la economía pública del liberalismo mexicano, 1850–1911*. 1st ed. Sección de obras de historia. México, D.F: El Colegio de México: Fondo de Cultura Económica.

Centeno, Miguel Angel. 2002. *Blood and Debt: War and the Nation-State in Latin America*. University Park, PA: Pennsylvania State University Press.

Centeno, Miguel Angel, and Agustín Ferraro, eds. 2013. *State and Nation Making in Latin America and Spain: Republics of the Possible*. Cambridge: Cambridge University Press.

Chamon, Marcos, and Márcio Garcia. 2016. Capital Controls in Brazil: Effective? *Journal of International Money and Finance* 61: 163–187.

Chamon, Marcos, Márcio Garcia, and Laura Souza. 2015. FX Interventions in Brazil: A Synthetic Control Approach. Texto para Disussão. Rio de Janeiro: Pontifícia Universidade Católica do Rio de Janeiro. Available at <http://www.econ.puc-rio.br/uploads/adm/trabalhos/files/td630.pdf>. Accessed 27 March 2018.

Christensen, John, Nick Shaxson, and Duncan Wigan. 2016. The Finance Curse: Britain and the World Economy. *The British Journal of Politics and International Relations* 18 (1): 255–269.

Christensen, Rasmus Corlin, and Martin Hearson. 2019. The New Politics of Global Tax Governance: Taking Stock a Decade after the Financial Crisis. *Review of International Political Economy* 26 (5): 1068–1088.

CIOT. 2018. 'Tax Gap' figures—Nearly six times as much lost to fraud as to avoidance. Press Release. London: Chartered Institute of Taxation. Available at <https://www.tax.org.uk/media-centre/press-releases/press-release-%E2%80%98tax-gap%E2%80%99-figures-%E2%80%93-nearly-six-times-much-lost-fraud-0>. Accessed 23 September 2018.

Cobham, Alex, and Petr Janský. 2017. Global Distribution of Revenue Loss from Tax Avoidance. Re-estimation and Country Results. WIDER Working Paper. Helsinki: United Nations World University World Institute for Development Economics Research.

Cohen, Benjamin J. 2013. Currency and State Power. In *Back to Basics*, edited by Martha Finnemore and Judith Goldstein, 159–176. Oxford: Oxford University Press. Available at <http://www.oxfordscholarship.com/view/10.1093/acprof:oso/9780199970087.001.0001/acprof-9780199970087-chapter-8>. Accessed 7 May 2018.

Collins, Michael. 1988. *Money and Banking in the UK: A History*. London: Croom Helm.

Committee of Public Accounts. 2013. *HM Revenue and Customs: Annual Report and Accounts 2011–2012*. London: House of Commons.

CONAIF. 2016. *Reporte Nacional de Inclusión Financiera*. Mexico City, D.F.: Presidente de la Comisión Nacional Bancaria y de Valores. Available at <http://www.cnbv.gob.mx/Inclusi%C3%B3n/Documents/Reportes%20de%20IF/Reporte%20de%20Inclusion%20Financiera%207.pdf>. Accessed 30 August 2017.

Cota, Isabella. 2015. Why Traders Love to Short the Mexican Peso. *Bloomberg*.

Crivelli, Ernesto, Ruud De Mooij, and Michael Keen. 2015. Base Erosion, Profit Shifting and Developing Countries. IMF Working Paper. Washington, DC: International Monetary Fund.

Cummins, Neil. 2022. The Hidden Wealth of English Dynasties, 1892–2016. *The Economic History Review*: ehr.13120.

Dahl, Robert A. 1957. The Concept of Power. *Behavioral Science* 2 (3): 201–215.

Damgaard, Jannik, Thomas Elkjaer, and Niels Johannesen. 2019. The Rise of Phantom Investments. Empty Corporate Shells in Tax Havens Undermine Tax Collection in Advanced, Emerging Market, and Developing Economies. *Finance and Development* 56 (3): 11–13.

Dharmapala, Dhammika and Hines, James R. 2009. Which Countries Become Tax Havens? *Journal of Public Economics* 93 (9–10): 1058–1068.

Daunton, Martin. 2002. *Just Taxes: The Politics of Taxation in Britain, 1914–1979*. Cambridge; New York: Cambridge University Press.

Daunton, Martin. 2007. *Wealth and Welfare: An Economic and Social History of Britain 1851–1951*. Oxford: Oxford University Press. Available at <http://public.eblib.com/choice/publicfullrecord.aspx?p=416039>. Accessed 5 November 2018.

Del Angel, Gustavo A. 2016. Cashless Payments and the Persistence of Cash: Open Questions About Mexico. Economics Working Paper. Stanford: Hoover Institution.

Dellepiane-Avellaneda, Sebastian. 2013. Gordon Unbound: The Heresthetic of Central Bank Independence in Britain. *British Journal of Political Science* 43 (2): 263–293.

Desan, Christine. 2014. *Making Money: Coin, Currency, and the Coming of Capitalism*. Oxford: Oxford University Press. Available at <https://oxford.universitypressscholarship.com/view/10.1093/acprof:oso/9780198709572.001.0001/acprof-9780198709572>. Accessed 10 January 2022.

Dettmer, Markus, and Sven Röbel. 2017. Das Ehrenwort. Der Spiegel.

Deutsche Bundesbank, ed. 2016. *Die Deutsche Bundesbank: Notenbank für Deutschland*. Frankfurt am Main: Deutsche Bundesbank, Zentralbereich Kommunikation, Redaktion Externe Medien.

Deutsche Bundesbank. 2017. *Monatsbericht*. Frankfurt: Deutsche Bundesbank. Available at <https://www.bundesbank.de/resource/blob/665284/c0eeb9d1460e0489c7b5f55cf98c98c6/mL/2017-04-monatsbericht-data.pdf>. Accessed 18 March 2022.

Díaz-Infante, Enrique. 2013. *La Reforma Financiera y Los Riesgos del Crédito*. Mexico City, D.F.: Instituto Mexicano para la Competitividad. Available at http://imco.org.mx/wp-content/uploads/2013/09/LaReformaFinancierayLosRiesgosdelCredito-3.pdf. Accessed 30 August 2017.

Dickens, Edwin T. 2005. The Eurodollar Market and the New Era of Global Financialization. In *Financialization and the World Economy*, edited by Gerald A. Epstein, 210–219. Cheltenham, UK; Northhampton, MA: Edward Elgar Publishing.

Dickson, P. G. M. 1993. *The Financial Revolution in England: A Study in the Development of Public Credit, 1688–1756*. Modern Revivals in History. Aldershot, Hampshire, England; Brookfield, VT: Gregg Revivals; Distributed in the United States by Ashgate Publ. Co.

Eccleston, Richard, and Felicity Gray. 2014. Foreign Accounts Tax Compliance Act and American Leadership in the Campaign against International Tax Evasion: Revolution or False Dawn? *Global Policy* 5 (3): 321–333.

Eich, Stefan. 2020. John Locke and the Politics of Monetary Depoliticization. *Modern Intellectual History* 17 (1): 1–28.

Emmenegger, Patrick. 2017. Swiss Banking Secrecy and the Problem of International Cooperation in Tax Matters: A Nut too Hard to Crack? *Regulation & Governance* 11 (1): 24–40.

Estellita, Heloisia, and Frederico Silva Bastos. 2015. Tax Exchange of Information and International Cooperation in Brazil. *Revista Direito GV* 11 (1): 13–36.

Falcao, Tatiana. 2012. Brazil's Approach to Transfer Pricing: A Viable Alternative to the Status Quo? *Tax Management Transfer Pricing Report* 20 (20), 2/23/2012.

Farnsworth, Clyde H. 1971. Germany shapes control on Eurodollar borrowing. The New York Times. New York.

Farquet, Christophe. 2019. Quantification and Revolution: An Investigation of German Capital Flight after the First World War. European Historical Economy Society Working Paper. Available at <https://EconPapers.repec.org/RePEc:hes:wpaper:0149>. Accessed 4 May 2021.

FATF and GAFILAT. 2018. Anti-money Laundering and Counter-terrorist Financing Measures—Mexico. Fourth Round Mutual Evaluation Report. Paris: Financial Action Task Force on Money Laundering. Available at <http://www.fatf-gafi.org/media/fatf/documents/reports/mer4/MER-Mexico-2018.pdf>. Accessed 22 May 2018.

Ferreira, Pedro Cavalcanti, and Marco Bonomo. 2006. *The Political Economy of Public Debt in Brazil*. São Paulo: Fundação Getulio Vargas. Available at <http://www.fgv.br/professor/ferreira/PolEconDebt.pdf>. Accessed 24 March 2018.

Ferslev, Hans-Peter. 2017. *Konzernentwicklung in der Deutschen Bank: 1985–1997*. Frankfurt a.M: Historische Gesellschaft der Deutschen Bank.

Fichtner, Jan. 2016. The Anatomy of the Cayman Islands Offshore Financial Center: Anglo-America, Japan, and the Role of Hedge Funds. *Review of International Political Economy* 23 (6): 1–30.

Findley, Michael G., Daniel L. Nielson, and Jason C. Sharman. 2014. *Global Shell Games: Experiments in Transnational Relations, Crime, and Terrorism*. Cambridge studies in international relations. Cambridge: Cambridge University Press.

Flores Zendejas, Juan. 2020. Explaining Latin America's Persistent Defaults: An Analysis of the Debtor–Creditor Relations in London, 1822–1914. *Financial History Review* 27 (3): 319–339.

Frieden, Jeffry A. 1987. The Brazilian Borrowing Experience: From Miracle to Debacle and Back. *Latin American Research Review* 22 (1): 95–131.

Friedman, Milton. 1971. *The Euro-Dollar Market: Some First Principles*. Selected Papers. Chicago: Graduate School of Business University of Chicago.

Gall, Lothar. 1995. The Deutsche Bank from its Founding to the Great War 1870–1914. In *The Deutsche Bank 1870–1995*, edited by Lothar Gall, Gerald D. Feldman, Harold James Carl-Ludwig Holfrerich, Hans E. Büschgen. London: Weidenfeld & Nicolson.

Gallie, W. B. 1956. IX.—Essentially Contested Concepts. *Proceedings of the Aristotelian Society* 56 (1): 167–198.

GAO. 1998. Private Banking. Raul Salinas, Citibank, and Alleged Money Laundering. Report to the Ranking Minority Member, Permanent Subcommittee on Investigations, Committee on Governmental Affairs, US Senate. Washingon, DC: United States General Accounting Office. Available at <https://www.gao.gov/archive/1999/os99001.pdf>. Accessed 11 June 2018.

Garcia-Bernardo, Javier, Jan Fichtner, Frank W. Takes, and Eelke M. Heemskerk. 2017. Uncovering Offshore Financial Centers: Conduits and Sinks in the Global Corporate Ownership Network. *Scientific Reports* 7 (1). Available at <http://www.nature.com/articles/s41598-017-06322-9>. Accessed 2 May 2018.

Gelemerova, Liliya. 2009. On the Frontline against Money-laundering: The Regulatory Minefield. *Crime, Law and Social Change* 52 (1): 33–55.

Genschel, Philipp. 2005. Globalization and the Transformation of the Tax State. *European Review* 13 (1): 53–71.

Genschel, Philipp, Hanna Lierse, and Laura Seelkopf. 2016. Dictators Don't Compete: Autocracy, Democracy, and Tax Competition. *Review of International Political Economy* 23 (2): 290–315.

Genschel, Philipp, and Peter Schwarz. 2011. Tax Competition: A Literature Review. *Socio-Economic Review* 9: 339–370.

Genschel, Philipp, and Laura Seelkopf. 2016. Winners and Losers of Tax Competition. In *Global Tax Governance. What Is Wrong with It and How to Fix It*, edited by Peter Dietsch and Thomas Rixen, 55–75. Colchester: ECPR Press.

Genschel, Phillipp, and Thomas Rixen. 2015. Settling and Unsettling the Transnational Legal Order of International Taxation. In *Transnational Legal Orders*, edited by T. C. Halliday and G. C. Shaffer, 154–184. Cambridge: Cambridge University Press.

Gerring, John. 2009. Case Selection for Case-Study Analysis: Qualitative and Quantitative Techniques. In *The Oxford Handbook of Political Methodology*, edited by Janet M. Box-Steffensmeier, Henry E. Brady, and David Collier. Oxford: Oxford University Press. https://doi.org/10.1093/oxfordhb/9780199286546.003.0028. Accessed 19 October 2022.

Gerschenkron, Alexander. 1979. *Economic Backwardness in Historical Perspective: A Book of Essays*. Cambridge, MA: Belknap Pr.

Giles, Chris, Guy Chazan, and David Keohane. 2021. Global Corporate Tax Deal Edges Closer after US Backs Minimum Rate. Financial Times. Available at <https://www.ft.com/content/35ce8c9d-d28a-49ad-b278-e7c49e06d7f9?shareType=nongift>. Accessed 14 April 2021.

Goertz, Gary, and James Mahoney. 2012. Concepts and measurement: Ontology and Epistemology. *Social Science Information* 51 (2): 205–216.

Goldberg, Linda, Craig Kennedy, and Jason Miu. 2010. *Central Bank Dollar Swap Lines and Overseas Dollar Funding Costs*. Cambridge, MA: National Bureau of Economic Research. Available at <http://www.nber.org/papers/w15763.pdf>. Accessed 19 November 2018.

Goldfajn, Ilan, and André Minella. 2005. Capital Flows and Capital Controls in Brazil. What Have We Learned? Working Paper. NBER Working Paper Series. Cambridge, MA: National Bureau of Economic Research. Available at <http://www.nber.org/papers/w11640.pdf>. Accessed 20 February 2018.

Goldfeld, Stephen M. 1976. The Case of the Missing Money. *Brookings Papers on Economic Activity* 7 (3): 683–740.

Goldsmith, Raymond W. 1986. *Brasil 1850–1984: Desenvolvimento financeiro sob um século de inflação*. São Paulo: Harper & Row.

Gravelle, Jane G. 2015. *Tax Havens: International Tax Avoidance and Evasion, Congressional Research Service*, Washington D.C. https://ecommons.cornell.edu/handle/1813/79373. Accessed 20 October 2022.

Green, Jeremy. 2016. Anglo-American Development, the Euromarkets, and the Deeper Origins of Neoliberal Deregulation. *Review of International Studies* 42 (3): 425–449.

Green, Jeremy. 2020. *The Political Economy of the Special Relationship: Anglo-American Development from the Gold Standard to the Financial Crisis*. Princeton, NJ: Princeton University Press.

Green, Jeremy, and Julian Gruin. 2020. RMB Transnationalization and the Infrastructural Power of International Financial Centres. *Review of International Political Economy* 28: 1–27.

Gruic, Branimir, and Philip Wooldridge. 2012. Enhancements to the BIS Debt Securities Statistics. *BIS Quarterly Review* December: 63–76.

The Guardian. 2016. Panama Papers: A special investigation. London. Available at <https://www.theguardian.com/news/series/panama-papers>. Accessed 21 September 2002.

The Guardian. 2017. The Paradise Papers: A special investigation. London. Available at <https://www.theguardian.com/news/2017/nov/05/paradise-papers-leak-reveals-secrets-of-world-elites-hidden-wealth>. Accessed 21 September 2018.

Guex, Sébastien. 2021. The Emergence of the Swiss Tax Haven, 1816–1914. *Business History Review* 96 (2): 1–20.

Haber, Stephen, Herbert S. Klein, Noel Maurer, and Kevin J. Middlebrook. 2008. *Mexico since 1980*. World since 1980. Cambridge: Cambridge University Press

Haber, Stephen, Noel Maurer, and Armando Razo. 2003. When the Law Does Not Matter: The Rise and Decline of the Mexican Oil Industry. *The Journal of Economic History* 63 (1). Available at <http://www.journals.cambridge.org/abstract_S0022050703001712>. Accessed 1 June 2018.

Haber, Stephen, and Aldo Musacchio. 2013. *These Are the Good Old Days: Foreign Entry and the Mexican Banking System.* Cambridge, MA: National Bureau of Economic Research. Available at <http://www.nber.org/papers/w18713.pdf>. Accessed 28 August 2017.

Haberly, Daniel, and Dariusz Wójcik. 2015a. Tax Havens and the Production of Offshore FDI: An Empirical Analysis. *Journal of Economic Geography* 15 (1): 75–101.

Haberly, Daniel, and Dariusz Wójcik. 2015b. Regional Blocks and Imperial Legacies: Mapping the Global Offshore FDI Network: Regional Blocks and Imperial Legacies. *Economic Geography* 91 (3): 251–280.

Hakelberg, Lukas. 2020. *The Hypocritical Hegemon: How the United States Shapes Global Rules against Tax Evasion and Avoidance.* Cornell Studies in Money. Ithaca, NY: Cornell University Press.

Hakelberg, Lukas, and Laura Seelkopf, eds. 2021. *Handbook on the Politics of Taxation.* Cheltenham: Edward Elgar Publishing.

Hall, Linda B. 1995. *Oil, Banks, and Politics: The United States and Postrevolutionary Mexico, 1917–1924.* Austin, TX: University of Texas Press.

Hall, Peter A., and Rosemary C. R. Taylor. 1996. Political Science and the Three New Institutionalisms. *Political Studies* XLIV: 936–957.

Hamilton, Nora. 1982. *The Limits of State Autonomy: Post-revolutionary Mexico.* Princeton, NJ: Princeton University Press.

Hampton, Mark P. 1996a. Creating Spaces. The Political Economy of Island Offshore Finance Centres: The Case of Jersey. *Geographische Zeitschrift* 84 (2): 103–113.

Hampton, Mark P. 1996b. Sixties Child? The Emergence of Jersey as an Offshore Finance Centre 1955–71. *Accounting, Business & Financial History* 6 (1): 51–71.

Hardie, Iain, and Helen Thompson. 2020. Taking Europe Seriously: European Financialization and US Monetary Power. *Review of International Political Economy* 28: 1–19.

Harding, Luke. 2017. The Global Laundromat: How Did it Work and Who Benefited? The Guardian. London. Available at <https://www.theguardian.com/world/2017/mar/20/the-global-laundromat-how-did-it-work-and-who-benefited>. Accessed 9 October 2018.

Harrington, Brooke. 2012. Trust and Estate Planning: The Emergence of a Profession and Its Contribution to Socioeconomic Inequality. *Sociological Forum* 27 (4): 825–846.

Harrington, Brooke. 2016a. Trusts and Financialization. *Socio-Economic Review* 15 (1): 31–63.

Harrington, Brooke. 2016b. *Capital Without Borders: Wealth Managers and the One Percent.* Cambridge, Massachusetts: Harvard University Press.

Hayek, Friedrich August von. 1990. *Denationalisation of Money: The Argument Refined. An Analysis of the Theory and Practice of Concurrent Currencies.* 3rd ed. Hobart paper Special 70. London: Inst. of Economic Affairs.

He, Dong, and Robert N. McCauley. 2010. Offshore Markets for the Domestic Currency: Monetary and Financial Stability Issues. *BIS Working Papers* (320).

He, Dong, and Robert N. McCauley. 2012. Eurodollar banking and currency internationalisation. BIS Quarterly Review: 33–46.

Hearson, Martin. 2021. *Imposing Standards: The North–South Dimension to Global Tax Politics.* Cornell Studies in Money. Ithaca, NY: Cornell University Press.

Helleiner, Eric. 1994. *States and the Reemergence of Global Finance: From Bretton Woods to the 1990s.* Ithaca, NY; London: Cornell University Press.

Henry, James S. 2012. *The Price of Offshore Revisited. New Estimates for 'Missing' Global Private Wealth, Income, Inequality, and Lost Taxes.* Tax Justice Network.

HMRC. 2018. Inheritance tax. Available at <https://www.gov.uk/inheritance-tax/print>. Accessed 4 October 2018.

Hodge, Margaret. 2016. *Called to Account: How Corporate Bad Behaviour and Government Waste Combine to cost us millions.* London: Little, Brown, an imprint of Little, Brown Book Group.

House of Lords. 2013. *Tax Avoidance—the Role of Large Accountancy Firms.* London: House of Lords.

Hüfner, Felix. 2010. The German Banking System: Lessons from the Financial Crisis. OECD Economics Department Working Papers. Paris: Organisation for Economic Co-operation and Development.

ICIJ. 2016. The Panama Papers: Exposing the Rogue Offshore Finance Industry. Available at <https://panamapapers.icij.org/>. Accessed 10 January 2017.

ILO. 2014. Informal Employment in Mexico: Current Situation, Policies and Challenges. Notes on Formalization. Lima: International Labour Organization. Available at <http://www.ilo.org/wcmsp5/groups/public/---americas/---ro-lima/documents/publication/wcms_245889.pdf>. Accessed 30 August 2017.

IMF. 2014. Spillovers in International Corporate Taxation. Washington, DC: IMF.

IMF. n.d. *Coordinated Direct Investment Survey.* Available at <http://cdis.imf.org/>.

Ingham, Geoffrey K. 2004. *The Nature of Money.* Cambridge, UK; Malden, MA: Polity.

James, Harold. 2004. *The Nazi Dictatorship and the Deutsche Bank.* Cambridge: Cambridge University Press.

Johannesen, Niels and Zucman, Gabriel. 2014. The End of Bank Secrecy? An Evaluation of the G20 Tax Haven Crackdown. *American Economic Journal: Economic Policy* 6 (1): 65–91

Joyce, R., and L. Sibieta. 2013. An Assessment of Labour's Record on Income Inequality and Poverty. *Oxford Review of Economic Policy* 29 (1): 178–202.

Kaina, Viktoria. 2004. Deutschlands Eliten zwischen Kontinuität und Wandel. Empirische Befunde zu Rekrutierungswegen, Karrierepfaden und Kommunikationsmustern. *Aus Politik und Zeitgeschichte* 10: 8–16.

Kilz, Hans Werner, and Joachim Preuss. 1983. *Flick: die gekaufte Republik.* Spiegel-Buch 48. Reinbek bei Hamburg: Rowohlt.

Knapp, G. F. (Georg Friedrich). 1924. *The State Theory of Money [4th ed]/by Georg Friedrich Knapp.* London: Macmillan & Co.

Knight, Alan. 1990. *Porfirians, Liberals and Peasants.* 1st ed. paperback print. The Mexican Revolution Volume 1. Lincoln: University of Nebraska Press.

Knight, Alan. 2013. The Mexican State, Porfirian and Revolutionary, 1876–1930. In *State and Nation Making in Latin America and Spain. Republics of the Possible.*, edited by Miguel Angel Centeno and Augustine E. Ferraro, 116–138. Cambridge: Cambridge University Press.

Knobel, Andres. 2017. *Trusts: Weapons of Mass Injustice?* Chesham: Tax Justice Network. Available at <https://www.taxjustice.net/2017/02/13/trusts-weapons-mass-injustice-new-tax-justice-network-report/>. Accessed 8 October 2018.

Koddenbrock, Kai. 2019. Money and Moneyness: Thoughts on the Nature and Distributional Power of the 'Backbone' of Capitalist Political Economy. *Journal of Cultural Economy* 12 (2): 101–118.

Kohl, Helumt. 1990. *Fernsehansprache von Bundeskanzler Kohl anlässlich des Inkrafttretens der Währungs-, Wirtschafts- und Sozialunion*. Bulletin. Bonn: Presse- und Informationsamts der Bundesregierung. Available at <www.helmut-kohl.de/index.php?msg=555>. Accessed 26 July 2018.

Kose, M. Ayhan, Eswar Prasad, Kenneth Rogoff, and Shang-Jin Wei. 2009. Financial Globalization: A Reappraisal. *IMF Staff Papers* 56 (1): 8–62.

Krasner, Stephen D. 1999. *Sovereignty: Organized Hypocrisy*. Princeton, NJ: Princeton University Press.

Kreicher, Lawrence, and Robert N. McCauley. 2016. Asset Managers, Eurodollar and Unconventional Monetary Policy. BIS Working Papers 578.

Lake, David A. 2008. *The State and International Relations*. Oxford: Oxford University Press. Available at <http://oxfordhandbooks.com/view/10.1093/oxfordhb/9780199219322.001.0001/oxfordhb-9780199219322-e-2>. Accessed 19 March 2021.

Lamby, Stephan, and Egmond R. Koch. 2017. Bimbes—die schwarzen Kassen des Helmut Kohl. *Das Erste*.

Langbein, John H. 1997. *The Secret Life of the Trust: The Trust as an Instrument of Commerce*. Faculty Scholarship Series. Yale: Yale Law School. Available at <http://digitalcommons.law.yale.edu/fss_papers/503>. Accessed 8 October 2018.

Leahy, Joe. 2015. BNDES: Lender of First Resort for Brazil's Tycoons. Financial Times. London, sec. The Big Read. Available at <https://www.ft.com/content/c510368e-968e-11e4-922f-00144feabdc0>. Accessed 25 April 2018.

Levi, Margaret. 1989. *Of Rule and Revenue*. Berkeley: University of California Press.

Linsi, Lukas, and Daniel K. Mügge. 2019. Globalization and the Growing Defects of International Economic Statistics. *Review of International Political Economy* 26 (3): 361–383.

Longo, Carlos Alberto. 1994. Federal Problems with VAT in Brazil. *Revista Brasileira de Economia* 48 (1): 85–105.

McCauley, Robert N. 2005. Distinguishing Global Dollar Reserves from Official Holdings in the United States. *BIS Quarterly Review* September: 57–72.

McCauley, Robert N., Patrick McGuire, and Valdyslav Sushko. 2015. Dollar Credit to Emerging Market Economies. *BIS Quarterly Review* December: 27–41.

Macdonald, James. 2003. *A Free Nation Deep in Debt: The Financial Roots of Democracy*. Princeton, NJ; Oxford: Princeton University Press.

McDowell, Daniel. 2017. *Brother, Can You Spare a Billion? The United States, the IMF, and the International Lender of Last Resort*. New York: Oxford University Press.

MacIntosh, Chris. 2017. *How the Financial Plumbing Got Broken and What This Means*. Capitalist Exploits.

McLeay, Michael, Amar Radia, and Ryland Thomas. 2014. Money Creation in the Modern Economy. *Quarterly Bulletin*. London: Bank of England. Available at <https://www.bankofengland.co.uk/quarterly-bulletin/2014/q1/money-creation-in-the-modern-economy>. Accessed 30 November 2020.

MacLeod, Dag. 2005. *Downsizing the State: Privatization and the Limits of Neoliberal Reform in Mexico*. University Park, PA: Pennsylvania State University Press.

Maurer, Noel, and Andrei Gomberg. 2004. When the State is Untrustworthy: Public Finance and Private Banking in Porfirian Mexico. *The Journal of Economic History* 64 (4): 1087–1107.

Maxfield, Sylvia. 2001. *Gatekeepers of Growth: The International Political Economy of Central Banking in Developing Countries*. Princeton, NJ: Princeton University Press.

Mehrling, Perry. 2011. *The New Lombard Street: How the Fed Became the Dealer of Last Resort*. Princeton, NJ: Princeton University Press.

Mehrling, Perry. 2012. The Inherent Hierarchy of Money. Available at <http://ieor.columbia.edu/files/seasdepts/industrial-engineering-operations-research/pdf-files/Mehrling_P_FESeminar_Sp12-02.pdf>. Accessed 23 May 2017.

Mehrling, Perry. 2015. Elasticity and Discipline in the Global Swap Network. *International Journal of Political Economy* 44 (4): 311–324.

Mehrling, Perry. 2016. The Economics of Money and Banking. Lecture Notes, New York City.

Mello, Eduardo, and Matias Spektor. 2014. How to Fix Brazil. Breaking an Addiction to Bad Governance. *Foreign Affairs* 95 (5): 102–110.

Melo, Marcus A., Armando Barrientos, and Andreé Canuto Coelho. 2014. *Taxation, Redistribution and the Social Contract in Brazil*. IRIBA Working Papers. Manchester: University of Manchester.

Meltzer, Allan H., and Scott F. Richard. 1981. A Rational Theory of the Size of Government. *Journal of Political Economy* 89 (5): 914–927.

Milne, Richard. 2018. Danske Bank Whistleblower was British Executive in Estonian Branch. Financial Times. London. Available at <https://www.ft.com/content/32d47fd8-c18b-11e8-8d55-54197280d3f7>. Accessed 9 October 2018.

Moore, Philip. 2004. Founding Fathers and 35-year olds. Euromoney Magazine June. Available at <https://www.euromoney.com/article/b1320s1gnyqn0n/founding-fathers-and-35-year-olds>. Accessed 26 July 2018.

Mügge, Daniel. 2020. Economic Statistics as Political Artefacts. *Review of International Political Economy* 29: 1–22.

Murau, Steffen, Joe Rini, and Armin Haas. 2020. The Evolution of the Offshore US-Dollar System: Past, Present and Four Possible Futures. *Journal of Institutional Economics* 16 (6): 1–17.

Musacchio Farias, Aldo, and Sérgio G. Lazzarini. 2014. *Reinventing State Capitalism: Leviathan in Business, Brazil and Beyond*. Cambridge, MA: Harvard University Press.

National Audit Office. 2010. HM Treasury: Maintaining the Financial Stability of UK Banks: Update on the Support Schemes. London: Stationery Office. Available at <http://www.official-documents.gov.uk/document/hc1011/hc06/0676/0676.pdf>. Accessed 11 January 2019.

NCA. 2018. *National Strategic Assessment of Serious and Organised Crime 2018*. London: National Crime Agency. Available at <http://www.nationalcrimeagency.gov.uk/publications/905-national-strategic-assessment-for-soc-2018/file>. Accessed 5 October 2018.

The New York Times. 1976. 18 banks arranging $800 million loan to bolster Mexico. New York City.

Norfield, Tony. 2016. *The City: London and the Global Power of Finance*. London; New York: Verso.

Obermayer, Bastian, and Frederik Obermaier. 2016. *The Panama Papers: Breaking the Story of How the Rich & Powerful Hide Their Money*. London: Oneworld Publications Ltd.

O'Brien, Patrick K., and Philip A. Hunt. 1999. England, 1485–1815. In *The Rise of the Fiscal State in Europe c.1200–1815*, edited by Richard Bonney, 53–100. Oxford: Oxford University Press. Available at <http://www.oxfordscholarship.com/view/10.1093/

acprof:oso/9780198204022.001.0001/acprof-9780198204022-chapter-3>. Accessed 24 October 2018.

OCCRP. 2014. The Russian Laundromat Exposed. Available at <https://www.occrp.org/en/laundromat/>. Accessed 9 October 2018.

OECD. 1998. *Harmful Tax Competition: An Emerging Global Issue.* Paris: Organisation for Economic Co-operation and Development.

OECD. 2013. *Addressing Base Erosion and Profit Shifting.* Paris: Organisation for Economic Co-operation and Development.

OECD. 2015. *Revenue Statistics in Latin America and the Caribbean 1990–2013.* Paris: OECD Publishing.

OECD. 2016. *OECD Statistics. Details of Tax Revenue—Brazil.* Paris: Organisation for Economic Co-operation and Development. Available at <http://stats.oecd.org/Index.aspx?DataSetCode=REVBRA>. Accessed 24 March 2018.

OECD. 2017a. *Revenue Statistics 2017—Germany.* Paris: Organisation for Economic Co-operation and Development. Available at <https://www.oecd.org/tax/revenue-statistics-germany.pdf>. Accessed 1 August 2018.

OECD. 2017b. *Revenue Statistics 2017—Mexico.* Paris: Organisation for Economic Co-operation and Development. Available at <https://www.oecd.org/tax/revenue-statistics-mexico.pdf>. Accessed 24 August 2017.

Ogle, Vanessa. 2017. Archipelago Capitalism: Tax Havens, Offshore Money, and the State, 1950s–1970s. *The American Historical Review* 122 (5): 1431–1458.

O'Malley, Chris. 2015. *Bonds without Borders: A History of the Eurobond Market.* Wiley finance series. New York City: Wiley.

Pacheco, Flávia. 2017. *Operation Car Wash. Understand the Investigation that Unveiled Brazil's Largest ever Corruption Scheme.* CreateSpace Independent Publishing Platform.

Palan, Ronen. 1998. Trying to Have Your Cake and Eating It: How and Why the State System Has Created Offshore. *International Studies Quarterly* 42 (4): 625–643.

Palan, Ronen. 2002. Tax Havens and the Commercialization of State Sovereignty. *International Organization* 56 (1): 151–176.

Palan, Ronen, and G. Mangraviti. 2016. Troubling Tax Havens: Tax Footprint Reduction and Jurisdictional Arbitrage. In *International Handbook of Wealth and Super-Rich*, edited by Iain Hay and Jonathan V. Beaverstock, 422–441. Cheltenham, UK; Northhampton, MA: Edward Elgar Publishing.

Palan, Ronen, Richard Murphy, and Christian Chavagneux. 2010. *Tax Havens: How Globalization Really Works.* Ithaca, NY: Cornell University Press.

Pape, Fabian. 2021. Governing Global Liquidity: Federal Reserve Swap Lines and the International Dimension of US Monetary Policy. *New Political Economy* 27: 1–18.

Passarinho, Nathalia, Fernanda Calgaro, and Lucas Salomão. 2015. Homem que soltou ratos na CPI é funcionário da Câmara, diz assessoria. O Globo. Brasília. Available at <http://g1.globo.com/politica/noticia/2015/04/funcionario-da-camara-soltou-ratos-em-sessao-de-cpi-diz-assessoria.html>. Accessed 21 February 2018.

Pessananti, Thomas P. 2008. The Politics of Silver and Gold in an Age of Globalization: The Origins of Mexico's Monetary Reform of 1905. *América Latina en la Historia Económica* 30.

Piketty, Thomas. 2014. *Capital in the Twenty-first Century.* Cambridge, MA/London: Belknap Press of Harvard University Press.

Pistor, Katharina. 2020. *The Code of Capital: How the Law Creates Wealth and Inequality.* Princeton and Oxford: Princeton University Press.

Pozsar, Zoltan, Tobias Adrian, Adam Ashcraft, and Hayley Boesky. 2010. Shadow Bank-ing. Federal Reserve Bank of New York Staff Reports. New York City: Federal Reserve Bank of New York. Available at <https://www.newyorkfed.org/research/staff_reports/sr458.html>. Accessed 22 March 2018.

Rawlinson, Kevin. 2014. UK Uncut Protesters Blockade Vodafone Stores across Coun-try. The Guardian. London. Available at <https://www.theguardian.com/uk-news/2014/jun/14/uk-uncut-vodafone>. Accessed 21 September 2018.

Rebenstorf, Hilke. 1995. *Die politische Klasse: zur Entwicklung und Reproduktion einer Funktionselite*. Campus Forschung Bd. 725. Frankfurt; New York: Campus.

Riding, Alan. 1977. Mexico Seeks $1.2 Billion Loan of Eurodollars, its Largest Ever. The New York Times. New York City.

Rigoni, João Marcus de Melo. 2014. A Brazilian View on Base Erosion and Profit Shifting: An Alternative Path. *Intertax* 42 (11): 730–742.

Rixen, Thomas. 2008. *The Political Economy of International Tax Governance*. Transforma-tions of the State. Basingstoke: Palgrave Macmillan.

Rocha, Geisa Maria. 2002. Neo-Dependency in Brazil. *New Left Review* 16 (July–August): 5–32.

Röper, Burkhardt. 1970. Entwicklung und Probleme des Eurodollarmarktes. *Jahrbücher für Nationalökonomie und Statistik* 4–5: 446–460. Available at https://www.degruyter.com/journal/key/jbnst/html?lang=de.

Roulot, Nicolas. 2013. Eurobonds: un vrai décollage de Luxembourg. *Paperjam–Business zu Lëtzebuerg*. Available at <http://paperjam.lu/news/eurobonds-un-vrai-decollage-de-luxembourg>. Accessed 5 July 2018.

Sabine, B. E. V. 2006. A History of Income Tax: The Development of Income Tax from its Beginning in 1799 to the Present Day Related to the Social, Economic and Politi-cal History of the Period. Available at <http://public.eblib.com/choice/publicfullrecord.aspx?p=1474695>. Accessed 22 November 2018.

Sahr, Aaron. 2017. *Keystroke-Kapitalismus: Ungleichheit auf Knopfdruck*. 1st ed. Hamburg: Hamburger Edition.

San Martín Reyna, Juan Manuel, Carlos Alberto Juárez Alonso, Jaime Díaz Martin del Campo, and Héctor Enrique Angeles Sánchez. 2016. *Evasión del Impuesto al Valor Agregado y del Impuesto Sobre la Renta*. Santa Catarina Mártir, Cholula, Puebla: Uni-versidad de las Américas Puebla. Available at <http://www.sat.gob.mx/administracion_sat/estudios_evasion_fiscal/Documents/IVA_ISR_%20DEFINITIVO.pdf>. Accessed 21 January 2018.

Sartori, Giovanni. 1970. Concept Misformation in Comparative Politics. *American Political Science Review* 64 (4): 1033–1053.

Schäfers, Bernhard. 2004. Elite. *Aus Politik und Zeitgeschichte* 10: 3–7.

Schenk, Catherine R. 1998. The Origins of the Eurodollar Market in London: 1955–1963. *Explorations in Economic History* 35 (2): 221–238.

Schmidt, Manfred G. 2012. *Der deutsche Sozialstaat: Geschichte und Gegenwart*. München: C.H. Beck. Available at <http://public.eblib.com/choice/publicfullrecord.aspx?p=4864278>. Accessed 1 August 2018.

Schularick, Moritz, and Thomas M. Steger. 2010. Financial Integration, Investment, and Economic Growth: Evidence from Two Eras of Financial Globalization. *Review of Economics and Statistics* 92 (4): 756–768.

Schumpeter, Joseph A. 1991. The Crisis of the Tax State. In *The Economics and Sociology of Capitalism*, edited by Richard Swedberg, 99–140. Princeton, NJ: Princeton University Press.

Scott, John. 1991. *Who Rules Britain?* Cambridge: Polity Press.

Seelkopf, Laura, Moritz Bubek, Edgars Eihmanis, Joseph Ganderson, Julian Limberg, Youssef Mnaili, Paula Zuluaga, and Philipp Genschel. 2021. The Rise of Modern Taxation: A New Comprehensive Dataset of Tax Introductions Worldwide. *The Review of International Organizations* 16 (1): 239–263.

Seibel, Karsten. 2014. Selbstanzeigen bringen dem Staat 4,3 Milliarden. Welt. Berlin. Available at <https://www.welt.de/wirtschaft/article127895284/Selbstanzeigen-bringen-dem-Staat-4-3-Milliarden.html>.

Seifert, Leonie. 2008. Mythos Sparkasse befeuert das Geschäft. Stern. Hamburg. Available at <https://www.stern.de/wirtschaft/geld/finanzkrise-mythos-sparkasse-befeuert-das-geschaeft-3747450.html>. Accessed 9 July 2018.

Selee, Andrew D. 2011. *Decentralization, Democratization, and Informal Power in Mexico.* University Park, PA: The Pennsylvania State University Press.

Sharman, Jason C. 2006. *Havens in a Storm: The Struggle for Global Tax Regulation.* Cornell studies in political economy. Ithaca, NY: Cornell University Press.

Sharman, Jason C. 2010. Offshore and the New International Political Economy. *Review of International Political Economy* 17 (1): 1–32.

Sharman, Jason C. 2011. *The Money Laundry: Regulating Criminal Finance in the Global Economy.* Ithaca, NY: Cornell University Press. Available at <https://books.google.de/books?id=cOIkdh9rtCcC>.

Sharman, Jason C. 2017. *The Despot's Guide to Wealth Management: On the International Campaign Against Grand Corruption.* Ithaca and London: Cornell University Press.

Shaxson, Nicholas. 2012. *Treasure Islands: Tax Havens and the Men Who Stole the World.* London: Vintage Books.

Sil, Rudra, and Peter J. Katzenstein. 2010. Analytic Eclecticism in the Study of World Politics: Reconfiguring Problems and Mechanisms across Research Traditions. *Perspectives on Politics* 8 (2): 411–431.

Skidmore, Thomas E. 2010. *Brazil: Five Centuries of Change.* 2nd ed. New York: Oxford University Press.

Skinner, Quentin. 2009. A Genealogy of the Modern State. In *Proceedings of the British Academy, Volume 162, 2008 Lectures,* edited by Ron Johnston, 324–370. British Academy. Available at <http://www.britishacademypublications.com/view/10.5871/bacad/9780197264584.001.0001/upso-9780197264584-chapter-11>. Accessed 13 August 2018.

Smith, Benjamin T. 2014. Building a State on the Cheap: Taxation, Social Movements and Politics. In *Dictablanda: Politics, Work, and Culture in Mexico, 1938–1968,* edited by Paul Gillingham and Benjamin T. Smith, 255–275. Durham, NC: Duke University Press.

Smith, Michael, Sabrina Valle, and Blake Schmidt. 2017. No One Has Ever Made a Corruption Machine Like this One. Bloomberg Businessweek. Available at <https://www.bloomberg.com/news/features/2017-06-08/no-one-has-ever-made-a-corruption-machine-like-this-one>. Accessed 20 February 2018.

Smith-Meyer, Bjarke, and Arnau Busquets Guàrdia. 2021. Europe's Brexit Dividend is a Small One. Politico, Online edition. Available at <https://www.politico.eu/article/brexit-financial-services-economy-europe-dividend-small/>. Accessed 27 April 2021.

Snider, Jeffrey. 2017. Eurodollar University—Part 2: What Goes up Must Come down. Slide deck. MacroVoices Podcast. Available at <https://www.macrovoices.com/macrovoices-research/guest-publications/2074-eurodollar-university-season-2-slide-deck>. Accessed 5 March 2019.

Snider, Jeffrey. 2018. MacroVoices PodCast to Eric Townsend. Eurodollar University, Season 2. Interview Transcript. MacroVoices PodCast. Available at <https://www.macrovoices.com/aia>.

Snider, Jeffrey, and Luke Gromen. 2019. Global U.S. Dollar Shortage Demystified. MacroVoices Podcast. Available at <https://www.macrovoices.com/683-macrovoices-184-luke-gromen-jeff-snider>. Accessed 9 October 2019.

Sobarzo, Horacio. 2011. Tax Reform in Mexico: A General Equilibrium Assessment. *Applied Economics Letters* 18 (7): 671–678.

Sotelo, María Eugenia Romero. 2008. El debate sobre la reforma monetaria de 1905 en México. *Iberoamericana* 8 (29): 63–84.

Sotero, Paulo. 2018. Petrobras scandal. Brazilian political corruption scandal. *Enyclopaedia Britannica*. Available at <https://www.britannica.com/event/Petrobras-scandal>. Accessed 21 February 2018.

Strange, Susan. 1994. *States and markets.* 2nd ed., Repr. London: Pinter.

Swank, Duane. 2003. The Effect of Globalization on Taxation, Institutions, and Control of the Macroeconomy. In *The Global Transformations Reader: An Introduction to the Globalization Debate*, edited by David Held and Anthony McGrew, 403–420. Cambridge: Blackwell Publishing.

Swank, Duane. 2016. The New Political Economy of Taxation in the Developing World. *Review of International Political Economy* 23 (2): 185–207.

Swiss National Bank. 2017. Swiss National Bank (SNB)—Banks in Switzerland. Available at <https://www.snb.ch/en/iabout/stat/statrep/id/statpub_bankench>. Accessed 22 August 2017.

Swissinfo. 2008. Salinas Funds Finally Head back to Mexico. *Swissinfo.ch.* Available at <http://www.swissinfo.ch/eng/salinas-funds-finally-head-back-to-mexico/6740256>. Accessed 11 June 2018.

Tax Justice Network. 2013. *Financial Secrecy Index—Results 2013.* Chesham: Tax Justice Network. Available at <http://www.financialsecrecyindex.com/introduction/fsi-2013-results>. Accessed 1 April 2015.

Tax Justice Network. 2018a. *Financial Secrecy Index—Germany.* Chesham: Tax Justice Network. Available at <http://www.financialsecrecyindex.com/PDF/Germany.pdf>. Accessed 11 July 2018.

Tax Justice Network. 2018b. *Financial Secrecy Index—Results 2018.* Chesham: Tax Justice Network. Available at <https://www.financialsecrecyindex.com/introduction/fsi-2018-results>. Accessed 4 July 2018.

Tax Justice Network. 2018c. *Narrative Report on USA.* Financial Secrecy Index 2018. Tax Justice Network. Available at <http://www.financialsecrecyindex.com/PDF/USA.pdf>. Accessed 2 May 2018.

Thompson, Helen. 2010. The Character of the State. In *New Directions in Political Science*, edited by Colin Hay, 130–147. Basingstoke: Palgrave Macmillan.

Thompson, Helen. 2017. How the City of London Lost at Brexit: A Historical Perspective. *Economy and Society* 46 (2): 211–228.

Tilly, Charles. 1990. *Coercion, Capital and European States: AD 990–1990.* Studies in Social Discontinuity. Cambridge, MA: Basil Blackwell.

Tomz, Michael. 2007. *Reputation and International Cooperation: Sovereign Debt across Three Centuries.* Princeton, NJ: Princeton University Press.

Tomz, Michael, and Mark L. J. Wright. 2013. Empirical Research on Sovereign Debt and Default. *Annual Review of Economics* 5 (1): 247–272.

Tooze, J. Adam. 2018. *Crashed: How a Decade of Financial Crises Changed the World.* London: Allen Lane.

Tørsløv, Thomas, Ludvig Wier, and Gabriel Zucman. 2018. *The Missing Profits of Nations.* Cambridge, MA. Available at <http://www.nber.org/papers/w24701.pdf>. Accessed 9 July 2018.

Trampusch, Christine. 2015. The Financialisation of Sovereign Debt: An Institutional Analysis of the Reforms in German Public Debt Management. *German Politics* 24 (2): 119–136.

Trampusch, Christine, and Dennis C. Spies. 2015. Was treibt Kommunen zu Spekulationsgeschäften? Eine Analyse der Swap-Geschäfte von Kommunen in Nordrhein-Westfalen. *Politische Vierteljahresschrift* 56 (1): 104–129.

Transparency International. 2017. Corruption Perception Index 2017. Available at <https://www.transparency.org/news/feature/corruption_perceptions_index_2017#table>. Accessed 8 October 2018.

Ullmann, Hans-Peter. 2005. *Der deutsche Steuerstaat: Geschichte der öffentlichen Finanzen vom 18. Jahrhundert bis heute.* Originalausg. Beck'sche Reihe 1616. München: Beck.

Ullmann, Hans-Peter. 2017. *Das Abgleiten in den Schuldenstaat: öffentliche Finanzen in der Bundesrepublik von den sechziger bis zu den achtziger Jahren.* V&R Academic. Göttingen; Bristol: Vandenhoeck & Ruprecht GmbH & Co.

UNCTAD. 2015. *World Investment Report 2015. Reforming International Investment Governance.* Geneva: United Nations.

Valerdi, Juan E. 2017. *La red de "Guaridas Fiscales" y su impacto negativo sobre la justicia fiscal en América Latina.* Lima: Latindadd and Red de Justicia Fiscal de América Latina y el Caribe. Available at <http://www.justiciafiscal.org/wp-content/uploads/2017/03/GuaridasFiscales_Valerdi__.pdf>. Accessed 16 February 2018.

van 't Klooster, Jens, and Clément Fontan. 2020. The Myth of Market Neutrality: A Comparative Study of the European Central Bank's and the Swiss National Bank's Corporate Security Purchases. *New Political Economy* 25 (6): 865–879.

Vogl, Joseph. 2015. *Der Souveränitätseffekt.* 1st ed. Zürich Berlin: diaphanes.

von Arnim, Hans Herbert. 2002. Strukturprobleme des Parteienstaats. In Aus Politik und Zeitgeschichte 16/2000, online ed, https://www.bpb.de/shop/zeitschriften/apuz/25648/strukturprobleme-des-parteienstaates/. Accessed 20 October 2022.

Wagner, Adolph. 1902. The National Debt of the German Empire. *The North American Review* 174 (547): 845–856.

Webber, Jude. 2019. Mexico Expects to Cover Most of its 2019 Financing in the Domestic Market. Financial Times. London. Available at <https://www.ft.com/content/75ac5eb6-1848-11e9-9e64-d150b3105d21>. Accessed 18 January 2019.

Weber, Max. 1994. The Profession and Vocation of Politics. In *Political Writings*, edited by Peter Lassman and Ronald Speirs, 309–369. Cambridge: Cambridge University Press.

Weber, Max. 1999. Politik als Beruf. In *Gesammelte Politische Schriften*, edited by Elisabeth Flitner, 396–450. Potsdamer. Potsdam. Available at <http://verlag.ub.uni-potsdam.de/html/494/html/PS.pdf>.

Weyland, Kurt. 1998. From Leviathan to Gulliver? The Decline of the Developmental State in Brazil. *Governance* 11 (1): 51–75.

Wibbels, Erik, and Moisés Arce. 2003. Globalization, Taxation, and Burden-Shifting in Latin America. *International Organization* 57 (1). Available at <http://www.journals.cambridge.org/abstract_S0020818303571041>. Accessed 10 January 2017.

Windecker Jr., George H. 1993. The Eurodollar Deposit Market: Strategies for Regulation. *American University International Law Review* 9 (1): 357–384.

Winkler, Heinrich August. 2005. *Weimar 1918–1933: die Geschichte der ersten deutschen Demokratie*. 4, Durchgesehene Auflage. München: Verlag C. H. Beck.

World Bank. 2018. World Bank National Accounts Data. Available at <https://data.worldbank.org/indicator/NY.GDP.MKTP.KD.ZG?locations=DE&year_low_desc=false>. Accessed 6 July 2018.

Zucman, Gabriel. 2013. The Missing Wealth of Nations: Are Europe and the U.S. net Debtors or net Creditors? *The Quarterly Journal of Economics* 128 (3): 1321–1364.

Zucman, Gabriel. 2014. Taxing Across Borders: Tracking Personal Wealth and Corporate Profits. *Journal of Economic Perspectives* 28 (4): 1–37.

Zucman, Gabriel. 2015. *The Hidden Wealth of Nations: The Scourge of Tax Havens*. Chicago; London: University of Chicago Press.

# Index